Aleksei

N. Kuropatkin, Walter Edward Gowan

Kashgaria - Eastern or Chinese Turkistan

historical and geographical sketch of the country, its military strength, industries

and trade

Aleksei

N. Kuropatkin, Walter Edward Gowan

Kashgaria - Eastern or Chinese Turkistan
historical and geographical sketch of the country, its military strength, industries and trade

ISBN/EAN: 9783337291938

Printed in Europe, USA, Canada, Australia, Japan

KASHGARIA:

[EASTERN OR CHINESE TURKISTAN.]

HISTORICAL AND GEOGRAPHICAL SKETCH OF THE COUNTRY; ITS MILITARY STRENGTH, INDUSTRIES AND TRADE.

BY

A. N. KUROPATKIN,

COLONEL ON THE GENERAL STAFF OF THE IMPERIAL RUSSIAN ARMY, ETC., ETC.

TRANSLATED FROM THE RUSSIAN

BY

WALTER E. GOWAN,

MAJOR, H. M.'S INDIAN ARMY.

CALCUTTA:

THACKER, SPINK AND CO.

BOMBAY: THACKER AND CO., LD. MADRAS: HIGGINBOTHAM AND CO.

LONDON: W. THACKER AND CO.

1882.

CONTENTS.

CHAPTER V.

CHAPTER VI.

CHAPTER VII.

CHAPTER VIII.

NOTE.

THE following eight Appendices appear in the original work, and although not without great political and military importance in view of any future operations in Kashgarian territory, they would have no special interest for the general reader. They have not, therefore, been incorporated in the present edition:

APPENDICES.

Appendix I.—Itineraries of the Route followed in 1876-77 by the Russian Embassy to Kashgaria, from the town of Osh to the town of Kashgar.

[Russ. text, pp. 219 to 253

Appendix II.—Do. do., from the town of Kashgar to the town of Aksu.
[Russ. text, pp. 255 to 273

Appendix III.—Do. do., from the town of Aksu to the town of Koorlia.
[Russ. text, pp. 275 to 296

Appendix IV.—(*a.*) Itinerary of the Route followed in 1877 by Second Captain Soonargooloff, from the town of Aksu to the town of Karakol, *viâ* Fort Ootch-Toorfan. [Russ. text, pp. 297 to 310

(*b.*) Karashar and Lake Bagratch-Kool. An excursion undertaken by Captain N. N. Kuropatkin and Mons. A. Wilkins.
[Russ. text, pp. 311 to 319

Appendix V.—(*a.*) Table of distances in the Route followed in 1876-77 by the Russian Embassy to Kashgaria, from the town of Osh to the town of Koorlia. [Russ. text, pp. 321 to 323

(*b.*) Table of distances in the Route followed in 1876-77 by the Russian Embassy on its way back from Kashgaria, from the town of Koorlia to the town of Osh. [Russ. text, pp. 324 to 326

Appendix VI.—Information relating to the trade between Russia and Kashgaria during the year 1876:

(*a.*) *Return 1.*—Of goods imported from Russian territory into the town of Kashgar, *viâ* Osh. [Russ. text, p. 328

Appendix VII.—(Continued.)

(*b.*) *Return II.*—Of goods imported into Russian territory from the town of Kashgar, *viâ* Osh. [Russ. text, pp. 329 & 330

(*c.*) *Return III.*—Of the number of caravaus which entered the town of Ootch-Toorfan from the Issikkul district. [Russ. text, p. 331

(*d.*) *Return IV.*—Of the number of caravans which entered the Isswik-kool district from Kashgar. [Russ. text, pp. 332 & 333

(*e.*) *Return V.*—Of the number of caravans which entered the Issik-kul district from Ootch-Toorfan. [Russ. text, pp. 334 & 335

Goods which form the principal part of the trade in the bazaars of Aksu and Kashgar. [Russ. text, pp. 336 to 345

(*f.*) *Return VI.*—Of the caravans which passed through the Tokmak district to Kashgar and back again. [Russ. text, pp. 346 to 427

Appendix VII.—The latitude and longitude east of Pulkoff's Observatory of some of the principal places in Kashgaria. [Russ. text, pp. 430 to 432

Heights of certain points in Kashgaria as ascertained barometrically. [Russ. text, p. 433

Appendix VIII.—Authorities consulted by Colonel A. N. Kuropatkin in his preparation of the map[1] of Kashgaria or Eastern or Chinese Turkistan. Cartographical materials other than the itineraries of the Embassy :[2]

i. Topographical survey of portions of the territory of the Diko-Kamenni or Wild Stone Kirghiz of the Trans-Ili and of the Chinese possessions, carried out in 1856, on a scale of 5 *versts* (3⅓rd miles) to the inch.

From this survey has been drawn the *eastern* end and neighbourhood of Lake Issik-Kul.

[1] A publication of the Cartographical Department of the Military Topographical Section of the Russian General Staff, compiled under the personal supervision of the Editor of Asiatic publications, Colonel A. A. Bolsheff.

[2] I. Itinerary of the route followed by the Russian Embassy to Kashgaria in 1876, prepared by Second Captain Startseff. Scale, 5 *versts* (3⅓rd miles) to an inch.

This itinerary includes the entire road from Osh, *viâ* Kashgar, to Koorlia and the prolongation thereof to Karashar (the latter portions from information furnished by N. Kuropatkin and A. Wilkins).

II. Eye and compass survey of the road from the town of Aksu, *viâ* Ootch-Toorfan, to the village of Slivkino, completed in 1877 by Second Captain Soonargooloff. Scale, 5 *versts* (3⅓rd miles) to the inch. —*Author.*

Appendix VIII.—(Continued.)

ii. Special 10 *versts* ($6\frac{2}{3}$rds miles) map of Western Siberia.

From this map has been drawn the *western* end and neighbourhood of Lake Issik-kul.

iii. Topographical survey of the *south-western* portion of Lake Issik-kul and of the highlands of the river Chu, carried out in 1860, on a scale of 10 *versts* ($6\frac{2}{3}$rds miles) to the inch.

From this map has been drawn a small portion of the country lying to the *south-west* of Lake Issik-kul.

iv. Map of the Narin tract, comprising a semi-instrumental survey carried out under the direction of Major-General Kraevski in 1868, and from *reconnaissances* effected by Sub-Lieutenant Petroff and Topographer Reingardt, on a scale of 5 *versts* ($3\frac{1}{3}$rd miles) to the inch.

v. Map of the Narin tract, from the *reconnaissance* of 1868-69 of Baron A. V. Kaulbars, on a scale of 30 *versts* (20 miles) to the inch.

This served to fill up the blanks in the preceding map.

vi. Map of the highlands of the Amu-Daria, compiled in the Military Topographical Section of the General Staff from the most recent information. Scale, 30 *versts* (20 miles) to the inch.

From this map was taken, amongst other information, the survey of the Alai Expedition, from the town of Osh to the Uz-Bel-Su pass. In connection with this survey is Startseff's itinerary from Sufi-Koorgan to Kashgar.

vii. Reconnaissance of the valley of the Tekes and of the Muzart pass under Colonel Poltoratski in 1867. Scale, 5 *versts* ($3\frac{1}{3}$rd miles) to the inch.

viii. Semi-instrumental survey of the Kuljan region, 1871-72. Scale, 5 *versts* ($3\frac{1}{3}$rd miles) to the inch.

From the southern portion of this survey have been noted the names, &c., of several rivers.

ix. Map of the Kuljan tract, compiled from semi-instrumental surveys carried out in 1872. Scale, 20 *versts* ($13\frac{1}{3}$rd miles) to an inch.

x. Captain Shepeleff's survey of the Muzart pass of 1873 (scale, 2 *versts* ($1\frac{1}{3}$rd miles) to an inch). Itinerary based on elicited information of the road from the Muzart pass to the town of Aksu (scale, 40 *versts* ($26\frac{2}{3}$rds miles) to an inch). The rivers met with on this route have been made to correspond with the course of those on the route of Captain Startseff from Aksu to Bai, and also with the description given thereof by A. N. Kuropatkin.

Appendix VIII.—(Continued.)

xi. Map based on elicited information of the valley of the Yeki-Su-Arasa, compiled in 1871. Scale, 5 *versts* ($3\frac{1}{3}$rd miles) to an inch.

This map served to amplify certain settled points in the Namangan district to the north of Osh and Urgentch.

xii. Semi-instrumental survey of the mountain region of the Namangan district and portions of the Chust districts of the province of Fergana, effected in 1877. Scale, 5 *versts* ($3\frac{1}{3}$rd miles) to an inch.

From the eastern portion of this map has been fixed the position of the river Narin.

xiii. Map of Lob-Nor, from the surveys of Colonel Prjevalski, effected in 1877. Scale, 40 *versts* ($26\frac{2}{3}$rds miles) to an inch.

xiv. Map of Turkistan, by Colonel J. T. Walker, R.E., 1875. Scale, 32 miles to one inch.

ERRATUM.

Through a misconception, which I regret, Major J. M. Trotter's name has been affixed to "Notes on Eastern Turkistan," *vide* note at foot of page 110.—W. E. G.

NOTE BY THE TRANSLATOR.

ALTHOUGH unforeseen causes have long delayed the publication of this work, I make no apology for presenting, at this time, an English translation of a valuable treatise on Kashgaria by a distinguished officer of the Russian General Staff. It is true, indeed, that Kashgaria has disappeared from the list (now rapidly decreasing) of the independent States of Central Asia and that another turn of the wheel of fortune has once more placed the Chinese in possession of that country. But it may be that ere long the further progress of that other Power, in whose movements both England and India have so great an interest, will divert to Kashgaria[1] some of the attention now given to Kuldja and the Turkman *oases*. The recent important step taken by the Russian Government, that of appointing a Consul-General at Kashgar, is full of meaning, and as such will, no doubt, attract the notice of other than those interested in the *trade* of Central Asia.

---

[1] It has been already shown that any occupation by Russia of the State of Yarkand-Kashgar would be most injurious to the long-established rights and interests of England in the north-western part of the Himalayas. Such an occupation would also affect the north-eastern boundary of Afghanistan, as already described. The Russians must be well aware of the just jealousy with which England would regard the interposition of a European power in Yarkand-Kashgar; but it is desirable that the weight of the English objections should be impressed upon the Russian Government.—*India in* 1880, *by Sir Richard Temple, Bart.*, &c., &c.

INTRODUCTION.

In the year 1876, there ceased to exist one of the most ancient of the independent Khanates of Central Asia, the Khanate of Kokan.[1] A Russian army, weak in numbers, but strong in spirit and in discipline, and led by experienced officers, defeated the huge masses of Kokandians, and occupied, one after the other, the most important towns of the country; whilst, in February 1876, the young General Skobeleff, who had so rapidly acquired such a wide celebrity, entered Kokan, the capital of the Khanate, at the head of his detachment.

During the several months of feverish activity which followed, Kokan was turned into a Russian province and renamed Fergana. The military national administration, which had stood a ten years' experience in the Turkestan tract, was introduced into the newly-conquered province.

Thanks to the successful choice of official personages, the settled population was quickly pacified; so that from April 1876, throughout the valley of Fergana, in which is collected the greater portion of this population, one could go everywhere alone, without a guard and without arms.

It was somewhat more difficult to subdue the nomad people of the Khanate, who wander over the majestic mountains of the Tian Shan range bordering on the Fergana valley.

Having been for a long time almost independent of the administration of the last weak Khans, the Kara-Kirghiz and a portion of the Kipchaks were at first but little disposed to recognize Russian rule.

Some Russian detachments that were sent to the mountains having defeated parties of Kirghiz, who tried by force of arms to bar our way to their fastnesses, compelled even the nomad population to declare submission and to acknowledge its fealty to Russia. Nevertheless, in time these movements disclosed

---

[1] The Russian way of spelling proper names has been adhered to in this translation.—*Trans.*

the fact, that not only could Kirghiz individuals but whole tribes easily avoid the pursuit of the Russians by passing over the Tian Shan range into Kashgaria, to the possessions of Yakoob Bek, where they met with a good reception.

The necessity, therefore, of establishing a border line between our newly-conquered possessions and Kashgaria was at once seen. The former boundary of the Khanate of Kokan had been ten years before upset by Yakoob Bek. Availing himself of the weakness of Khoodoyar Khan, the Khan of Kokan, he had extended to the north the sovereignty established by him in the fight, and by degrees had seized the greater portion of the mountain tract that separates the province of Fergana from Kashgaria.[1]

In May 1876, the Governor-General of Turkestan, General Aide-de-Camp Von Kaufmann 1st, appointed an Embassy to Kashgaria, with the object of opening negotiations with Yakoob Bek, relating to the re-arrangement of the border line between his possessions and the province of Fergana.

I was nominated chief of this Embassy, to which were also appointed my brother N. Kooropatkin, captain of Artillery, and Second Captains N. Startseff and A. Soonargooloff. To the Embassy was attached an escort of fifteen Cossacks.

In consequence of our little knowledge of the mountain tract, along which it was proposed to carry the new frontier, certain points favourable for our border line in this region were defined, and instructions accordingly were given to the Embassy.

In addition to this, the Embassy was directed to collect various particulars relating to Kashgaria, especially to her trade, and all information concerning the warlike strength and resources of Yakoob Bek.

The knowledge of Kashgaria that we possessed at the time was not merely incomplete, but it, to a considerable degree, exaggerated the real powers of the ruler of the country and the importance of the State which he had founded. We saw in Kashgaria a powerful Mussulman State, to which, as to a centre

[1] Or, in other words, the Fergana valley from the basin of the Tarim.—*Author.*

would be drawn the sympathy of the population, not only of the weak Mussulman States which had preserved their independence, but also that of the population of the provinces which we had conquered. The importance of Kashgaria in our eyes was, moreover, increased in consequence of the attempts of the English to draw this country to their side so as to incorporate it, (1) in a neutral zone of countries, which was to separate Russia from India, and (2) to acquire in Kashgaria a fresh market for the sale of their manufactured goods.

The immense personal successes of Yakoob Bek, who had risen from the profession of a 'batcha,'[1] and his boundless power over a vast country, had surrounded his person with a halo not wholly undeserved. Suffice it to say that in him many saw, owing to the number of his successes and the grandeur of his designs, a second Tamerlane. The resources of this ruler were likewise greatly exaggerated. The authentic information regarding the purchase by Yakoob Bek of a large consignment of quick-shooting rifles in Constantinople, as was supposed through the agency of Englishmen, gave a solid basis to these exaggerations.

It was imperative, therefore, to go and ascertain on the spot how far the real resources and power of Yakoob Bek could be dangerous to us.

Our Embassy to Kashgaria would not be the first. The basin of the Tarim, locked in on all sides by gigantic mountains, had served for more than twenty years as an alluring object to European travellers in their explorations. Since the year 1868, Yakoob Bek had, too, received several embassies both from Russia and from India, and he had himself equipped embassies in return.

Let us here give a summary of the Europeans who have visited Kashgaria in the course of the last twenty years:

In 1857, Adolphus Schlagintweit reached the town of Kashgar, where he was murdered by order of the then ruler, Hadji Vali-Khan-Tura.

In 1859, Lieut. Valikhanoff made his way from the town of Vairnoye to the town of Kashgar in the guise of a trader.

[1] A pretty boy, who dances before the public in female apparel.—*Author.*

In 1835, Mr. Johnson, who was engaged in topographical works on the confines of Kashmir, made his way to the town of Khotan, where he was kindly received by the temporary ruler of the place, Habbiboolla Hadji.

In 1868, Mr. Shaw appeared at Kashgar, with a consignment of goods from India, and he, too, was welcomed by Yakoob Bek.

In the same year, Mr. Hayward visited Kashgar, and was later on murdered at Yasin.

In this year, too, our Embassy under Captain Reintal arrived in the same town, but it was not received in a thoroughly friendly manner.

In 1870, the first Embassy under Forsyth came to the country. Its members were Messrs. Henderson and Shaw. This Embassy went as far as Yarkend.

In 1872, the Embassy of Baron Kaulbars, captain on the General Staff, was received at Kashgar. The members of this mission were Captain Sharngorst and Lieutenants Startseff and Kolokoltseff and Mons. Chanwisheff.

In 1873-74, Forsyth's second Embassy was received at Kashgar, and its members, in the character of sportsmen, got as far as Fort Maral-Bashi.[1]

In 1875, the second Embassy of Captain (now Colonel) Reintal was received at Kashgar.

Let us now add the years in which Yakoob Bek sent corresponding missions to various countries.

In 1868, Mirza Shadi went to Russia.

In 1869, the same personage was sent to the Viceroy of India.

In 1872, Said Yakoob Khan was accredited to the Viceroy of India and to the Turkish Sultan.

In 1875, the mission of Toorab Hadji arrived in St. Petersburgh.

The southern and south-western portions of Kashgaria were explored by our Embassies and by those sent from India, and the following towns were visited by them: Yarkend, Kashgaro and Khotan. There yet remained a considerable tract of country, to the east of the town of Kashgar, and as far as Koonya-Toorfan

[1] Halfway between the towns of Kashgar and Aksu.—*Author.*

and Lob-Nor, which had not been searched out. It was this portion of the country then that our Embassy hoped to visit after passing from the town of Osh, in the province of Fergana, to the town of Kashgar, and on beyond to Aksu, Koocha, Bai, Koorlia, Fort Kara-Shar and lake Bagratch-Kool.

Almost contemporaneous with our Embassy, the celebrated traveller, Prjevalski, colonel on the General Staff, reached Lob-Nor from Kuldja going by way of Koorlia.

The work, which is now offered to the public in the shape of this book, gives the result of our travels to Kashgaria, and it affords also, in several chapters, a complete history of our mission based on the report which I presented to the Governor-General of Turkestan on our return to the town of Tashkent.

In this book is given, in great detail, information regarding our researches in those places alone which we personally visited. The difficulty of collecting data, in the face of the universal suspicion on the part of the natives, was aggravated still more by the official position which I occupied during my stay in Kashgaria. These unfavourable conditions could not but detract from the completeness of some sections of my work in that excursions off the line of the route followed by our Embassy were almost impossible.

Neither did our Embassy start propitiously. After leaving Tashkent, in the month of May, we passed through Khodjent, Kokan and Margelan to the town of Osh, whence, on the $\frac{16th}{28th}$ July, we set out for Fort Gulcha. The day following when we were halfway between Osh and Gulcha, the Embassy had to withstand an unexpected attack from behind an ambuscade, delivered by a gang of Kara-Kirghiz. We were not massacred, thanks only to a happy accident, which enabled my brother to slay the leader of the gang, a known Kirghiz, by name Ishem Bek. In the struggle, I was wounded in the right arm, and had to return to Osh to undergo an operation. I was only able to start again on the $\frac{7th}{19th}$ October.

In addition to the persons before appointed, there were added to our party Mons. Eren, a doctor, and Mons. Wilkins, a naturalist. The escort, too, was made up to twenty-five Cossacks and mounted riflemen. Together with the native translators who were to collect information, the 'Djigits,'[1] the personal servants of members of the Embassy, and the mule-drivers, &c., the total number of persons in and attached to our mission amounted to sixty-four. There were also 104 saddle and pack-horses. In order to acquaint the reader with the form and character of the negotiations which I was to carry on with Yakoob Bek, and also with the tone which I, as Russian Envoy, was to adopt with the ruler of Kashgaria, I will give an extract from the despatch which accompanied the report of the Embassy as furnished by me to the Governor-General of Turkestan.

Proceeding by easy marches from the town of Osh, *viâ* the Terek-Davan pass, the Embassy arrived at the town of Kashgar, on the $\frac{\text{25th October}}{\text{6th Novr.}}$ 1876. 373 versts (248⅔rds miles) were traversed in eighteen marches.

Our Embassy remained at Kashgar until the $\frac{\text{20th November}}{\text{2nd December}}$ in expectation of the permission of the 'Badaulet'[2] for us to proceed onwards.

During the first three days of our stay in Kashgar, our movements were greatly hampered by order of Yakoob Bek's son, Bek-Koolwi Bek. But, on my threatening to return without entering into any sort of negotiations, we attained perfect freedom, of which we availed ourselves by going several times to the bazaar in the town, and by studying the infantry, artillery and the troops equipped and drilled in the Chinese style.

On the $\frac{\text{19th November}}{\text{1st December}}$, the permission, which had been asked for, came, and on the day but one following, we started on our onward route with the intention of going to Fort Togsoon, where Yakoob Bek was staying at the time. The onward route of the Embassy was as follows:—

On the $\frac{\text{10th}}{\text{22nd}}$ December, after passing Fort Maral-Bashi, we came to the town of Aksu, having done 436 versts (390⅔rds

[1] The 'Jigit,' or 'Djinghite,' or 'Djigit,' is a name derived from that given to the horse-soldiers of the army of Kashgar. See Boulger's Kashgar, page 143.—*Trans.*

[2] As Yakoob Bek is called in Kashgaria.—*Author.*

miles) in nineteen marches. At Aksu we remained a week, in order to become acquainted with the town and its bazaar, and to determine various doubtful points.

On the $\frac{18th}{30th}$ December we left Aksu and, proceeding *viâ* Bai and Koocha, arrived at Koorlia on the $\frac{10th}{22nd}$ January 1877, having performed 487 versts (324⅔rds miles) in nineteen[1] marches. The entire distance from Osh to Koorlia, which we had ridden, was 1,296 versts (864 miles).

The day following we were presented to the 'Badaulet,' when I, in the name of the Governor-General of Turkestan, offered him greeting and delivered my letters and gifts.

During the 'dastar-khân' (or usual entertainment)[2] I addressed the 'Badaulet' in a speech which was almost word for word as follows:—

"At your desire, Badaulet[3] of High Dignity,[4] we are the first Russians who have accomplished such a long journey in your dominions.

"The rulers at all the points which we have passed, and the persons attached to us have, by your orders, made all the necessary arrangements so as to render our route as little fatiguing as possible, and in this they have completely succeeded.

"On our part we have, during our journey, used every endeavour to acquaint ourselves with the localities which we have passed through, to discover the roads leading from the towns, at which we have stopped, into Russian territory, to gain a knowledge of these towns, and the requirements of their inhabitants with a view to bringing to bear from everything that we have seen and learnt, all that could possibly aid in the extension of our reciprocal trade relations, and through them of friendly intercourse.

"Whilst performing so long a journey, we have met places both fruitful and barren: we have seen towns both large and small; populations both rich and poor. We have noticed too the extreme cheapness of all the principal articles of food and of

1 *Sic* in original, 20 (?).

2 At which the guest is plied with various dishes.—*Trans.*

3 See Author's note at foot of page 8.—*Trans.*

4 Title given to Asiatic Khans.—*Trans.*

domestic use. From this circumstance, we have formed the conclusion that every subject of the 'Badaulet' of High Dignity, if only he be not lazy, can live without want. We could not but turn our attention likewise to the exact fulfilment by the subjects of the 'Badaulet' of all the ordinances and orders imposed upon them. This was done with the same exactitude in villages, the most removed from the town of Koorlia, as though the 'Badaulet' himself were there present.

"In conclusion, after making this long journey through his dominions, we are still more assured that the 'Badaulet' of High Dignity has not only created for himself a vast sovereignty, but that he possesses the power of wisely ruling it."

This speech Second Captain Soonargooloff translated by periods, whereupon Yakoob Bek said in reply that we were his dear guests; that he had nothing to hide from us; that he had only one wish, and that was to preserve the friendship of the Governor-General of Turkestan; that he was a humble individual, and must rely upon the Russians.

I then, in the name of General Aide-de-Camp Von Kaufmann, thanked Yakoob Bek for the good reception which he had given to our famous traveller Mons. Prjevalski, and I officially requested that he would, in the future, afford him all possible assistance. Finally, on rising to take leave, I expressed the hope that this occasion of the arrival of a Russian Embassy would strengthen our friendship with the people of Kashgaria—a friendship which had not been interrupted for so many years.

During the interview, Yakoob Bek deported himself simply and kindly, without that exaggerated importance (with which, for example, his son, Bek Kooli Bek, received us in Kashgar). He himself arranged the dishes spread out before us on the 'dastar-khân,' offered them to us, and hastened the servants by remarking that we were displeased.

Some days afterwards, Zaman-Khan-Effendi came to us. He was entrusted by Yakoob Bek with the conduct of preliminary negotiations. Our surprise was very great when it appeared that Zaman Khan could speak Russian beautifully, and that he was well educated. (We conversed with him about England, with which country he appeared to have no sympathies, and about European affairs. He evinced very correct notions, and displayed an acquaintance with the situation of affairs in Tunis, Algeria and Egypt).[1] He conveyed to us some details about his past, from which we gathered that he was an exile from the Caucasus; that he had received his education in Russia; and that for some political reason or another he had been obliged to fly to Constantinople. Thence, three years later, Zaman Khan had come to Kashgar, and from that time he had been with Yakoob Bek in the capacity of trusted Councillor. Zaman Khan has strong sympathies towards the Russians, and has, in fact, shewn the bent of his feelings by deeds. It was only by his influence that Colonel Prjevalski was allowed to go to Lob-Nor. Prior to the arrival of Zaman Khan in Koorlia our traveller remained in that town under a sort of honourable arrest. Zaman Khan himself offered to accompany Prjevalski to Lob-Nor, and afterwards, in his letters to me, our friend expressed his hearty thanks to Zaman Khan for his true friendship and co-operation in all the difficult circumstances under which the expedition was placed. Notwithstanding, however, my great faith in Zaman Khan, I did not consider it possible to open negotiations with him relative to the establishment of a border line, and so I demanded a personal interview with the 'Badaulet.' After several visits from Zaman Khan, in which he, amongst other things, several times repeated that Yakoob Bek had disconnected himself from the English, as he well understood what sort of people they were; that he had not paid attention to them when they sought to sow enmity between the Russians and himself; and that he now understood the advantage of depending on the Russians alone.

At length, on the morning of the $\frac{\text{20th January}}{\text{1st February}}$ Zaman Khan informed us that at 8 o'clock that evening the 'Badaulet' wished us to go to him in order to conduct our negotiations. Zaman Khan added that an evening reception on the part of the 'Badaulet' was a great favour, as in the evening he was always in good spirits, and at that time only received his nearest and most valued friends.

---

[1] Singular coincidence, for these are the very countries that have attracted, and are now attracting, so much interest in Europe.—*Trans.*

Setting out at the appointed hour, accompanied by Second Captain Soonargooloff only, I was received as affably as on the first occasion. After inviting us to sit down, Yakoob Bek said that he was ready to hear what we had to communicate on the subject of the establishment of a border line.

I then made the speech which I had prepared beforehand. This Second Captain Soonargooloff translated in short periods according to the measure of my elocution.

The speech was almost *verbatim* as follows:—

"The chief object of my coming is to thoroughly strengthen the friendly relations between Russia and Kashgaria, which, thanks be to God, have not been interrupted for so many years. The second object consists in establishing the main point of a boundary line betwixt what was the Khanate of Kokan and what is now the Province of Fergana and the possessions of the 'Badaulet' of High Degree.

"Mons. the Governor-General of Turkestan, before despatching me as his envoy to you, has indicated to me certain points through which it is necessary that this frontier line should pass.

"The assent of your Highness to the acceptance of this line, in accordance with the wishes of the Governor-General of Turkestan, will serve as the strongest testimony on your part of your wish to strengthen as much as possible the friendly relations with powerful Russia.

"The fate of sovereignties, as of individuals, is directed by the Divine will. The Divine will ordains that with wise government some rulers shall establish the power of their States, and shall also extend their boundaries, whilst others, through their own defects, not only do not establish that power, but even lose that which has been acquired by their forefathers and predecessors in the course of many centuries.

"Thus it is only thirteen years since the Khanate of Kokan was the most powerful State in Central Asia. Its boundaries on the west reached to the town of Chemkent; on the east to the Narwin tract, where Fort Koortka was established; on the south it embraced the whole of the mountain region as far as the exit on to the plains of Kashgaria. Koorgashin-Kani and Tash-Koorgan were considered its frontier advanced posts.

"Internal discord arose, and a series of mistakes were made by Khoodoyar Khan, the last ruler of this Khanate, so that he had at first to put up with the loss of several towns, and then during last year the possessions formerly comprising the Khanate of Kokan were incorporated in the Russian Empire.

"The chief strength and richness of the former Khanate of Kokan consisted in its settled population, which is confined to the valley of Fergana and to the large towns and villages therein.

"The inhabitants of the mountainous region of the Kokan Khanate, *viz.* Kipchaks, and particularly the Kara-Kirghiz, have always served as the source, not of strength, but of weakness.

"As long as the Government was strong, it maintained in the mountains a line of forts, with the aid of which it kept in check the mountain population. The weakening of the power of the Government was felt first of all in the mountains; whereupon, whole tribes of Kara-Kirghiz and Kipchaks, not only refused to pay the small tribute charged upon their flocks and herds, but, after chosing leaders, descended into the plains, and finally overturned the Government which had begun to grow weak.

"During the past thirteen years, the mountain tract, separating the Fergana valley from Djitwishar and belonging almost entirely to the Khanate of Kokan, began by degrees, in consequence of the weakness of the Government of this Khanate, to be incorporated by your Highness in the possessions of Kashgaria.

"Its incorporation was forced upon you, and had for its sole object the deliverance of the peace of your subjects from the inroads of the Kara-Kirghiz.

"With this object you established in the mountains the posts of Ooksalwir, Mashroop, Ooloogchat, Nagra-Chaldwee, Yegin and Irkeshtam. After this your posts along the road to the town of Osh reached as far as the natural boundary of Noor and along the road to the town of Oozgent to the natural boundary of Oi-Tal, in the valley of Alai-Koo.

"It is indisputable that if the dissension in the Khanate of Kokan had not been put a stop to by the appearance of the Russians, your Highness would have found it necessary to continue to extend your dominions in the direction of the north as far as the exit from the mountains into the valley of Fergana opposite the towns of Osh and of Oozgent.

"With the occupation by us of the Khanate of Kokan, Russian power has taken upon itself the obligation of introducing peace into the incorporated possessions and of defending the life and property of its new subjects. To this end, therefore, the Russians have advanced into the mountains just as far as it appeared at first to be necessary. We thus occupied Isfara, Ootch-Koorgan and Goolcha.

"But soon events showed that this line was not sufficient. The insurrection of the Kara-Kirghiz called for a difficult and costly expedition into the mountains. This expedition need not have taken place if the Russian advanced posts had in the first instance been thrown out further to the south than was the case.

"In August of last year, Mons. the Governor-General of Turkestan, being desirous of introducing peace into the province of Fergana, visited all the towns of that province and also rode out into the mountains beyond Fort Goolcha, in order to make himself better acquainted with the boundary line of this region.

"After a personal inspection of the mountainous country, and after a consideration of the report sent to him by the ruler of the province of Fergana, Mons. the Governor-General of Turkestan considered it indispensable, for the future peace of the entire population of that province, to arrange with your Highness the main points of the following boundary line between Kashgaria and the province in question.

"From the Sooyek pass, which is the extreme point on the south-west of the boundary between the province of Semiraitchensk and the possessions of the 'Badaulet,' this border line should pass to Fort Ooloogchat and further on to mount Maltabar.

"Forts Ooloogchat, Nagra-Chaldwee, Yegin and Irkeshtam should be made over to us.

"The detailed settlement of this border line should be left to a special commission to be composed of persons appointed both by the Governor-General of Turkestan and by your Highness.

"On me has been imposed the presentation to your consideration of this determination on the part of Mons. the Governor-General of Turkestan, and so also has been left to me the arrangement, in the spirit of this determination, of a project for a treaty to be ratified both by your Highness and by Mons. the Governor-General of Turkestan."

Between the several periods of this speech the 'Badaulet' made observations relating to his own weakness in comparison with the power of Russia and to his wish to preserve always a peace with her. He went on to add, that it was only by the aid of friendship on the part of Russia that he had reached the height to which he had attained.

When I proceeded to speak of Ooloogchat and Maltabar as future boundary points, Yakoob Bek's agitation became very manifest, but he restrained himself until the termination of my speech, when he began to point out with fluency his own rights to the possession of these points.

He said that he had established Ooloogchat before Khoodoyar Khan had become the Khan of Kokan; that all the other posts were established under his own immediate superintendence; that the Russians, during Abdoola-Bek's insurrection, had learnt how far he was able to protect the boundary which he had himself laid down, seeing that not a single Kirghiz had crossed this boundary, &c.

In answer I replied to him, that, in the year 1869, when we were establishing Fort Narwin, the 'Badaulet' had declared his rights in like manner to all the left bank of the Narwin river. We had extended the boundary considerably further to the south than he had wished, and this fact had, in consequence, brought about the friendly relations which had not been interrupted up till now.

After this and some unimportant observations the 'Badaulet' said:

"I beg that you will intercede for me, and be my brother, in the presence of the Governor-General of Turkestan. If he desires to show me his friendship, let him leave to me the forts which I have built and which I have held for fourteen years."

I maintained that I could not recede one step from the points which I had indicated.

Then the 'Badaulet' proposed that a letter should be written to the Governor-General of Turkestan to ask of him some abatement in his demands. I dissented from this proposition, saying that, after having journeyed 2,000 versts (1,333⅓rd miles), I could not await an answer, and that I had been personally entrusted with the settlement of the business.

After continued assurances that he would agree to less heavy conditions and after my refusal to make any sort of concessions, the 'Badaulet' asked me to think over the matter for some days. And so we arose on my receiving a promise from him that he would send Zaman Khan to us next day for the purpose of continuing the conference.

Zaman-Khan-Effendi and Pansat-Moolla-Yakoob (who was attached to us during the whole sojourn of our Embassy) had taken no part in our conference; only once had the 'Badaulet' turned towards them and said with warmth, as he pointed to me, "He requires that I should give up to the Russians Nagra-Chaldwee and Ooloogchat."

The following day Zaman Khan, on behalf of the 'Badaulet,' made some further concessions, but I held to the surrender of Ooloogchat and further demanded a categorical answer.

At last, on the $\frac{\text{30th January}}{\text{11th February}}$ Zaman Khan brought me the following answer from the 'Badaulet:'

"I accept the proposal of the Russian Envoy to carry the boundary through Sooyek, Ooloogchat and Maltabar, because I do not consider it possible to act in opposition to the will of Mons. the Governor-General of Turkestan.

"But I will send with you my own envoys for the purpose of requesting the powerful Yarwim-Padishah[1] to make some abatement in his demands and to leave in my hand places in the construction of which I have laboured for fourteen years. If he will not consent to this my petition, then I must leave it entirely to Mons. the Governor-General of Turkestan to establish a boundary

[1] As General Aide-de-Camp Von Kaufmann is called in Central Asia.—*Author.*

line wherever he may consider necessary, and I will accept his decision."

Considering the instructions which I had received to be fulfilled,—*viz.*, to bring about the acceptance of some sort of an arrangement of the kind, I announced my Embassy at an end, and appointed the $\frac{6th}{18th}$ February for a farewell interview with the 'Badaulet,' and the $\frac{7th}{19th}$ idem for our departure. This was arranged.

During the march through Kashgaria as far as the town of Koorlia, and in all our halts at the several towns en route, I and the members of the Embassy collected as complete particulars as possible in answer to the questions dictated in the instructions which had been delivered to me. The collection of these particulars could not be concealed from the Kashgarian officials attached to our suite, and therefore we, from the first, decided not to hide our intentions of acquainting ourselves in the minutest particular with Kashgaria. At every step we interrogated the people of the country, and then openly jotted down in our note-books our own observations. On entering the various towns we summoned experienced merchants and agriculturists for the purpose of cross-questioning them. In like manner, along the road we openly inquired the names of the various points of the locality through which we passed. Without venturing to interfere with our collection of information, the Kashgarian officials who accompanied us nevertheless considered it their duty to convey to Yakoob Bek an extremely exaggerated account of our actions, and therefore, at the first interview with Yakoob Bek after our arrival at the town of Koorlia, I openly told the 'Badaulet' that we were endeavouring to take advantage of the journey which we were making throughout his dominions, to become acquainted both with them and with all the roads leading from Kashgaria into Russian territory. In like manner, during our stay of seven days in the town of Koorlia, I expressed a wish to become acquainted with the town of Kashgar and with lake Bagratch-Kool, and in order that I might do this, I asked Yakoob Bek's consent to my sending to these places some members of my Embassy, captain of Artillery N.

Kooropatkin and Mons. Wilkins. After some hesitation this consent was given. During this trip, my brother openly carried out an itinerary survey. Since we had already come through the Terek-Davan pass and possessed a description of the roads into Kashgaria from the Narwin direction by way of the Tooroogart and Terektwee passes and from India by the Karakorum and Kooen-Loon ranges, one route alone remained unknown to us,—*viz.*, that from the town of Aksu (by way of Ootch-Toorfan) and the Badal pass to the town of Karakol.[1] At our final interview, I obtained the consent of the 'Badaulet' to the despatch along this road of a member of the Embassy, *viz.*, Second Captain Soonargooloff, under the pretext of sending thereby to the Governor-General of Turkestan the earliest information regarding the Embassy.

In demanding of Yakoob Bek the cession to us of Ooloogchat and other posts, I was guided by two considerations:

1st.—Prior to the time of our stay in the town of Koorlia, we had succeeded in convincing ourselves that Yakoob Bek's position was a very difficult one; that he did not possess strong sympathies either on the part of the army or amongst the people. Hence the forces that he had collected for a fight with the Chinese were insufficient, provided the latter were to carry on the war in any sort of energetic manner. Finally, that the monetary resources of Yakoob Bek were very bad.

Therefore, in my conferences with the 'Badaulet' I considered it possible to assume a tone somewhat different to that which the Russian Embassies to Kashgaria prior to mine had adopted. I, in addition to the open declaration that we were exploring his country, spoke to Yakoob Bek of the necessity of "subjecting himself to the will of Mons. the Governor-General of Turkestan," and I requested him to surrender without any indemnification on our part several posts which, in the opinion of Yakoob Bek, had a very important military significance.

2nd.—The boundary along the river Koksoo, which already existed according to previous agreements, sufficiently satisfied us,

[1] The road from the town of Aksu through the Moozart pass to Kuldja is not practicable for marching.—*Author.*

and I, therefore, did not consider it necessary, having regard to the uncertainty of the issue of the struggle between the Chinese and Yakoob Bek, to make any special haste in coming to a settlement of that boundary question.

Our Embassy, which set out on its return journey on the $\frac{\text{6th}}{\text{18th}}$ February, arrived safely in the town of Osh on the $\frac{\text{28th March}}{\text{9th April}}$, having accomplished 1,300 versts ($866\frac{2}{3}$rds miles) in 42 marches (or, including halts, 51 days). From the time of our setting out from Tashkent we had traversed in all 3,000 versts (2,000 miles).

The following were the results obtained by the labours imposed on the members of the Mission:

An itinerary of the route from the town of Aksu, through the towns of Ootch-Toorfan and Karakol, worked out by Second Captain Soonargooloff, and notes by Mons. Wilkins[1] on Karashar and lake Bagratch-Kool."

Moreover, Second Captain N. P. Startseff, known in Turkestan as one of the most experienced and skilful topographers, carried on from day to day, in spite of bad weather and fatigue, a route map [5 versts ($3\frac{1}{3}$rd miles) to the inch] of the entire country which we had traversed.

These route maps afforded the principal material in the preparation of the map of the country which we now have. Independently too of Mons. Startseff's labours, Mons. N. N. Kooropatkin made a survey of the route lying between the town of Koorlia, Fort Karashar and lake Bagratch-Kool, whilst Mons. A. N. Soonargooloff prepared one of the road lying between the town of Aksu and the town of Karakol.

Over and above all this every member of the Embassy and likewise many of the Cossacks and natives endeavoured with all their power to lighten the task imposed upon me by bringing me various information, some in the form of notes and some by word of mouth.

Throughout the whole of our journeyings all the Russians, as well as the natives of the party, formed one friendly family,

[1] Mons. Wilkins likewise furnished a short article, entitled "The nature of the basin of the Tarim" to the journal called *Nature*, No. 3 for 1877.—*Author.*

living with one common interest, and sharing the same joys and the same sorrows. The time spent among this family will for me remain ever memorable. The friendly accord of the members of the Embassy and their readiness to labour for a common object, were a support amid all the severe moments in the time passed by the Embassy, and will always call forth in my mind the warmest reminiscences of each of our recent fellow-travellers,

A, KOOROPATKIN.

CHAPTER I.

Geographical sketch of Kashgaria — Character of the Kashgarian valley — Its mountains, rivers, soil, oases and deserts — View of the natural wealth of Kashgaria — Communications — Population of Kashgaria, occupations of its inhabitants, their dress, food, language and religion.

Geographical sketch of Kashgaria.

UNDER the name of Kashgaria is known the country which lies between 43° and 35° North Latitude, and between 72° and 90° East Longitude.[1]

Character of the Kashgarian valley.

As a whole, Kashgaria is in the form of a crater, the flat bottom of which towards the west rises to a level of 4,000 feet above the sea, whilst, on the eastern side, its height does not exceed 2,500 feet, which is the height of lake Lob-Nor. Kashgaria has a surface of 19,000 square miles.

Its mountain ranges.

Mountain ranges of the first class enclose the valley of Kashgaria. On the north, there is the Tian Shan range; on the west are the Pamir peaks; on the south, the Kooen-Loon chain, and to the east tower the Altwin-Tag mountains, so recently discovered by Colonel Prjevalski. All these mountains are covered with perpetual snow, and their peaks exceed a height of 20,000 feet above the sea. They are approachable only by narrow tracks, whilst parts of them are altogether inaccessible during the winter season. The passes over them are very difficult, and often lie at a height of 14,000 feet.

Its rivers.

Thousands of swift streams carry their waters towards the Kashgarian plains, and some of these, before issuing from the mountains, are grouped in several well-defined river systems. For instance, there are the Khotan-Darya, the Yarkend-Darya, the Kashgar-Darya, the Aksu-Darya, the Koocha-Darya, the Haidoo-Gola.[2] All these streams, after joining together, form

---

[1] Pulkoff's reckoning. The Observatory of Pulkoff is 30° 19′ 40·5″ east of Greenwich.—*Trans.*

[2] Otherwise called the Haidwin-Kooya. This river passes under Fort Karashar, and hence formerly was wrongly called the Karashar-Darya.—*Author.*

the volume of the river Tarim, which loses itself in the marshes surrounding lake Lob-Nor.

The course of the principal rivers of Kashgaria exceeds 1000, and even 1,400 versts ($666\frac{2}{3}$rds and $933\frac{1}{3}$rd miles respectively), but in volume and depth they are far behind the Central Asian rivers,—*i.e.*, the Sir-Darya and the Amoo-Darya. In their upper courses, the Kashgarian rivers are swift and stony, and flow through steep gorges; whilst in their middle and lower streams, that is, after they have reached the plains, their currents are less rapid, and their banks are low and marshy, so that in some parts their waters go to form lakes and bogs overgrown with coarse reeds.

In illustration of this description, let us here give some detailed particulars concerning the rivers Kashgar-Darya, Tarim and lake Lob-Nor. The river Kashgar-Darya (Kwizwil-Soo) at 500 versts ($333\frac{1}{3}$rd miles) from its source, and at 800 ($533\frac{1}{3}$rd miles) from lake Lob-Nor, *i.e.*, at station Koopruk (which is on the road from the town of Kashgar to the town of Aksu, at a distance of 300 versts (200 miles from the former), has a width of 11 'sajens,'[1] a depth of 2 'sajens' (14 feet), and a velocity of 200 feet per minute.

The river Tarim, according to Mons. Prjevalski's measurements, has, at the western extremity of lake Lob-Nor, near the village Abdalla, a width of 18 'sajens' (42 yards), a depth of 2 'sajens' (14 feet), and a velocity of 140 feet per minute. Near lake Lob-Nor it narrows to 3 or 4 'sajens' (21 and 28 feet respectively), and loses itself in the reed-growths about the lake where the Tarim receives the waters of the Oogen-Darya[2] at a distance of more than 300 versts (200 miles) from lake Lob-Nor; it then becomes a very wide stream, with a width of 60 'sajens' (140 yards), and a depth of 3 'sajens' (21 feet). That the Tarim is less wide at its mouth than at the point where it receives the waters of the Oogen-Darya, is explained by the fact that the course of the river towards its mouth lies through marshes and lakes.

[1] $25\frac{2}{3}$rds yards.—*Trans.*

[2] 80 versts ($53\frac{1}{3}$rd miles) to the south of the town of Koorlia.—*Author.*

Lake Lob-Nor has, according to Prjevalski's account, a length of 100 versts (66⅔rds miles), and a width of 20 versts (13⅓rd miles). This lake, or, to speak more correctly, this marsh, is thickly overgrown with reeds rising to a height of as much as 21 feet. On its southern bank only is there a narrow strip of clear water, the width of which is from one to three versts (⅔rds mile to 2 miles). The depth of the lake is ordinarily 6 feet, but in certain places it is as much as from 12 to 13 feet. Its water is clear and fresh.

The soil of Kashgaria.

The soil of the Kashgarian plains is brackish throughout the entire country. Oases afford the only fruitful land. In the southern portions of the valley there are vast tracts of crumbling sands. In the northern and central parts the sandy tracts are less frequent. They here take the form of narrow and low rows of hillocks. In the neighbourhood of the mountains the soil is covered with pebbles.

The climate of Kashgaria.

The climate of Kashgaria is in the highest degree dry, with severe heat in summer, and comparatively warm weather in winter. During the autumn of 1876, which we spent in Kashgaria, there was not one fall of rain. During the winter snow fell but three times, and even then it immediately melted. In the spring of 1877, the sky was frequently overcast, but rain fell only once during the whole season. The winds in the spring are very strong, and usually begin about 11 o'clock in the morning, and last till the evening. Fogs are very frequent in Kashgaria. They obscure for a whole day the entire horizon, leaving but a clear circle in the zenith.

The cultivation of Kashgaria.

The arable portion of Kashgaria is confined to a narrow belt, which is shut in by the highlands of the Tian Shan, the Pamir and the Kooen-Loon mountains.

The oases of Kashgaria.

The country, outside this region, consists of an almost uninhabited desert. But the belt above spoken of is not wide, and does not, throughout its extent, present a surface of fruitful land; such fruitful portions as are cultivated and dwelt upon are situated within oases. The largest of these, beginning from the east, are Koonya-Toorfan, Karashar, Koorlia, Koocha, Bai, Aksu, Maral-Bashi, Kashgar, Yangi-Hissar, Yarkend, Khotan and Keriya. Their situation depends on the course of the principal rivers of Kashgaria. Each of these oases is a circle of green corn cut off from the remainder by a sandy waste in some cases over a hundred versts (66⅔rds miles) wide. Through all of the above enumerated oases there passes a road, which is the main road of the whole country. In the desert parts of the country small settlements exist along this road, and there have been built, throughout its course, several stations, in all of which there is a garrison of a few men.

Its cultivation and system of irrigation.

Cultivation in the oases is kept up by means of irrigation. Each of the principal rivers of Kashgaria, *viz.*, the Khotan-Darya, the Yarkend-Darya, the Kashgar-Darya, the Aksu-Darya, &c., are diverted (before they issue from the mountains), by the aid of dams, into several main streams. These streams are in turn diverted into courses from which the water is let out on to the fields. A very complicated irrigation system is thus formed in all parts of the oases. Each small field must have its own watercourse, otherwise cultivation could not be carried on. The system of dykes makes it possible to evenly distribute the water in every direction. The water thus let out on any particular field lies on it for several days. The boundaries of these oases are very clearly marked. Wherever there is water there is life; where the water ceases, there is a desert. On the other hand, it pays to let the water out on to the desert, as in this way barren and even brackish tracts are made available for cultivation.

There is water in Kashgaria sufficient to irrigate a considerably larger tract of country than is now in use. It may be affirmed with accuracy that the sparseness of the population of Kashgaria is the principal cause for the relatively small portion of land now under cultivation, whilst the amount of land that is suited to irrigation and cultivation is not small, and might be taken up by a considerably larger number of inhabitants.

The route followed by the Russian Embassy to Kashgaria.

Our Embassy, after leaving the town of Osh (in the province of Fergana), crossed the Tian Shan by the Terek-Davan pass and so reached the town of Kashgar. Then passing through the towns of Aksu, Bai, Koocha and Koorlia, it reached Fort Karashar, traversing by this route a great portion of that part of Kashgaria which is embraced within the cultivated tracts. Going by the main road, we came across the following oases and desert regions. Between Kashgar and the village of Faizabad there is an oasis of 70 versts (46$\frac{2}{3}$rds miles). Between Faizabad and Fort Maral-Bashi there is a desert stretching over 150 versts (100 miles). The length of the Maral-Bashi oasis is 20 versts (13$\frac{1}{3}$rd miles). Between this, and as far as the borders of the Aksu oasis, there intervene 165 versts (110 miles) of desert country. The length of the Aksu oasis by the road is 85 versts (56$\frac{2}{3}$rds miles). From the latter, up to the oasis around the town of Bai, there is a desert of 65 versts (43$\frac{1}{3}$rd miles). The length by the road across the Bai oasis is 25 versts (16$\frac{2}{3}$rds miles). Between this to the Koocha oasis lies a desert of 60 versts (40 miles). The length of the Koocha oasis by the road is 25 versts (16$\frac{2}{3}$rds miles). Between this again and the oasis surrounding the hamlet of Boogoor, there is a desert of 70 versts (46$\frac{2}{3}$rds miles). The extent of the Boogoor oasis is 15 versts (10 miles). Between it and the Koorlia oasis intervenes a desert of 150 versts (100 miles). The length of the Koorlia oasis by the road is 10 versts (6$\frac{2}{3}$rds miles), and, between it and the Karashar oasis, there is a desert of 45 versts (30 miles).

Each of these extensive oases contains one comparatively large town, which forms the centre of a district, comprising a greater or less number of villages. According to the conditions of soil and of irrigation, the rural population is either distributed over large villages or scattered over small farms. Between the several villages and farms considerable tracts of waterless country are frequently met with.

Appearance of the country.

The barren portions of Kashgaria present several phases. There are crumbling sands (to the south), there are again rocky tracts or country covered with loose stones, and there are brackish soils. The last mentioned are the most common of all. Salt impregnates the clayey soil of the country, and renders it spongy and brittle. Sometimes the fields look white as with snow from the quantity of salt exuding to the surface.

In the brackish parts of Kashgaria, amongst other scanty kinds of vegetation, tamarisk and a peculiar kind of poplar, called "Toograk," grow.

Immediately after issuing from the oasis of Kashgar, a brackish and level salt tract begins, along which are scattered conical hillocks of a salt-like soil. These hillocks are sometimes several feet high. On their summits grow tamarisks, the long and numerous roots of which bind together the interior of the hillocks in every direction.

Whole generations of this plant intermingle one with the other on the same hillock, thus adding to the mass of roots. In order to get fuel, the natives burrow under some of the hillocks, and extract from each several loads of roots.

In going to the town of Aksu from Kashgar, after passing the village of Koopruk, and before crossing the river Kwizwil-Soo, we met with the first separate "Toograk" trees. Beyond these, again, we came to a forest of the same kind. This forest forms a narrow belt by the river Kwizwil-Soo, and reaches to Tarim and lake Lob-Nor. According to the natives, "Toograk" forests also skirt the rivers Yarkend-Darya and Khotan-Darya.

In the "Toograk" forests we found no decayed soil, such as is an indispensable characteristic of other forests. According to the investigations of one of the members of the Embassy, Mons. A. Wilkins, the leathery leaves of this kind of tree dry on the twigs, and the wind then disperses and reduces them to dust. Hence the leaves do not go to form the vegetable soil spoken of.

In "Toograk" forests the soil is composed of a clay impregnated with salt, such as is characteristic of the greater portion of the surface of Kashgaria. In moving through a "Toograk" forest clouds of a brackish dust are raised, which is very injurious to the eyes.

Some of the properties of a "Toograk" tree are noticed in the irregular form of its leaves, so that on one and the same tree several shapes will be found.

On the branches of such trees, especially on such branches as have been broken, masses of a white powder will appear. From this a kind of glue is prepared.

The rivers of Kashgaria have thick reed-growths on both banks. These reeds are thickest at the place where the particular river enters a lake.

The height of these reeds is sometimes as much as 21 feet.

Fauna of Kashgaria.

The poor but, from a scientific point of view, very interesting fauna of Kashgaria is still but little known. Those who wish to become, in some measure, acquainted with it, are recommended to refer to the work of N. M. Prjevalski, entitled "From Kuldja across the Tian Shan to Lob-Nor;"[1] also to an article by Mons. A. Wilkins, headed "The Nature of the Basin of the Tarim;"[2] and to an article by Mons. Valikhanoff on "the Condition of Altwishar, or the Six Eastern Towns of the Chinese Province of Nan-Loo."[3]

Natural wealth of Kashgaria.

The natural riches, too, of Kashgaria have been also but little explored. Mineral wealth that has ever drawn the Chinese towards this country must be very considerable. Gold is found in the neighbourhood of Keria; and there is copper in Aksu, Sairam and Koocha. The latter place too yields iron, coal, sulphur, alum and sal ammoniac. In the neighbourhood of Kashgar, there is coal and lead. Khotan yields naphtha; Kalpin[4] sulphur; and the vicinity of Bai saltpetre.

Of raw products, after grains of all kinds, the principal things that Kashgaria produces, are wool and silk. Besides that which goes to supply local requirements, masses of 'mata' (a coarse cotton web) are exported from Kashgaria to Semiraitchensk and the province of Fergana, and even to Orenburgh, for sale to the Kirghiz. The production of this 'mata' is confined principally to the neighbourhood of Kashgar. Wool is produced chiefly in the Khotan and Koonya-Toorfan districts; silk, too, is raised in the first of these. During the last year, raw silk formed a very important item in the export trade of Kashgaria. The local silk manufactures are not exported with the exception of 'mashroop' (a semi-silken web). "Hashish"[5] from Yarkend forms an important item in the exports to Kashmir and the

[1] "From Kuldja across the Tian Shan to Lob-Nor." An account of the expedition of Col. N. M. Prjevalski, in Central Asia, in 1876-77. *Vide* "Intelligence of the Imperial Russian Geographical Society for 1877," Vol. XIII, Sec. II, pages 263 and following. This compilation has appeared in the form of a separate book. (An English translation of which has been published. W. E. G.)—*Author.*

[2] See the Journal called "Nature," for 1877, No. III.—*Author.*

[3] See Journal of the Imperial Russian Geographical Society for 1861, No. III, Sec. II, pages 1 to 76.—*Author.*

[4] A row of settlements north of the road from Ootch-Toorfan to the town of Kashgar.—*Author.*

[5] A drug similar in its effects to opium.—*Trans.*

Punjab. Moreover, amongst the exports, the carpets from Khotan, the slippers from Yarkend, the leathern and copper-wares from Aksu, the iron manufactures from Koocha, are renowned. Yarkend is celebrated for its fruit, Aksu for its tobacco, and Koonya-Toorfan for its wool and cotton.

Domestic animals of Kashgaria.

Of domestic animals, the following are bred in Kashgaria: horned cattle, horses, sheep, mules and donkeys. In respect of horses, on which all the articles of trade are carried, and especially of sheep, there is amongst the settled population of the country a great deficiency. Sheep are procured from the Kirghiz of the mountain tracts, bordering on Kashgaria; and horses from the inhabitants of Fergana. There are but very few camels in the country.

Roads in Kashgaria.

We have already said that the principal road of Kashgaria is the cart-road which connects the towns of Koonya-Toorfan, Karashar, Koorlia, Koocha, Bai, Aksu, Kashgar, Yarkend and Khotan. This road is the chief trade and military route of the whole country. Not far from the town of Koonya-Toorfan, it is joined to the Chinese trade route (also a cart-road), which passes through the Celestial Empire, *viâ* Choogoochak, to Gootchen, Hami, Lan-Djei-Foo, Hankoi, to Nankin. After this the road runs parallel with the mountains, and meets a number of bridle paths that intersect the Tian Shan, Pamir and Kooen-Loon. The principal of these, beginning from the north, are:—

1. The road from the town of Koorlia, along the Yuldoos and Koonges valleys, to the town of Kooldja. This road, which was traversed during the year 1877 by Colonel Prjevalski, is 530 versts (353⅓rd miles) long. The highest passes on it are the Habtsagai-Gol, 9,360 feet, and the Narat, 9,800 feet, above the sea. The first of these leads from the Haidwin-Kooya (Haidoo-Gola) valley to the Yuldoos valley. This road is not practicable in winter time on account of the drifts of snow.

2. The roads from the town of Bai and Aksu to the Moozart pass, and thence to the town of Kooldja. From the town of Bai to the Moozart pass is about 170 versts (113⅓rd miles),[1] and

[1] According to the information which we collected in answer to questions put the road from the town of Bai to the Moozart pass lies by the following villages: Davanchik (400 houses), Oosten and Kari (each from 50 to 100 houses),

to the town of Kooldja about 300 versts (200 miles). The road from Aksu to the Moozart pass joins on to the road from the town of Bai to the Moozart guard-house. From Aksu to this guard-house the distance is about 80 versts (53⅓rd miles). To the Moozart pass it is 60 versts (40 miles) more. The entire distance from the town of Aksu to the Moozart pass is about 140 versts (93⅓rd miles), and to the town of Kooldja, about 440 versts (293⅓rd miles). There is another and somewhat circuitous road, which, first of all, follows the main road to Bai as far as the Djoorga station, whence it turns off to the mountains, and at the Oostan-Booi settlement, emerges into the valley of the river Moozart, which is distant from the Moozart guard-house from 40 to 50 versts (from 26⅔rds to 33⅓rd miles).[1]

3. The road from Aksu to the town of Ootch-Toorfan and beyond lies by way of the Badal pass and Fort Kara-Kol. This route was traversed in the year 1877 by a member of our Embassy, Captain Soonargooloff. The distance by it from the town of Aksu to the Russian settlement of Slivkino, near Kara-Kol, is 309 versts (206 miles).[2]

Charkchi (200 houses), Karabakh (Kara-Bagh ?) (500 houses). From Bai to the latter is 4½ 'tash' (36 versts or 24 miles). From Karabakh to the Moozart guard-house is about 80 versts (53⅓rd miles), and thence to the Moozart pass is about 60 versts (40 miles). The whole distance from the town of Bai to the Moozart pass is about 175 versts (116⅔rds miles). On the summit of this pass a small guard-house has been built, and lower down a fort, which contains 300 men.—*Author.*

[1] The road from Aksu to the Djoorga station, the Embassy marched over by the following stages:—From Aksu to the Ishlianchi settlement, 18 versts (12 miles); from Ishlianchi to Kara-Yulgoon, 36 versts (24 miles); from Kara-Yulgoon to Djoorga, 36 versts (24 miles): total, 90 versts (60 miles). I do not know the distance from Djoorga to Oostan-Booi along the valley of the river Moozart, but I suppose that it is from 25 to 35 versts (16⅔rds to 23⅓rd miles). This would make the whole length of the road from Aksu to the Moozart guard-house, 150 versts (100 miles).—*Author.*

[2] The marches by this route are as follows:—From Aksu to Barin, 32 versts (21⅓rd miles); from Barin to Achatag, 26 versts (17⅓rd miles); from Achatag to Ootch-Toorfan, 24 versts (16 miles); from Ootch-Toorfan to Bash-Yagma, 27 versts (18 miles); from Bash-Yagma to Agatch-Kool, 51 versts (34 miles). The road then ascends the Badal pass and reaches a height of 14,000 feet above the sea, and so passes to the Tepe guard-house, distant from Agatch Kool 24 versts (16 miles). From Tepe to Djau-Djoorek the distance is 50 versts (33⅓rd

4. There are several roads from Fort Narwin to the town of Kashgar. The most practicable of these lie across the Terektwi and Tooroogart passes. The road from the town of Kashgar to Fort Narwin, by the first of these, is 260 versts (173⅓rd miles); and by the second, 270 versts (180 miles). As far as Fort Narwin, a cart-road has already been made. From this to Kashgar there are, at present, only bridle paths. Apparently the fittest of these for conversion into a cart-road was traversed by Colonels Kaulbars and Reintal in 1870 and 1875 respectively. This road runs from Fort Narwin, across the Tash-Rabat pass to lake Chatwirkool, and thence across the Tooroogart pass to Fort Chakmak, and so on by the village of Artoosh to the town of Kashgar. According to descriptions given of it, this road could, with very inconsiderable alterations, be easily converted into a cart-road.

5. There are several bridle paths leading from the towns of Osh and Oozgent (the province of Fergana) to the town of Kashgar. The first of these, along which passes the trade between Kashgaria and the Central Asian states, goes by way of the Terek-Davan pass. This route has been traversed by our Embassies on two occasions—in October 1877, and in March 1878. It embraces, from the town of Osh to the town of Kashgar, an extent of 372 versts (248 miles), including the passes over the parallel branches of the Alai range. The heights of these are as follows: The Chigirchik, 7,000 feet; the Terek-Davan, 12,000 feet; the Ike-Ikezyak, about 10,000 feet; and the Shoor-Boolak, above 8,000 feet. This road, before it could be turned into a cart-road, would require the expenditure of vast sums of money—money that could scarcely be recovered. From four to five months in the year,—*i.e.*, from the middle of April to the middle of September,—this route is abandoned by traders in consequence of the flooding of the rivers and the rocky nature of the country.

---

miles); from Djau-Djoorek the road ascends the Kashka Soo pass, and then descends into the valley of the river Zooka, along which it goes as far as the Russian settlement of Slivkino, lying distant from the town of Karakol, 33 versts (22 miles); from Djau-Djoorek to Slivkino, the distance is 75 versts (50 miles).—*Author.*

During these months, caravans select the road across one of the following passes, which lead on to the plains of Alai.[1]

The roads from Fergana into Kashgaria, *vid* the Alai range, lie across the following passes, beginning with those leading across the Narwin tract,—*i.e.*, the part of the country nearest to Semiraitchensk: (i) the road across the Koogart pass; (ii) the road across the Chitta pass; and (iii) the one across the Bogooz pass. These three passes are very steep. The movements over them begin in the middle of April, and go on to the beginning of October (old style), when snow drifts begin to interrupt the communications. (iv) the road across the Belyaooli pass, which diverges from the main road across the Terek-Davan pass, near Yangi-Arwik, and again joins it at the valley of the river Kok-Soo. Along all these passes only Kirghiz and Kirghiz traders go. After these follow in the order given, (v) the pass across the Terek-Davan, of which we have already spoken. (vi) The Kolmak-Atoo pass, which is very high and steep, is followed only by Kirghiz; (vii) the Shart pass; (viii) the Archatwi; (ix) the Taldwik; (x) the Toorook. The last four lead from the province of Fergana to the valley of the Greater Alai, whence they emerge by the Toongoobooroon pass, near the Irkeshtam post, on to the caravan road across the Terek-Davan. Movements across these passes begin only from the middle of April and continue to the middle of September, or sometimes to the beginning of October (old style). During the other months there are no movements across these passes in consequence of the deep snow drifts from

[1] The distances along the route from the town of Osh to Kashgar, *vid* the Terek-Davan pass, are as follows: from the town of Osh to the entrance of the Taldwik pass 18 versts (12 miles); from the Taldwik pass to Fort Goolcha 49 versts (32⅔rds miles); from Fort Goolcha to Kwizwil-Koorgan 16½ versts (11 miles); from Kwizwil-Koorgan to Sarwi-Koochook 36 versts (24 miles); from Sarwi-Koochook to the river Kok-Soo 28 versts (18⅔rds miles); from the river Kok-Soo to the Kashgarian post of Irkeshtam 23 versts (15⅓rd miles); from Irkeshtam to Igin 20 versts (13⅓rd miles); from Igin to Fort Ooloogchat 18 versts (12 miles); from Ooloogchat to Ooksalwir 40 versts (26⅔rds miles); from Ooksalwir to Koorgashin-Kani 27 versts (18 miles); from Koorgashin-Kani to Kan-Djoogan 22 versts (14⅔rds miles); from Kan-Djoogan to Min-Yul 30 versts (20 miles); from Min-Yul to Fort Yangi Shar 44 versts (29⅓rd miles); from Fort Yangi-Shar to Kashgar 7 versts (4⅔rds miles) —*Author.*

the direction of the vast Alai plateau, and also owing to the want of fuel. Along the northern slopes of the passes there is fuel in the shape of 'archa' (the pencil cedar) in abundance; whereas, on the southern slopes and in the valley of the Alai, the only fuel to be got is dung. The best of the four passes last mentioned is the Taldwik, along which caravans of goods are sent when the communications across the Terek-Davan pass are interrupted.

Trade between Kashgaria and Fergana is almost entirely carried on by means of horses. Sometimes the smaller caravans have camels and mules. The latter animal is, however, met with in every caravan, but it is ridden only by the muleteers who precede the caravans. With regard to the route across the Terek-Davan, an insufficiency of fuel is only met with on the southern slopes of the Tian Shan. In winter time caravans take with them dried corn for fodder. In the encampments on the southern slopes the horses find enough grass to munch throughout the year. On the northern slopes, however, they only get such fodder as can be carried. Water of good quality is everywhere met with. In the warmer weather the various natural boundaries are made use of for encamping grounds and also in winter time by such nomad Kirghiz as remain in the mountains. Beyond the Terek-Davan pass, in the Kashgarian dominions, a row of small road-side forts and posts have been built by Yakoob Bek. Near these small quantities of forage can be procured. Food for the persons accompanying a caravan must, however, be carried for the whole journey, as along the road it is only possible to occasionally buy sheep.

During the winter time communications are only practicable by way of the Terek-Davan pass. This pass is often deep in snow, and then movements are impeded for several days, and sometimes for weeks together. Kara-Kirghiz of the Sartlar tribe, who roam about the pass, have the monopoly of conducting caravans across it, and for doing this they receive the principal part of their earnings. As a rule, when the pass is blocked with snow, caravans approaching from the town of Osh stop at Soofi-Koorgan, which is in the centre of the nomads of the Sartlar tribe, while those approaching from the direction of Kashgar, halt at the

Irkeshtam post, and there make arrangements with the Kara-Kirghiz for the conduct of their caravan across the pass.

The Sartlar-Kirghiz, when the snow is deep, bring out several 'yaks' (oxen of a Tibetan breed) to tread down a roadway and the caravans are then conducted over the track.

The population of Kashgaria.

Passing to a review of the population of Kashgaria, let us say some words regarding the peoples composing the aborigines of this country.

From the information we possess, it may be supposed that originally Eastern Turkestan was inhabited by peoples of Aryan origin.

From the Second Century B.C., races of Mongol descent began to pour into Eastern Turkestan. These people either drove out the aborigines of the country, or mingled with them, and so formed the peculiar race inhabiting Kashgaria. The incessant wars waged between the dwellers in Eastern Turkestan and the Chinese, left behind them that Chinese type in the admixture that now predominates in the country. This is especially noticeable in those parts of Kashgaria bordering on China. In like manner are still found traces of those Arabs who invaded Eastern Turkestan in the Eighth Century.

At the present time the purer types of Aryan people are, according to the researches of our Asian explorers, only to be found in the inaccessible mountains that border Kashgaria on the west and south-west. The Mongol race has been well maintained amongst the Kalmucks, a few of whom dwell in the neighbourhood of Karashar and in the valley of the Haidwin-Kooya.

The occupiers of the several oases compose the settled population of Kashgaria, and they have adopted for their tribal designations the names of these oases. Thus we find in the country Kashgarians, Yarkendians, Khotanese, Aksutians, Koochayans, and Toorfantians. They in reality all belong to the one ugly type into which at present enters, in a more marked manner—now the Turkish race (amongst the inhabitants of the west and south-west)—now the Mongol race (amongst the dwellers in the eastern portions of the country).

The more modern inhabitants of Kashgaria are composed of

Chinese, Doongans and emigrants from Western Turkestan, and especially from the late Khanate of Kokan. These people are called Andijantians. Hindoos are met with too, but in considerably less numbers; they appear chiefly in the character of traders. The Kara-Kirghiz compose the nomad population which occupies the mountain tract encircling Kashgaria.

The total number of the inhabitants of Kashgaria can only be determined in a very approximate manner. It may be supposed that in the whole country there are 1,200,000 souls, and that there are 65 persons to the square mile.

The settled population of Kashgaria is chiefly agricultural,—reaping their crops of wheat, barley, maize, millet, rice and cotton. By reason of the system of irrigation in vogue, very good harvests are obtained. The nomad portion of the population also adds agriculture to its flock-rearing. The crops raised by it consist chiefly of barley. Thanks to the frequent falls of rain in the mountains, all these crops are obtained without the aid of irrigation.

Industries and manufactures of Kashgaria.

Mountain industries do not occupy a very considerable place. Small quantities of coal and of metals are obtained, but, generally speaking, such industries in Kashgaria are in their infancy, and this too in spite of the known mineral wealth of the country.

Prior to the conquest of Kashgaria by Yakoob Bek, the Chinese used to engage themselves to a great extent in the working of gold and in extracting naphtha in the province of Khotan. Now it is said that the working of gold has fallen off, but even at present it brings in to the ruler of Khotan a large revenue.

The various industries of Kashgaria are, comparatively speaking, very advanced, and still they can only be considered to be mediocre. The first place is taken by the produce of 'mata' (see page 27), articles of apparel and slippers, carpets and silk. Then come the working of metals, the shaping of wood into articles for domestic use, the manufacture of agricultural implements and of arms, the working in leather. Speaking generally, with the exception of 'mata' and of other articles of dress, all these productions only suffice for the not too exorbitant needs of the local population.

Further on we shall speak of the trade of Kashgaria in greater detail. Now we will only remark, that the articles of export from Kashgaria are as follows:—Of raw goods—silk, cotton, opium, alum, sal ammoniac and sulphur: of manufactured wares—'mata,' prints, 'mashroop' (a semi-silken and very durable material), carpets, slippers and coloured linens. Of these 'mata' is exported in very considerable quantities, and forms the principal item in the export trade of the country.

Exports from Kashgaria.

They import into Kashgaria from Russia, chintzes, cloth, tinsel, iron and ironwares, pewter, tea, sugar, dyed articles of various kinds, matches, saddles, leather straps, glue, fruits and tobacco.

Imports into Kashgaria.

Russian manufactured wares predominate in the markets of all the towns that we visited, whereas the English goods that get into Kashgaria from India (*viâ* Ladak and Yarkend) cannot as yet compete with them. The specimens of English chintzes that we collected, although very pretty in design, are not lasting in quality, and are moreover faded, and far more highly priced than the same sort of Russian articles. Indian muslins are fairly well distributed throughout Kashgaria, and indeed everywhere in Central Asia. Of late the importation into Kashgaria of tea from India has greatly increased. The chief articles of export from Kashgaria to India are opium and silver in the form of bars (or 'yambs').

Condition of the people of Kashgaria.

Inasmuch as Kashgaria cannot be called a country richly endowed by nature, her inhabitants are not to be held as opulent people. But then their requirements are but very few. Their dwelling places are poor, being built of sun-burnt bricks, and without windows. They have earthen floors, and are generally of the same type of architecture as obtains throughout Central Asia. But then, on the other hand, it must be observed, that there are, for example, in our own Central Asian possessions, very many comparatively rich houses in the towns—houses, the inner walls of which are made of alabaster, and the ceilings adorned with carvings and rich modelling, whilst the exteriors are but of burnt brick. In Kashgaria the abodes of the rulers of the country present the appearance of simplicity almost approaching to poverty. The walls are not merely left unplastered, but are without white-wash. Towns thus look poor and dirty. The

Their dwellings.

absence, too, of imposing buildings like mosques, strikes the eye at first sight. Several buildings that have still remained from the times of the Arab rule, are almost the only memorials deserving of the attention in an architectural sense. The interior arrangements of most of the houses fully correspond with their exteriors. The household furniture is of the most primitive order. A few benches, low wooden tables, some wooden and earthen utensils, the whole presenting an air of poverty, and often of filth.

State of the sciences in Kashgaria.

It should be added, that if architectural science in Kashgaria remains at such a low ebb, so too are all the other sciences found to be in the same primitive condition. They are more likely to disappear than to improve. Literature in Kashgaria does not exist with the exception of some works of Bokharian and of Arab writers. After going through the greater portion of the country we nowhere saw a single bookshop.

Dress of the people of Kashgaria.

The dress of the people of Kashgaria is similar to that worn by the people of all the Central Asian Khanates. They have the same long shirt made of 'mata,' trowsers of sheepskin, the 'choga,' morocco leather slippers, and on their heads the customary turban. The comparative poverty of the inhabitants of Kashgaria is revealed to a certain extent by the sort of calico material which they wear. As a rule, on *fête* days, one will meet in the bazar of Central Asian towns, many people attired in semi-silken, silken, and even brocaded materials; whilst there are few really poor persons who do not wear chintzes. In Kashgaria, however, the number of people clad in chintzes ornamented with embroidery are very rare, whilst those dressed in silk are in the minority. In winter time, they add to the number of their garments by placing one over the other. Their chintz coverings are then wadded or covered with sheepskin or other furs.

Their food.

The daily food of the mass of the people consists of a dish of 'tooppa,' a thick kind of vermicelli, cut up with a greater or less quantity of meat, or with an admixture of grease, and 'shoorpa' or mutton broth with vegetables, to which meat is added according to the means of the good man of the house.

On festive occasions the most favourite dish of all Central Asian peoples is prepared,—*viz.*, the 'plov' or 'pilau,' a mixture of rice, mutton and spices.[1] From Chinese *cuisine*, the people of Kashgaria have learnt to make 'el-kazan,' a kind of soup prepared in a peculiar vessel shaped like a 'samovar' (or Russian tea urn), and divided into several compartments. Into the composition of this very complicated dish various sorts of meat enter, also vermicelli, pepper, cloves and laurel leaves. But this kind of food is only within the reach of rich people. From the Chinese the people of Kashgaria have also borrowed various kinds of jellies. Their drink at meals is generally water, and occasionally milk. In Kashgaria, during the autumn and winter, fruits are a great addition to the food of the population. Amongst these, the first place is taken by various sorts of melons and of water-melons, grapes, pears and apples. Of sweetmeats the confectionery imported from Russia occupies a very perceptible place. Their drink.

The language of Kashgaria is almost everywhere Turkish, and throughout the entire country all speak one and the same dialect.

This dialect is, in some respects, different to that in use in the other Central Asian Khanates. The difference partly arises in consequence of an admixture of Chinese words, and partly because different names are given to the various articles. There is yet another distinction. The Kashgarians pronounce words with scarcely opened lips and with closed teeth, and hence do not divide either one sound or one syllable from another. Amongst the Kashgarians, too, there are many words that obtain likewise amongst our own Tatars, words which are not used generally in Turkestan. An inhabitant of Tashkent would not understand these words, whilst an Orenburgh Tatar would do so, although with difficulty, in consequence of the manner of pronouncing them, and the substitution of certain letters for others. The Chinese words used by Kashgarians in conversation become mutilated in the process. The language of Kashgaria.

The names of the weights and measures that are used in the country are borrowed from the Chinese, as are also the divisions

1 'Pilau,' 'shoorpa' and 'tooppa' are the principal dishes of the inhabitants of our own Central Asian possessions. In Tashkent 'tooppa' goes by the name of 'oogra.'—*Author*.

of time. As a general rule, the difference in the dialects of Kashgaria and those of Turkestan is not so great as to prevent a Turkestanese from acquiring within the space of some weeks that which distinguishes his own patois from the Kashgarian dialect.

Religion of the people of Kashgaria.

The bulk of the population of Kashgaria professes the Mahometan religion.

General administration of the country.

Since the introduction of Yakoob Bek's power into the country, no other religion has been tolerated. Those Chinese who were allowed to live, were turned into Mahometans, for they had but the choice between death and a change of their religion. An exception was made in favour of the Kalmucks, who remained idol-worshippers. In the time of the Chinese dominion, the people were left free to follow their own faith. In those days the severity and fanatacism of the teaching of Mahomet was very skilfully circumscribed by the sons of the Celestial Empire. One of the results of their influence was the great freedom given to women. Women were even allowed to walk about in the streets with unveiled faces. Moreover, the Chinese allowed themselves great latitude in morals—a latitude which approached often to depravity, and gave license in the matter of marriage. Marriage, which can, by the law of Mahomet, be so easily dissolved in Kashgaria, was set aside with even fewer formalities; and besides this, amongst the Chinese there is a kind of marriage in vogue, which is contracted for a term—this term may be for a week only. These temporary marriages which are entered into with all the usual ceremonial rites are principally contracted by those traders who are residing but for a time in the country. Fasts are irregularly kept, and prayers are still less frequently said. Since the seizure of power by Yakoob Bek, he, in the matter of religion, has placed his heavy hand on the people. The former strict observance of religious ceremonies, such as fasts and public prayers, has again appeared. In order to insure the uninterrupted observance of religious rites, a class of clergy has been established. Women, too, have been directed to walk in public with veiled faces. The most favourite *fête* day of Asiatics—the 'baiga'—at which the men show their skill in horsemanship and their strength in personal encounters has been forbidden. Licensed houses which, during the Chinese rule, became so numerous, have been closed throughout the towns of Kashgaria. Yakoob Bek has himself given an example of devoutness and of simplicity of life, and has strictly required the like from others. He has acted as though he would turn the country into one vast monastery, in which the new monks must, whilst cultivating the soil with the sweat of their brow, give as much as possible—nay, the greater part of their earnings—into the hands of the Government, to devote to warlike impulses. Plurality of wives in Kashgaria, as in other Mussulman countries, is open to all, and yet in practice it is a custom that is within the reach of the opulent alone. Yakoob Bek, whilst leading an exceedingly chaste life, and living in no better style than any thriving native, prefers to dwell in a caravanserai rather than in a house, and maintains in his ordinary harem as many as 300 women, six of whom accompany him in all his wanderings.[1]

Severe punishments, often that by death, overtake those disobedient to the will of Yakoob Bek. Of late years, however, having succeeded in making his name terrible, this potentate has, in spite of the generally-received opinion to the contrary, very seldom resorted to capital punishment. Being in need of money, he has more frequently punished offenders and those in disgrace by declaring their possessions confiscated to the State.

Diseases prevalent in Kashgaria.

Of diseases that are most ordinarily met with in Kashgaria, the first place must be assigned to those connected with the eyes. Blindness is very common, as are also affections of the lungs, scrofula, itch, tumours and goitre. Affections of the eye are explained by the saline properties of the dust that fills the air, and by the glare arising in summer time from the salty soil. The natives attribute the frequency of goitre to the use of water. One must also call attention to those diseases which arise from the very extended use of opium. Dr. Bellew, Forsyth's colleague, has observed that such diseases impair the digestive organs and produce hypochondria and manias of various kinds. The use of opium is common to both men and women.

[1] The chaste life notwithstanding.—*Trans.*

CHAPTER II.

Division of Kashgaria in an administrative sense — Hakims — Collection of taxes, direct and indirect — Sirkars—Yuz-Bashis, Kazis and Raises — Proportion of taxation to the Circles of Kashgar, Maral-Bashi, Aksu, Bai, Koocha and Koorlia — Abuses in the collection of taxes — Dissatisfaction of the population with Yakoob Bek — Causes of the dissatisfaction of certain classes: Agricultural, Priestly and Military — Its consequences.

Division of Kashgaria in an administrative sense.

IN an administrative sense, Kashgaria is divided into ten principal, and a considerable number of lesser, units. To the principal belong the Circles of Kashgar, Yangi-Hissar, Yarkend, Khotan, Aksu, Ootch-Toorfan, Bai, Koocha, Koorlia and Koonya-Toorfan. Amongst the lesser divisions are classed the Circles, or, more properly, the Sections of Maral-Bashi, which lies on the road from Kashgar to the town of Aksu; Kalpin, situated between Kashgar and the town of Ootch-Toorfan; Ooloogchat, which embraces a part of the mountain region between the province of Fergana and Kashgaria; Kargalwik, situated on the road between the town of Yarkend and Khotan; Tash-Koorgan, which embraces the mountain region and the highlands of the Yarkend-Darya. To the same divisions belong those cultivated tracts which have an administration independent of the Circles above enumerated. Of these we only know the following, which adjoin the Circle of Kashgar, *viz*., Oopal, Tash-Malwik, Artoosh, Argoo, Tazgoon and Khan-Arwik.

Each Circle contains one town and a greater or less number of villages. Thus, to the Kashgar Circle belong the villages of Sarman, Togoozak, Koorgan, Kara-Kwir, Bish-Karam, Abat, Kwizwil-Booi, Yandam, Shaptali, Ak-Yar, Yar-Masan, Lower Yandam, Bai-Tookai, Khosh-Abat (Hosh-Abat), Faizabad, Koop-Sangir, Toopryak, Karabag, Parratch, Boovia-Kitai, Nanchook, Davlet-Bag and Kwizwil-Doobya.

To the Aksu Circle belong the villages of Koom-Bash, Sai-Arwik, Bish-Arwik, Chook-Tal, Igartchi, Asook, Baldan, Djam,

Abdali-Kavoonoosh, Taldadwi (or as some call it Taz-Langar), Sooget, Koom-Tam, Ishlantchi. The six villages last noted share the common name of Yar-Bashi.

To the Maral-Bashi Section are attached the villages of Char-Bag, Toomshook, Chadwir-Kool, Psyak-Swindwi, Yaka-Koodook.

To the Bai Circle belong the villages of Kooshtam, Davantchik, Charktchi, Kara-Bag, Yaka-Arwik, Mirza-Tam, Oon-Bashi, Djig-Dali, Yangabad, Oot-Bashi, Azgan, Yukagwir-Balwiktchi, Itartchi, Yangi-Langar, Kaptchi, Ak-Ooili, Choodja-Balwikchi, Aral, Togto-Soon, Boogan, Chigan, Kwizwil and others. The twelve villages last mentioned are grouped together and form the large settlement of Sairam, which on the maps is represented as a town.

In the Koocha Circle are included the town of Sha-Yar and the villages of Kara-Kash, Kooutchi-Makhabya, Tag-Arwik, Boostan, Pailu, Toi-Booldwi, Sooleiman, Togoos-Tama, Khodja-Kambar, Davlet-Bag, Swirak-Toograk, Shik-Tari, Kok, Goombat, Shemal-Bag, Mazar-Bag, Ootchar, Mazar-Khodja, Shoomoot, Yaka-Yarwik, Sakatchi, Oozgoon, Tagetchi, Krish and others.

To the Koorlia Circle belong the villages of Boogoor, Yangi-Hissar, Yangobad, Tesh-Arwik, Yaigi, Chimpakh, Arol Alasai (the four last mentioned form a group around Boogoor), Kargaboik, Takhtwi, Bagdjida, Maloo, Booloon, Koodook, Tala-Boolak, Ak-Sarai (the last eight are grouped around Yangi-Hissar), Doorbin, Kosh-Arwik, Toorba, Sailwik, Sai-Bag (the last five are close to the town of Koorlia), Danzil, the fort and village of Karashar and others.

The *Hakims*, or rulers of each Circle, are designated *Beks*[1] by the 'Badaulet,' and the rulers of the Sections are called *Beks, Togsobas*,[2] *Pansatis*,[3] and also *Yuz-Bashis*.[4] All the Hakims are Hakims.

[1] *Note.*—In explanation of the titles refered to in this para. the following may here suffice :—

Beh or *Beg* is a chief or governor of a province.

[2] *Togsoba* or *Toghatchi* is a headman or chief of an encampment or village. One possessed of the *togh* or *tugh*, *i. e.*, entitled to carry the insignia of military rank—a yak's tail fastened at the top of a long stick and used as the standard of a military officer of rank.—*Vide* Shaw's Sketch of the Language of Eastern Turkestan.

[3] *Pansat* or *Pansad* is the chief of five hundred.

[4] *Yuz-Bashi* is a centurion or chief of a hundred.—*Trans.*

independent the one of the other, and are directly answerable to Yakoob Bek himself. Each rules his district as though he held it on lease. He is obliged to furnish to the treasury a certain fixed quantity of produce and of money. Anything that remains over and above this quota he can keep for himself. The Hakims do not receive any personal allowance nor any State contributions towards the government of their provinces. Each ruler is, moreover, required to maintain at the expense of his Circle or Section a greater or less number of soldiers to furnish the garrisons of the towns, also a staff of police officials and postmen or messengers.

In consequence of these arrangements on the part of Yakoob Bek, the Hakims receive territorial possessions of greater or less extent either for a time or in perpetuity. Each, moreover, besides furnishing the treasury with a certain fixed quantity of grain and of money, is obliged to make yearly offerings to the 'Badaulet.' The nature and value of such tribute are strongly influenced by the good or bad state of the ruler's relations towards the donors. The gifts may consist of a large number of horses, of bales of robes, of carpets, of silken webs, of packages of tea, and of sugar, of plates containing gold and silver money or bars or ingots. The number 'nine' plays a considerable part in the amount of these gifts. It is usual, for example, to send as an offering one or several sets, of nine horses each, of nine bales of robes (or in case of the donor's poverty of only nine robes), of nine boxes or loaves of sugar, of nine 'yambs' (bars of the value of 108 roubles[1] each), &c. These offerings are either sent by the hands of accredited personages, or are personally made by the Hakims on bended knee before the 'Badaulet.'

The 'Badaulet' bestows on his Hakims in return for their gifts a greater amount of his favour than of material articles having intrinsic value. Robes of various colours, girdles and fire-arms are generally the things that he gives both to the Hakims of high rank as well as to the messengers of more humble position.

Before we speak of the administration, we had better first

[1] A rouble is worth now about 2*s*. 6*d*.—*Trans.*

explain what the duties of the several individuals, who belong to the administrative '*personnel*,' are. Let us, therefore, briefly refer to the taxes and imposts that exist in Kashgaria.

The taxes and imposts of Kashgaria.

The taxes that obtain in Kashgaria are the same as those in other Asiatic States. Amongst them the first place is occupied by the *heradj* tax. This consists of 1-10th part of the produce of the soil. Then follows the *tanap* tax on gardens, sown fields, cotton, clover and orchard produce. Each *tanap* is assessed separately, and amounts to 20 'tengas.'[1] Lastly, there is the *ziaket* tax on cattle and merchandise, amounting to about 2½ per cent.

Direct and indirect.

The *heradj, tanap* and *ziaket* are the direct taxes. Amongst the numerous indirect taxes are—

Saman-pool.—This is a *batman* (or 10 lbs. weight) of grain (generally wheat) with two sacks of straw. Now, in place of straw, money is exacted at discretion, but often to a considerable amount.

Kiyafsen.—As the tax on grain is called, which goes to recompense the tax-gatherers when they collect the several taxes. The amount of this is likewise discretionary, and depends on the greater or less degree of avarice on the part of the 'Beks' and their tax-gatherers.

Tari-Kara.—After the death of a native of the country, his property is appraised, and from 2½ to 5 per cent is taken for the use of the State.

Amongst the indirect imposts too must also be classed the demands made on the population for money, for produce, and for fuel to supply the demands of foreigners and their embassies, when these arrive at the several stages on their route through the country. Likewise the furnishing of *materiel* to meet the burdens of war, the gratuitous supply of fuel for heating soldiers' barracks, State and public buildings, and the compulsory and unrequited labour of those employed on earthworks.

Division of Circles and of Sections.

Each Circle or Section, in an administrative sense,—*i. e.*, for the collection of taxes,—is divided into a greater or less number of

[1] A 'tenga' = 10 Russian 'kopaikas;' and a 'kopaika' = about 1⅛th farthing. —*Trans.*

parts, 'volosts,' or 'aksakalstvas,' and each of these contains one or more villages.

The 'Sirkars' and the 'Yuz-Bashis.'

In the 'volosts' the principal official personages are the *Sirkars* and the *Yuz-Bashis.*

Duties of the 'Sirkar.'

The duties of the *Sirkar* are to collect, to hold, and to account to the treasury for the *heradj* imposts. He likewise superintends the State victualling stores, from which he issues to the various troops on the march the necessary provisions and forage. This system is pursued by means of contracts entered into with the *Hakims.*

Duties of the 'Yuz-Bashis.'

The *Yuz-Bashis* see to the collection of the *ziaket* tax and to all the indirect taxes, with the exception of the *saman-pool* and *kiyafsen,* with which the *Sirkar* only is concerned. On the *Yuz-Bashis* are imposed the maintenance of order in their villages, the keeping up and repairing of the roads, the reception of official personages and of troops, the assigning to these of halting-places, the collection from the people of the requisite carriage for troops, and the making over of this and of other requirements to the military authorities.

Every Hakim has attached to his suite one *principal Sirkar* and several *Mirzas* (secretaries or writers).

As we have said above, the collection of the *heradj* and *ziaket* taxes is carried out in each 'volost' by the local officials, *viz.,* the *Sirkars* and *Yuz-Bashis.* The collection of the *tanap* tax, on the other hand, is under the immediate superintendence of the Hakims themselves, and for the purpose of collecting this tax the Hakims send forth their *Mirzas.*

The *heradj* tax is either farmed out to the *Sirkars,* who are then obliged to furnish to the treasury a certain fixed quantity of grain, apart from the harvest gathering, or its value in money, or the *Sirkars* themselves send into the treasury yearly an amount of grain reckoned in connection with the harvest supply.

In the former case, a person is appointed to the office of *Sirkar* by the *Hakim.* In the latter, the *Sirkar* must be an inhabitant of the place, from whom the *Hakim* will require a guarantee for the fulfilment of his duties, and a security that the full amount of the fixed contribution is exacted from the more wealthy inhabitants.

The administration of justice in Kashgaria is entrusted to *Kazis*, who are appointed by Yakoob Bek. There is one or more *Kazi* for each of the several 'volosts' according to the density of the population and the extent of country embraced in the particular 'volost.' With each *Kazi* is associated a *Mooftia*, or interpreter of the law. And in each settlement there is at least one *Rais*, who is selected from among the most moral and devout of the local inhabitants. The rights of these *Raises* are very extensive, and they are exercised and extended in the majority of cases, so as to bear on the population not less heavily than does the latitude allowed to the *Sirkars* and *Yuz-Bashis* in the collection of taxes. According to the spirit of the law and to custom, the *Rais* is the guardian of the public morals, and of the purity of the ceremonials of the Mahometan religion.

Administration of justice in Kashgaria.

Armed with the symbol of his power—a knotted rope—the *Rais* visits the people at any hour of the day or night, since he has the right to enter every house. Men, women and children are all subject to his orders. He has to see that there are no dissensions in families; that every one, children included, regularly attends the appointed prayers; that the children are sent to school; that just weights and measures are adhered to in the shops; that the articles sold in the bazars are of good quality; that the women do not appear in the public streets with unveiled faces; and that by eight or nine o'clock at night every member of a household has gone off to bed. The *Rais* can punish offenders, or even those suspected of crime, with stripes on the back, shoulders and head. For certain offences, which are specified, a fixed number of stripes are awarded. For example, a weaver, who sells *mata* in pieces of less than the usual length, will receive 39 stripes.

The measured progress of the *Rais* along the streets, attended by the police, calls forth a panic amongst those whom he meets. The men, as a rule, stand still with lowered head and wait until the strict guardian of the law has passed by; women and children, on the other hand, on beholding the dreaded *Rais*, rush off anywhere in headlong flight. Every person so met, even if he shall have committed no fault, and provided he is not of the richer sort, may certainly reckon on the receipt of several blows with the thong carried by the *Rais*.

Religion and education in Kashgaria.

The ceremonials of religion are carried on in the mosques by *Moollahs.* These persons are likewise appointed by the 'Badaulet.' The individuals chosen are generally taken from the higher classes at the colleges. Failing these, they are selected from the most religious and respected individuals amongst the local inhabitants. The schools attached to the mosques are of two kinds,—the lower or *Maktab,* and the higher or *Madressas.* The teachers in the former are styled *khalifas,* and in the latter *moodarisses.*

At the head-quarters of every Circle, in addition to the officials above referred to, there reside a *Kazi-oskar,* or special judge appointed to try persons in the military profession; a *Kazi-Kazyan,* or elder of all the *Kazis;* and a *Kazi-Rais,* or elder of all the *Raises.* These three officials are personally appointed by Yakoob Bek, and are independent of the Hakims. Not one of all the personages who have been mentioned, beginning with the Hakim, receives from the State any stipend. The Hakims remunerate themselves out of the taxes which they collect, and judging from the nature of the presents which they find it possible to make to the 'Badaulet,' this remuneration must be something very considerable.

The remuneration of the several officials in Kashgaria.

Those *Sirkars* to whom the *heradj* tax is farmed out, receive no remuneration. But the *Sirkars* who collect the same tax in conjunction with the harvest, have the right to a *kiafsen,—i. e.,* to a certain portion of grain, as a remuneration for themselves and for those assistants associated with them in the collection of the tax.

The *Yuz-Bashis,* who are chosen from amongst the local inhabitants, as a rule, own land on the spot where they are serving, and in that case they make the people attend to it without payment.

The *Kazis* and *Mooftias* exact from litigants or offenders a certain fixed remuneration for every case that they settle. This remuneration, beginning at 20 kopaikas,[1] goes up to figures that are very large. Those police officials, too, who attend on the *Kazi,* and all persons summoned to his Court, also demand from the litigants or offenders a stipulated amount.

[1] About 6*d.* in English money.—*Trans.*

The *Raises* are likewise in the habit of accepting voluntary contributions made to induce them to be less strict. These offerings are sometimes very large. Besides this, the *Rais*, who officiates at all funerals, enjoys the right of taking for himself the best robe of the deceased which, according to custom, is always placed on the body during the ceremonies prior to interment.

The remuneration of the *Moollahs* likewise falls on the people, and consists of voluntary offerings, of payments made for the instruction of children in the schools, if, that is, the school is in charge of a *Moollah*, and of fixed sums for conducting marriages, making out divorces, attending funerals, and the like.

The remuneration of the school teachers depends on the number of their pupils and the degree of wealth of the pupils' parents. Generally speaking, it is very little, and is paid partly in kind and partly in money.

Character of the style maintained by the Ruler and by the officials of Kashgaria.

Notwithstanding that none of the official personages of Kashgaria are in the receipt of any fixed income, they live, as compared with the people around them, in a very affluent way.

With regard to the ruler himself and the modesty of his own personal requirements, Yakoob Bek may serve as an example not only to all Asiatic potentates, but to certain of his own Beks. His residences are simple even to poverty. His own dress and food and that of all his followers are of the same quality. His sole extravagance appears to take the form of a large harem, in which there are three hundred women. His marching harem, as has been said above, consists of six wives. The court display of Yakoob Bek little resembles in its limited extent that kept up by either the Amir of Bokhara or the late Khan of Kokan.

Yakoob Bek's method of transacting business and of giving his orders.

All the arrangements for the administration of the country and all his correspondence, Yakoob Bek carries on through his *chancellerie*, which is composed of four *Mirzas*. These *Mirzas* serve Yakoob Bek both as secretaries and as clerks. One of them, Makhsoom by name, was sent as envoy to Tashkent in the year 1872, and enjoyed the greatest influence in affairs.

On every possible occasion, Yakoob Bek's orders are issued verbally.

Every morning at dawn, the ruler takes his accustomed seat on a carpet placed near the door of his audience chamber.

All the correspondence which has been received during the previous day, he peruses line by line. After reading through in this way every paper, he immediately dictates his orders, and these are written out by the *Mirza* on the back of each paper. Every day mounted couriers, who ride at a speed of from 140 to 200 versts (from 90 to 130 miles) in the 24 hours, carry the several papers to their destination. At every 40 or 50 versts (26 to 30 miles) the couriers change horses at stations built for the purpose.

The swiftness of Yakoob Bek's decisions and their severity are known to all, and hence all his subjects learn to tremble at his name even when they are hundreds of versts away.

The amount of taxes in kind paid by the several Circles or Sections.

I only know with approximate accuracy the amount of the taxes in kind paid by the several Circles or Sections which I visited (from Kashgar *viâ* Aksu, Bai, Koocha, Koorlia and Karashar). Of the amount of the taxes paid in the Yarkend and Khotan Circles I have not even approximate information.

Nevertheless, the question as to the paying powers and resources of the population of Kashgaria is so important and so interesting that I produce below, in spite of its incompleteness, all the information which we collected on the subject.

Kashgar Circle.

We will begin with the Kashgar Circle. The Hakim of this Circle, Aldash-Datkha, a Tashkent merchant, sent in to the treasury from the town of Kashgar and from all the above enumerated villages of the same Circle a *heradj* tax of 900,000 *chariks*[1] of different grains, chiefly maize and wheat.

Of this quantity the amounts that came from the villages lying along the main road to Maral-Bashi were as follows:—

From Shaptali, with its 600 families, 2,000 *chariks*. From the village of Faizabad, with from 400 to 500 families, 60,000 *chariks*.

[1] According to calculations which we made in the town of Aksu, the weight of a *charik* = 24 lbs. wheat, or 26 lbs. of maize, or 25 lbs. of barley.—*Author*.

Mr. Shaw, in his vocabulary of the language of Eastern Turkestan, says: "There are three distinct *characks* in Eastern Turkestan,—one used for raw silk, certain colouring materials, spices, tea, &c.: it is equal to 4 *jings* or 5 *lbs*. The second is used for all manner of goods, and is called *ashligtashi*, 'food weight,' also *tört-tash*, 'four weights:' it weighs 12¼ *jings* or nearly 16 *lbs*. This is distinguished from the third sort recently introduced by the Amir, which is called *besh-tash*, 'five weights,' and weighs 16 *jings* or 20 *lbs*."—*Trans*.

This village, together with that of Khanarwik, is the chief centre of the *mata* industry. From the village of Yangobad, with from 70 to 100 families, 400 *chariks*. Since the previous year Yangobad has been incorporated in the Maral-Bashi Circle.

The total amount of the *tanap* tax is not known. From certain villages, in which horticulture is more highly developed, there were collected from Bish-Karam 100,000 *tengas*;[1] from Abat, 32,000; from Togoozak, 64,000; from Koorgan, 16,000; from Kwizwil-Booi the *tanap* and *ziaket* taxes together 90,000; from Nanchook, 25,000; and from Davlet-Bag, 18,000 *tengas*. The amount of the *ziaket* tax from the same places is not known.

From the Sections that are independent of the Kashgar Circle, the collections are as follows:— Sections independent of the Kashgar Circle.

From Khan-Arwik the *heradj* tax amounts to 220,000 *chariks*, and the *ziaket* and *tanap* taxes to 118,000 *tengas*. The taxes from Khan-Arwik were fixed by Yakoob Bek in favour of his eldest son, Bek-Kooli Bek, and they, therefore, do not go to the State.

From Tazgoon the *heradj* tax amounts to 90,000 *chariks*, and the *tanap* and *ziaket* to 88,000 *tengas*.

This Section consists of from 13 to 15 small settlements, which bear the common designation of Tazgoon. The Hakim of this

---

[1] Without taking into account the exchange on silver, one may reckon a Kashgar *tenga* at 10 *kopaikas*.—*Author*. Ten *kopaikas* would be equal to about 3*d*. English.—*Trans*.

Mr. Shaw, in the work previously quoted, says:—"A *tangah*, or *tenga*, consists of 25 small copper 'coins' (of Chinese make with square holes through them) called *dah-chân*, each of which is worth two *pul* (imaginary coin). The value of the *tangah* varies constantly in the bazars according to the number of them that may be given for a *kurs* (a Chinese silver ingot weighing about 2 lbs and worth about 170 rupees). Sometimes the number reaches 1,100 and sometimes falls as low as 800. The Amir of Kashgar has lately supplied the lack of small silver coinage, by issuing in the name of the Sultan of Turkey silver coins worth a *tangah* each, and called *ak-tangah* (white tangahs) after the model of the Khokan and Bokhara coins of the same name. These are current at a small premium. The Khotan *tangah* consists of 50 copper *shu-chan*, which are only slightly smaller than the Yarkend *dah-chan*. Consequently, a Khotan *tangah* is worth nearly twice as much as a Yarkend or Kashgar one." The word *tenga* is also used for the *scales* of a fish.—*Trans*.

Section is one Islam Bek, a native of Kashgar. The inhabitants are principally husbandmen, and their chief crop is maize. The population of Tazgoon amounts to about 10,000 families.[1]

Artoosh yields a *heradj* tax of 83,000 *chariks*. The amount of the *tanap* and *ziaket* taxes is not known. The principal article of industry of its inhabitants is *mata* of an inferior quality. Husbandry occupies a secondary place. The population of Artoosh is above 10,000 families.

From Tash-Malwik they collect—

A *heradj* tax of 64,000 *chariks* and a *ziaket* tax of 40,000 *tengas*. To this Section belongs the mountain region near lake Sari-Kol. Its inhabitants are for the most part Kirghiz, who pay, by means of the cattle which they possess, the *ziaket* tax to the amount above named. Their occupations are husbandry to a limited extent and digging for coal. The number of the inhabitants is not known. The Hakim of this section is Abdul Rahman-Moorza-Bardar, a Kara-Kirghiz of the Naiman tribe from the Margelan district.

In Argoo, three years ago, the *heradj* tax amounted to 48,000 *chariks*. Its inhabitants are workers in *mata* of an inferior kind. They also prepare soap, cultivate gardens, and carry on a trade with the Kirghiz. The population, according to Chinese reckoning, consists of 300 families.

Oopal produces a *heradj* tax of 80,000 *chariks*. The amount of its contributions to the *tanap* and *ziaket* taxes is not known. Its population is agricultural. The Hakim of this place is Rahim-Baba-Togsoba, an inhabitant of Pskent. On him has been conferred the right to make use of the revenue from Oopal for the maintenance of the garrisons of the forts in the mountain districts between the province of Fergana and Kashgaria.

In the Maral-Bashi Section, the *heradj* tax amounts to 40,000 *chariks*. Its population is reckoned at 3,000 families. The people of this Section are *Doolans*, a Mongol race, which migrated to Kashgaria about 150 years ago, during the Djoongar rule. The race took up its abode along the course of the rivers

[1] According to the first census carried out by the Chinese in the year 1760, there were in Tazgoon only 700 families.—*Author*.

Kashgar-Darya, Yarkend-Darya, Khotan-Darya, and in the neighbourhood of lake Lob-Nor.

Their poor little villages exist along these rivers up to this time. The Doolans are divided into three tribes: (1) The *Chash-Shirin*, who dwell along the road from the village of Chadwir-Kool to the town of Aksu and in the village of Psyak-Swindwi, which lies to the south of the main road along the river Kash-gar-Darya. They sometimes call themselves Mogols. (2) the *Bachook*, who dwell along the road from Maral-Bashi to Yarkend; and (3) the *Boogoor*, who occupy the village of Chadwir-Kool only.

The Kalpin Section brings in a *heradj* tax amounting to 14,000 *chariks*, a *tanap* tax of 20,000 *tengas*, and a *ziaket* tax of 25,000 *tengas*. It has a population of 3,000 families. The village of Kalpin stretches in a long line several versts to the north of the road from the town of Kashgar to Ootch-Toorfan, and lies close to the latter place.

The Aksu Circle yields a *heradj* tax of from 1,500,000 to 2,000,000 *chariks*, a *tanap* tax of 100,000 *tengas*, and a *ziaket* tax, from its cattle, of 60,000 *tengas*. The population of the Aksu Circle amounts to 30,000 families. **Aksu Circle.**

The Bai Circle brings in a *heradj* tax of 80,000 *chariks*, a *tanap* tax of from 26,000 to 30,000 *tengas*, and a *ziaket* tax of from 45,000 to 50,000 *tengas*.[1] The population of the town of Bai is 390 families. That of the village of Sairam and of the adjoining hamlets is 800 families. **Bai Circle.**

The Koocha Circle yields a *heradj* tax of 250,000 *chariks*, a *tanap* tax of 70,000 *tengas*, and a *ziaket* tax of 150,000 *tengas*. Into these figures enter the same taxes from the town of Sha-Yar. **Koocha Circle.**

The Koorlia Circle gives a *heradj* tax of 200,000 *chariks*, a *tanap* tax of 120,000 *tengas*, and a *ziaket* tax of 150,000 *tengas*. To these figures must be added the contributions from the village of Boogoor and of the neighbouring hamlets—a *heradj* tax of 40,000 *chariks*, a *tanap* tax of 20,000 *tengas*, a *ziaket* tax of 25,000 *tengas*. The population of the Koorlia Circle is 2,000 families. **Koorlia Circle.**

[1] Of this quantity the yield of the village of Sairam and the surrounding hamlets is as follows: *heradj* tax 30,000 *chariks*; *tanap* tax from 13,000 to 14,000 *chariks*; *ziaket* tax 14,000 *tengas*.—*Author.*

The village of Yangi-Hissar and the settlements belonging to it contribute a *heradj* tax of 42,000 *chariks*, a *tanap* tax of from 18,000 to 21,000 *tengas*, and a *ziaket* tax, from cattle, of 60,000 *tengas*. The population is 2,000 families. The inhabitants are very rich in cattle in consequence of the excellent grazing grounds that they own.

The village of Charchi yields a *heradj* tax of 1,500 *chariks* and a *tanap* tax of 600 *tengas*. Its population amounts to 22 houses.

The village of Doorbin brings in a *heradj* tax of 12,000 *chariks*, and a *tanap* tax of 6,000 *tengas*. Its population amounts to 300 houses.

The town of Koorlia with the villages belonging to it yields a *heradj* tax of 85,000 *chariks*, a *tanap* tax of 65,000 *tengas*, and a *ziaket* tax of from 45 to 48,000 *tengas*.

Tax-paying capabilities of the population of Kashgaria not shown by the figures above given.

But the figures above given do not express to the full either the tax-paying capabilities of the population, or the actual quantity of money and of grain collected from the inhabitants of Kashgaria.

Official abuses.

The abuses of the officials who are employed to collect the taxes are the normal state of affairs not only in Kashgaria but in all the other independent Asiatic States. The people are accustomed to them. They bear them patiently as long as they can pay such unjust demands. On the other hand, the officials, to whom the general administration of the country is farmed out, consider that they have the right to squeeze from the land in their charge as much as possible over and above their legitimate income.

Abuses in the collection of taxes are then what obtain generally. The offenders rank throughout all the persons engaged in the administration of the country, beginning with the *Beks* and ending with the *Sirkars* and *Yuz-Bashis* subordinate to them.

Thanks to this sort of oppression, the taxes lie like a heavy burden on the impecunious masses. The more well-to-do persons do indeed manage somehow or other (generally by means of bribes), and, having got round the tax-collector, contrive to contribute to the treasury less than their poorer neighbours.

Of the innumerable indirect taxes nothing has been said. Some persons succeed either in evading payment of these altogether or in paying but a small percentage on their earnings from crops or from cattle. Thus, whilst from the richer folk the *heradj* tax, in place of yielding 10 per cent., will yield but 2 per cent., from the poorer it will amount to 20 per cent. and more. The more indigent classes are in this way made to contribute 75 per cent. of the whole taxation of the country, since the same remark applies to taxes of all kinds. Now and then the indirect taxes lie as heavily on the people as the direct taxes, and this because the discretion exercised in their collection is wider. For example, the amount of the remunerations exacted by the tax-gatherers (on account of *kiyafsen* and *saman-pool*) entirely depends on the extent of their avarice, since by no law is a measure put to their demands. But in a country like Kashgaria, even were a law for the purpose in force, the collectors of the taxes would not be kept within it. When a demand is made for carriage for army transport purposes, those who possess horses in large numbers contrive to buy the officials off, and then the poor people are obliged to give up their last animal in order to make up the number that may be required.

The indirect taxes.

In like manner, when a foreign embassy is in progress through the country, all the villages *en route* are obliged to furnish gratis fuel, forage, cattle, and whatever provisions that may be necessary in the way of bread, eggs, sweetmeats, tea, sugar, &c. All such articles are of course exacted in a two-fold or three-fold proportion, and the overplus is sold by the native officials, who are attached to the embassy in question,—it may be to the very persons from whom the articles were in the first instance taken.

Every additional impost of taxes on the part of Yakoob Bek is made not with reference to the tax-paying capabilities of his subjects, but to incidental causes arising principally out of war expenses.

The Beks, on the receipt of orders to furnish a supplementary amount of grain or, oftener, of money from their respective Circles, are seldom themselves out of pocket. After ordering several times over the amount of the grain or of the money demanded, they put the surplus in their pockets. The other members of the administration follow their example. The people alone are the sufferers, since they have to pay at least double what has been called for by the ruler of the country.

Condition of affairs in Kashgaria.

Let us now try to form a conclusion as to how far the existing order of things in Kashgaria may be considered durable, and to what degree Yakoob Bek succeeded in gaining the sympathy of the people during the last thirteen years of his rule.

Past history of the country.

We will first examine that which Kashgaria needs above everything. We shall at the same time see what the history of the country was many years before the Christian era. The dominion of the ruling race in Kashgaria has given place to that of another very many times,—Chinese have ousted Mongols and Mongols again Chinese. Then have followed Arabs and again Mongols, who have once more given way to Djoongarians and to Chinese.

In the intervals, between the inroads of the peoples abovementioned, internal dissensions have divided the country against itself. The Circles of Kashgar, Yarkend, Khotan, Aksu and others have at one time become independent each of the other, and have again fallen under the yoke of one another in turn.

The struggle for political supremacy gave way, in the Sixteenth Century, to religious strife between the two parties under the Khodjas, who then made their appearance in the country—the *white mountaineers* and the *black mountaineers*. This strife divided the country into two hostile camps, and it was owing to this state of things that Kashgaria fell so easily under the power first of the Djoongarians and then of the Chinese. The period of Chinese sovereignty from 1760 to 1825, uninterrupted as it was by *émeutes* of any kind, gave some repose to the country, and with that repose the condition of the population improved.

The mistakes made by the Chinese, and their weakness and inability to gain, if not the sympathy, at least the respect and fear of the people whom they had conquered, called forth the insurrection of 1825. Then began afresh the bloody period in the history of Kashgaria—a period that has not terminated up to the present time. A slight glance at the simple abstract of events which we give below will be sufficient for us to see through how many agitations Kashgaria has passed during the last fifty years. From what has been already said we can, too, perceive how much blood has been shed during those periods of agitation.

In the year 1825 there took place in Kashgaria the rising of Djengir-Tura. In 1830 there was a rebellion of the Kokan troops followed by the insurrection under Khodja Med-Yusoof. In 1847 there was the rebellion of the seven Khodjas (Katta-Tura). In 1857 occurred the insurrection of Valikhan-Tura. In 1862-63 Kashgaria rose up against the Chinese. In their insurrection the Djoongans Rashedin-Khodja, Abdoola-Khodja and Habiboolla-Khodja took part. From 1864 to 1868 the conquest of Kashgaria at the hands of Yakoob Bek was proceeding.

In 1869 Yakoob Bek marched against the rebels of the province of Sarwi-Kol.

In 1872 there was a Doongan insurrection against Yakoob Bek, which was suppressed by Yakoob Bek's son, Bek-Koolwi-Bek.

In 1876-1877 began and ended the struggle between Yakoob Bek and the Chinese. After every rising the state of the country became worse, since each rising was promoted for the sake of individuals, who succeeded only because the Chinese commanders were inefficient and their armies small and of inferior quality. After the suppression of each insurrection, the chief offenders contrived, as a rule, to get away, at least for a time, with the booty which they had acquired, whilst the people paid for the actions of their leaders with their possessions and with their lives.

The people of Kashgaria desire peace.

From this it will be understood that what the people of Kashgaria most desire is peace and the advantages of such enjoyments as may still be left to them.

This the rule of Yakoob Bek has not given them.

With regard to their demands for peace, we have already seen from the simple chronological statement of events during the past fourteen years, that Yakoob Bek did not fulfil this desire of the population; and hence for this cause alone, he called forth dissatisfaction against himself.

Dissatisfaction of the population with Yakoob Bek and its causes.

But dissatisfaction against Yakoob Bek was called forth by other causes as well. First of all, he became the ruler of Kashgaria not by the popular desire, but from being a usurper, and one who, by taking advantage of the weakness of those in authority and by gaining an influence over the army, took the power into his own hands.

We have seen above that Yakoob Bek succeeded in possessing himself of the sovereignty. But how did he labour to this end? He captured Yangi-Hissar, Yarkend and Khotan. In the last-named place he slaughtered numbers of the inhabitants and treacherously murdered the Hakims of Khotan and of Koocha—Habiboolla and Rasheddin. He destroyed also the rebel Kipchak, whom he had promised, with an oath on the Koran, to free and to send out of Kashgaria. He administered poison to Katta-Tura, observing as he did so, that his victim was not in a position to render unquestionable obedience to him, &c.

In such a way, then, did Yakoob Bek gain possession of his throne. Hence he created many bitter animosities. But his people would have forgiven all, if only, after becoming supreme ruler of the country, he had finally given them the desired peace and enabled them to obtain the rest they so much wished for, by introducing order and security for their property and labour.

But Yakoob Bek could not fulfil these expectations.

Whilst unconvinced of the durability of his sovereignty from inward causes—a sovereignty acquired at the price of the blood of many thousand inhabitants, Yakoob could be no less uncertain as to the dangers which beset Kashgaria from without.

He, therefore, made it his object to seek for the necessary security. As the best means of arriving at peace within the State he held that strong garrisons should be established in all the towns. As the best method of securing the safety of his possessions from without, he considered it wise to set in hand the extension of his border line beyond the limits that Kashgaria had ever possessed. Accordingly, he pushed his borders far into the mountains that shut in Kashgaria on the north, west and south, and built many forts and posts on all the roads leading to his country through this mountain region. On the east, whence Kashgaria was threatened with the danger of a Doongan invasion, or, after the subjugation of these people, an inroad of the Chinese, he seized the Doongan towns of Koonya-Toorfan, Ooroomchi, Manas and others, and so carried his borders far towards the east.

Thus, working to secure, by means of troops, both interior order and the safety of his kingdom, Yakoob Bek could not devote much time towards introducing order into his country; and he, therefore, established a system for the government of Kashgaria, which, whilst it was easy for himself, was at the same time most oppressive to his people.

All his provinces were farmed out, and the Hakims, who were bad tenants, began to collect from the people more than they really could afford to pay. Thus, all possibility of recovering themselves was completely withheld from the people. The minor officials, such as *Sirkars* and *Yuz-Bashis*, acted in the same way as their superiors, each thought only of his profits, and, being aware of the insecurity of his own position, endeavoured to enrich himself with all possible speed.

Let us now glance at the causes of the discontent amongst the population of Kashgaria, and let us examine each principal condition separately:—

Causes of dissatisfaction of the agricultural class.

(1.) The agricultural class, the most numerous and important in Kashgaria, could not be satisfied with the existing state of things in the country, because for their hard work they were only allowed to receive not nine-tenths (as the Mussulman law allows), but from one-fourth to half.

The orders of Yakoob Bek, as addressed to the Hakims direct, ruled that the principal part of the *heradj* tax should be paid not in kind but in money, and so the condition of the agriculturists became still further injured. The Hakims, who were always alive to their own gains, appointed prices which were far above those obtaining in the bazaar; and these, of course, quickly fell only when there was an extra supply of grain-produce.

Besides this, the greater percentage of recruits for the army came from among the agriculturists.

Of the trading class.

(2.) The trading class had likewise several well-founded grounds for dissatisfaction with Yakoob Bek. Trade in Kashgaria did not enjoy the perfect freedom that was indispensable to it. The seasons for despatching caravans across the border were appointed by Yakoob once every four months, and sometimes less frequently.

Especially of late, had they begun to restrict the despatch of caravans into Russian territory, and this because to these caravans many young people were in the habit of attaching themselves as muleteers with the object of leaving their native land for good and all. Besides this, demands were made from traders in the shape of *douceurs*. Further, they were either paid but insufficiently for their goods, or were not paid at all. Moreover, the state of trade in Kashgaria could not but be affected by the poverty of its principal dealers—the agriculturists.

The insecurity of the right of enjoying their own belongings had induced many, who had still some property left, to hide it.

Of the priestly class.

(3.) Finally, the priesthood had also sufficient reason to be dissatisfied with Yakoob Bek.

Notwithstanding his outward piety (for thirteen years he had not omitted a single prayer, and his relatives boasted of the same), Yakoob Bek, in all his quarrels with the priestly class, had acted very harshly.

The church lands, which had never paid any sort of tax, were included by Yakoob Bek in the same category as other property with regard to the payment of the *heradj* and *tanap* taxes.[1] And this, notwithstanding that the voluntary contributions of the people, burdened already with intolerable impositions in support of the priesthood, could not be otherwise than considerable.

Consequent policy of Yakoob Bek.

Thus, Yakoob Bek could never count on the sympathy of the people towards him. Knowing this very well, he, from the first day of his coming to Kashgaria, began to form around himself a party, to whose advantage it would be to support him. To this party belonged those persons from Kokan, Tashkent, and also from Kashgaria itself, who had succeeded in obtaining the goodwill of the new ruler.

To them were given all the most lucrative posts in the country. Perceiving their support, however, to be insufficient, Yakoob Bek made friends with a more powerful stay—the army.

By placing the army in a privileged position, by forming a pseudo-aristocracy of the country of members of the army, by liberally rewarding their services and by giving the first places

[1] This information requires confirmation.—*Author.*

in the administration to those persons who had served therein, Yakoob Bek could, at first, reckon on the sympathy and support of the troops. But, afterwards, the too manifest preference evinced by Yakoob Bek for exiles from Tashkent, Kokan, Afghanistan, India and other places, over recruits from amongst his own subjects, and the more recent increase of military levies, coupled with his first failure against the Chinese, all made the troops even dissatisfied with Yakoob Bek.

Indications of the breaking up of Yakoob Bek's power.

The desertions, which of late became very numerous, clearly proved what has been said. Several individuals, too, who occupied high positions in the administration, and on whose fidelity Yakoob Bek had previously always reckoned, now began to change towards him. They ceased, in fact, to believe in the star of Yakoob Bek, and they endeavoured to make off, whilst there was yet time, with the booty they had obtained.

It may be believed, then, that, by opening a war with the Chinese, Yakoob Bek, notwithstanding a few successes, only hastened his own fall.

Comparison between Yakoob Bek and other rulers in Asia.

Such, then, were the results that thirteen years of feverish activity had brought upon Kashgaria. Meanwhile, it must be undoubtedly admitted that this ruler possessed many qualities which made him stand out from amongst all the rulers of Asia.

His military accomplishments, his powers of organization, his personal bravery, his chaste life, his power of will, his iron energy in the attainment of those objects which he had marked out,—all seemed a guarantee, that, under the direction of this, by nature, richly-gifted personage, the country would obtain rest, and would recover from, and outlive, its poverty. But there are obstacles of such a kind, which so operate on a Central Asian potentate, that, even in the face of favourable qualities, a combination of political, religious, economical, and social conditions make his rule unstable, his activity but of little use, and the sovereignty, which he has founded, but of short duration.

CHAPTER III.

Trade of Kashgaria — Trade treaty with Yakoob Bek — Position of traders in Kashgaria — Russian traders — Their complaints — Currency of Kashgaria — Units of weights and measures — Trade-dues — Brokers — Foreign trade of Kashgaria — Imports into Kashgaria—Principal articles of import: chintzes, cattle, tea, iron, iron-wares, dyeing materials, cotton — Exports from Kashgaria — Disproportion between imports and exports — Exchange of Russian raw products for Kashgarian prepared goods — Danger to Russia of reciprocity in trade — Way of avoiding it — Kashgarian woollen and cotton webs — *Mata*, dyed *biaz*, printed linen, *chakmen* — Silk and silken manufactures — Robes, felts, alum — Trade with India.

Trade of Kashgaria.

THE information that we possess regarding the trade of Kashgaria relates only to later times, and begins with the consolidation of Yakoob Bek's power in the country. It corresponds also to the period of the Russian occupation of the town of Tashkent.

Russian goods penetrated into Kashgaria, and, with some exceptions, even now arrive there through the instrumentality of Russia's newly-acquired Central Asian subjects, *viz.*, Bokharian, Kokan and Tartar merchants. Those Russian traders who attempted to personally superintend the transport of their goods into Kashgaria met with an inhospitable reception, and suffered from exactions even greater than those to which the native traders were subjected.

The ruler of Kashgaria, Yakoob Bek, looked upon trade in the light of his own monopoly. He appraised goods after having inspected them himself, and took a considerable portion of them at his own prices and on credit for indefinite periods. Besides this, a portion of the imported wares passed to him, according to custom, in the form of 'offerings.' Payment for selected goods proceeded very slowly, and sometimes extended over many years. Protests on the part of the traders ended sometimes in refusal to discharge the debt, and sometimes in their imprisonment and in the confiscation of their property, and sometimes even in their death. The despatch of caravans from Kashgaria was stopped for months together. The personal freedom of the traders was subjected to restraint. Many of the first Russian merchants, who reached Kashgaria in the early part of the year 1870, suffered in a special manner. These persecutions caused the Governor-General of Turkestan to despatch a mission to Kashgaria with the object of concluding a trade-treaty with the 'Badaulet.'

An experienced and energetic officer of the General Staff, Colonel Baron Kaulbars, was placed at the head of this mission. The mission was received in 1872 by Yakoob Bek, in the town of Kashgar. In spite of innumerable difficulties, Kaulbars succeeded in inducing the 'Badaulet' to agree to the following conditions:—

Trade treaty.

"*Article I.*—To all Russian subjects, whatsoever be their religious belief, is allowed the right to travel for the purposes of trade in 'Djitwishar'[1] and in all places and towns subject to the ruler of this country, wherever they will, just as it is now allowed, and in the future will be allowed, to the inhabitants of 'Djitwishar' to trade throughout the whole of the Russian Empire. The respected ruler of 'Djitwishar' undertakes to carefully protect from danger and to guard all Russian subjects who may be found within his dominions and to extend the same protection to their caravans and to all their property generally.

"*Article II.*—Russian merchants will be allowed to have in the towns of 'Djitwishar,' if they themselves desire it, their own caravan-serais in which they shall be able to store their goods. The same right shall be enjoyed by 'Djitwishar' merchants trading in Russian towns.

"*Article III.*—In order to insure the regular progress of trade and the lawful collection of all dues, to Russian merchants will be accorded the right to have, if they wish it, in all the towns of 'Djitwishar,' trade agents (*Karavan-Bashis*). This right will also be accorded to 'Djitwishar' merchants in the towns of Russian Turkestan.

"*Article IV.*—From all goods entering 'Djitwishar' from Russian territory or entering Russian territory from 'Djitwishar,' there shall be exacted a tax of 2½ per cent. on the cost of the

[1] A name by which Yarkand-Kashgaria is often known. The word signifies the seven cities.—*Trans.*

goods. In no case shall more be demanded. This agreement will also apply to the Mussulman and 'Djitwishar' subjects of both the contracting parties.

"*Article. V.*—To Russian merchants and their caravans will be accorded a free and safe conduct throughout 'Djitwishar' territory and the possessions adjoining thereon. The same privileges will be extended to 'Djitwishar' caravans travelling through Russian territory."

Extent of the value of this treaty.

Although this treaty was never strictly adhered to by Yakoob Bek, still it brought with it some advantages to Russian traders. Later on, in proportion as external and internal affairs became worse for Yakoob Bek, he became more and more disposed to respect the interests of Russian subjects. Whilst bringing but little material advantage to our trade relations, this treaty would still possess one other importance. The non-observance of it on the part of Yakoob Bek would always afford us the pretext of going to war with him, if we desired, to extend our Central Asian possessions further to the south, towards Kashmir, or to the east towards China.

Position of traders in Kashgaria.

Russian traders.

During our stay in Kashgaria in 1876-77, we found in Kashgar a Russian agent, a Mons. Shkokoff, member of the firm of Bwikovski. This person was the sole representative of Russian commerce in the whole country. According to his statements he had sold off all the various goods which he had brought with him for ready-money without being subjected to extortion on the part of the Kashgarian authorities. But concerning his personal freedom, Mons. Shkokoff had to submit to great restraint. He was obliged to live in the caravanserai under constant supervision. He had not the right to travel to other towns from Kashgar. He even could not leave the outskirts of the town without the permission of Bek Aldash, the Governor of the Kashgar Circle. We had great difficulty in obtaining for Shkokoff permission to visit us at the house which we were occupying near Fort Yangi-Shar. Shkokoff's departure from the country was subject, moreover, to the personal will of Yakoob Bek. With regard to the Sarts and Tartars, Russian subjects and traders from Tashkent and Kokan, both Yakoob Bek and his officials, in their dealings towards them, were very exacting.

When we visited the bazars of the towns of Kashgar, Aksu, Koocha and Koorlia, the officials tried to prevent Russian merchants from speaking to us. On each occasion we had to urgently demand that such traders should be allowed to come, and we never concealed the fact that the object of their coming was to enable us to collect information with regard to trade and to their own grievances. The complaints made by almost all the traders whom we questioned were against Yakoob Bek himself, his son Bek-Kooli-Bek, and his officials generally, for failing to pay a given price, within a stipulated term, for the goods they had taken.[1]

Their complaints.

[1] As a specimen of these complaints, the following translation of two made to me will suffice:—

(*a.*) To Captain Kooropatkin of the General Staff. The petition of Doda-Baba-Bai and Mir Fazwilbaeff:

"The Hakim of Kashgar has taken from me goods to the value of 200 *tillas*" (a golden coin worth about 4 Russian roubles or 10 shillings English.—*Trans.*)

"Of that sum he has kept 80 *tillas* for himself. It is now three years since I have failed to receive from the *Datkha* (a military title) this money. Be so kind as to aid me in recovering it."

(*b.*) To the Russian Envoy. The petition of natives of Tashkent dwelling in the town of Aksu:

"We beg to inform the Envoy of high rank that it is now a year since we arrived at this place for purposes of trade, and, during that time, we have utterly failed to get away. Nowhere in any business are traders so oppressed and hindered as they are here. Five months ago one of us, the son of the merchant Mir Hamid, was taken for a soldier and attached to the suite of an official. We beg the Gracious Envoy to take us under his powerful protection.

"We yesterday conversed with your people and they noted down what we said, but we are now afraid that, after your departure, they will kill us. We request that you will take Mir Hamid's son with you to Tashkent. Signed by Mir Halwik, Mir Salikhbaeff, Mir Alim Bai, and Abdoo-Kadwir Bai."

After inquiring into the second of these petitions, I found it necessary to write a sharp letter to the *Datkha* of the town of Aksu, in which I called his attention to the condition of the trade-treaty, and I made over the petitioners to his especial solicitude, on the understanding that he would be held responsible concerning them.

With regard to the son of Mir Hamid, aged 17, the Russian subject, who had been taken as a soldier—in spite of protests and requests—I demanded his extradition and I took him with a view of sending him to Kooldja, where his father was living. Later on I learnt that all the petitioners had safely returned to Russian territory.—*Author.*

Amongst others, I was informed of many acts of oppression in the town of Kashgar.

Moolla-Yar-Mahomet, a merchant of Tashkent, complained that Bek-Kooli-Bek, the 'Badaulet's' eldest son, had taken cattle from him to the value of 2,200 *tillas,* and that for three years he had not been paid for them.

Mahomet-Omar-Mirza-Baeff complained that Aldash-Datkha, Bek of Kashgar, had taken cattle from him to the value of 800 *tillas,* and that for two years he had not been paid for them.

Besides this, I was informed, through the natives attached to the Embassy, that as many as forty agents of Tashkent and Kokan merchants were ready to make me a collective complaint; but they were prevented from doing so by the local officials, who threatened that, were a petition presented, their property would be confiscated, and they themselves killed.

The exactions for the army and for military purposes—exactions so immensurate with the resources of the country and the means of the population—pressed heavily on the traders of Kashgar. In addition to the impost of taxes on all articles of import and export, to compulsory 'offerings,' to the surrender of a portion of their property to the State, to the giving of credit for indefinite and very often for protracted periods, merchants were harassed with especial and extraordinary exactions on unforeseen occasions of want of money. And as Yakoob Bek developed his military resources, his periods of necessity occurred with greater frequency.

Thus, during our stay in Kashgaria, breech-loading cannon, rifles on the Snider system, ammunition of all kinds that were purchased by Yakoob Bek in Constantinople, were detained in Kashmir until taxes to the amount of 30 silver *yambs,* or 4,000 roubles,[1] had been paid. This money was taken by Yakoob Bek's orders from merchants and sent by 'express' messenger to Kashmir.

Similar unexpected charges had to be met very often.

As a rule, the insecurity of property and even of life in Kashgaria caused capital to be concealed and trade to be stifled.

---

[1] About £500 in English money.—*Trans*

The currency of Kashgaria is the following: *pool* or *kara-pool*,[1] a Chinese copper coin with four angular holes through the middle. In size it is larger than the Russian *2-kopaika* piece. Currency of Kashgaria.

Fifty *pools* are equal to a *tenga*,[2] which is a silver piece coined by Yakoob Bek. This coin, in size and weight, is somewhat larger than the Russian *10-kopaika* piece.

Twenty-five *tengas* are equal to a *chorvónets*,[3] or ducat, a coin which varies very much in size and value.

Forty ducats are equal to a *yamb*. *Yambs* are bars of silver of three different sizes, used by the Chinese in their monetary system. The largest size is about 4¾ lbs. in weight, and though their bazaar value is 1,100 *tengas*, they are received into the treasury for 1,000 *tengas* only.[3] In Russian money, the exchange being at the rate of 10 per cent on silver, a *yamb* would cost about 130 roubles.[4] Besides the above, they have in circulation, in Kashgaria, Bokharian and Kokan *kokanis*, a silver coin which answers to the Russian *20-kopaika* piece,[5] and *tillas*, a gold coin, worth about 4 roubles[6] in Russian money.

Although *kokanis* are equal in weight to two Kashgar *tengas*, they are nevertheless not received into the treasury except at the compulsory rate of 1½ *tengas*. Yakoob Bek, by taking advantage of this depreciation of the price, bought up *kokanis* in exchange for the *tengas* coined by himself, and recast them with his new *tengas*, thus gaining by a crafty contrivance a considerable profit.

The principal measures of weight in Kashgaria are the *djin*,[7] borrowed from the Chinese and equal to 1½ lbs.: and the *charik*,[8] which is of two sizes. There is the *charik* of 16 *djins*, or 24 lbs., and the *charik* of 12½ *djins*, or 18¾ lbs. Units of weights and measures.

[1] Shaw says that the *pool* is the 50th part of a *tenga*, and is about 5*d*. English.—*Trans.*

[2] See note, page 43.—*Trans.*

[3] See note, page 49.—*Trans.*

[4] About £16·5.—*Trans.*

[5] Worth about 6*d*.—*Trans.*

[6] About 10 shillings English.—*Trans.*

[7] Shaw says, the *djin* or *ling* is a weight equal to about 1·275 lbs.—*Trans.*

[8] Or charak, see note, page 48.—*Trans.* A *charik* of wheat weighs 24 lbs.: a *charik* of maize, 26 lbs.; and a *charik* of barley, 25 lbs.—*Author.*

All the necessaries of life are measured by the first of these, whereas imported goods, metals and liquids are weighed by the latter kind of *charik*.

The Russian *arshin* (alchin)[1] serves as a long measure. They measure with a wooden rule of about ½ arshin long.

Trade-dues.

On articles imported into Kashgaria a *ziaket* tax at the rate of 2½ per cent on the value of the goods is imposed. The articles are taken to the *ziaket* post and are there valued by merchants appointed for the purpose. They are always valued above their actual cost. Thus, goods valued at 48 ducats would be appraised at 50 ducats. The *ziaket* tax forms the heaviest item in trade expenses, and in addition to it there is a levy on goods on behalf of the proprietor or lessee of the warehouse to which the goods are taken to be valued or stored.

This charge, if a shop is hired in the serai, varies from a *yamb* to six *tengas,—i.e.*, about ¼ per cent.

Protection of goods.

For the protection of merchants' wares payment is made according to agreement.

Daily hire of labourers.

The daily hire of a labourer was, during 1876, from 35 to 40 *pools* (less than 10 *kopaikas*).[2]

Hire of shops.

The hire of shops in a caravanserai is not dear. It is about 1½ ducats a year for a square *sajen*[3] on the groundfloor.

Wholesale trade.

Wholesale trade is sometimes carried on for ready-money, but more often on credit for various periods, but even then, from various causes, as has been shown above, payment is not accurate.

Brokers.

In wholesale trade, merchants take the place of the brokers appointed by Government. The brokers' fees amount to about $\frac{1}{25}$th per cent.

Particulars as to trade in Kashgaria.

Kolesnikoff, a Tashkent merchant, who accompanied Colonel Kaulbars to Kashgaria, says in his circumstantial account[4] of the trade of that country:

---

[1] 28 inches English.—*Trans.*

[2] *i. e.*, 3*d*. English.—*Trans.*

[3] A sajen = 7 feet English.—*Trans.*

[4] *Vide* Report compiled in the "Labours of the Society for the Support of Russian Trade and Industry" for the year 1873, Part II.—*Author.*

"For sale on credit no documents are demanded. The business in question is arranged on a given word. In case of any inexactness in payment, complaint is made to the Bek. The debtor is then put in prison and his property is confiscated. The son has to answer for the father, after the father's death. This fact shows what strong ideas as to the sanctity of debt prevail amongst the natives, and how debtors can never deny their just liabilities. Hence, cases of failing to meet them are rare."

Without disputing this testimony on the part of Mons. Kolesnikoff, I would only observe that, according to my experience, traders in Kashgaria, whether Russian or Central Asian, suffer from many hindrances. Indeed, Mons. Kolesnikoff himself thus writes in an earlier passage in his account:

"On the expiration of the term agreed upon, they pay the money very irregularly. This irregularity, with almost all Asiatics, has more to do with the time than with the method of payment."

Foreign trade of Kashgaria.

The foreign trade of Kashgaria is carried on with those portions of the former Khanate of Kokan that lie adjacent to it, with too the province of Semiraitchensk, and on the south with Kashmir and Hindoostan.

I have only information as to the extent of the trade of Kashgaria for the year 1876, and this refers to the imports and exports of the country for that year.

This information has been obligingly furnished to me by the governors of the provinces adjacent to Kashgaria,—*viz.*, Fergana, Osh, Semiraitchensk, Tokmak, and Karakol. I have no particulars as to the amount of the interior trade of the country.

Imports into Kashgaria.

Let us now examine the import trade of Kashgaria.

IMPORT OF GOODS INTO KASH

From European Russia and Russian Turkestan, through the Districts of Tok

Description of Goods.	Through Tokmak.			Through Karakol.		
	Quantity	Value in Russian money.	Value in English money.	Quantity	Value in Russian money.	Value in English money.
		Roubles.	*£sterling*		*Roubles.*	*£sterling*
Russian chintzes ...	...	73,375	9,172	...	2,697	337
Red fustian	...	......	...	...	700	87
Plush	...	......	...	20 pieces	180	22
Black cloth	...	......	...	150 arshins 116⅔rds yds.	300	37
Grey cloth	...	......	...	250 arshins 583⅓rd yds.	250	31
Iron, wrought and cast, and iron-wares	...	9,085	1,135	...	......	...
Pewter and tin ...	...	......	...	...	......	...
Tea	...	30,800	3,850	...	......	...
Sugar	...	2,085	260	48 poods 1,728 lbs.	940	117
Tobacco	...	......	...	...	......	...
Dyeing materials ...	...	......	...	...	......	...
Pepper	...	......	...	...	......	...
Matches, brimstone and gall-nuts ...	...	......	...	...	......	...
Pistachio nuts ...	...	......	...	...	......	...
Dried apricots and grapes	...	......	...	...	......	...
Honey ...	60 poods 2,160 lbs.	300	37	...	......	...
Cotton	...	......	...	...	......	...
Leather straps ...	...	......	...	...	......	...
Saddles	...	......	...	...	......	...
Tinsel	...	......	...	...	......	...
Ghee	...	......	...	...	......	...
Coral	...	......	...	...	......	...
Miscellaneous goods ...	...	24,000	3,000	...	......	...
Sheep	22,000 hd	50,000	6,250	...	......	...
Total	...	189,645	£23,705	...	5,067	£633
Percentage of each district	...	76½ %	...	...	2%	...

GARIA DURING THE YEAR 1876.

mak, Karakol and Osh, and the Provinces of Semiraitchensk and Fergana.

Through Osh.			Sum-total in Russian money.	Sum-total in English money.	Percentage.
Quantity.	Value in Russian money.	Value in English money.			
Horse-loads.	*Roubles.*	*£ sterling*	*Roubles.*	*£ sterling.*	
132	30,480	3,810	106,552	13,319	43%
......	......	......	700	87	...
......	......	......	180	22	...
......	......	......	300	37	...
......	......	......	250	31	...
121½	3,124	390	12,209	1,525	5%
14	900	112	900	112	...
......	......	......	30,800	3,850	12½%
18	3,180	397	6,205	775	2½%
119	1,790	223	1,790	223	...
228½	4,900	612	4,900	612	2%
14	1,120	140	1,120	140	...
38	1,771	221	1,771	221	...
11	295	37	295	37	...
10	200	25	200	25	...
......	......	......	300	37	...
104½	2,120	265	2,120	265	...
5	310	38	310	38	...
27½	2,120	285	2,120	285	...
4	400	50	400	50	...
29½	336	42	336	42	...
2	310	38	310	38	...
......	......	......	24,000	3,000	9½%
......	......	......	50,000	6,250	20½%
......	53,356	£6,669	248,068	£31,008	95%
......	21½%	......	......	......	100%

By examining the tabulated statement on the previous page, it is seen, that the following is the percentage of some of the products named—

Russian chintzes	43	per cent.
Sheep	20½	„
Tea	12½	„
Iron and iron-wares	5	„
Sugar	2½	„
Dyeing materials...	2	„
The percentage of miscellaneous goods is ...	9½	„
And the percentage of the rest of the goods amounts to less than 1 per cent, but collectively to	5	„
Total ...	100	per cent.

Chintzes.

Chintzes.—Generally speaking, this class of Russian manufactures has a better sale in Kashgaria than the English kinds. The latter are a little dearer than the Russian; whereas in quality they are inferior. English chintz fades soon and is not durable, being too soft in texture. Hence it does not please the natives, who are very fond of the rustling of a new dress.

There are many inferior kinds of chintz in circulation. The average kinds come from the manufactories of Napolkoff, Graitchin, Karetnikoff, Goraylin, Razorenwei, Fokin, Mindovski and Kaloojski. The best specimens, such as those which come from Tretyakoff's manufactory and from the manufactories of Tver, are not in the market.

The price in Kashgaria for chintzes of an inferior kind is from 2 to 2½ Kashgarian ducats[1] for a piece of 42 *arshins.*[2]

The crimson chintzes of Baranoff, Yelagin, Boorkoff and Zimin sell at the following rates: For a piece of 50 *arshins*[2] from 4½ to 5½ ducats, *i. e.*, from 11¼ to 13¾ roubles. The dearer chintzes have to yield in price to the less expensive. Cotton

[1] *i. e.*, from 5 roubles to 6¼: a Kashgarian ducat = 25 *tengas* = 2½ roubles. See page 65. In Tashkent a piece of chintz of the same description would cost 6 roubles = 15 shillings.—*Author.*

[2] About 32 yds. 1 ft. and 38 yds. 2 ft. 8 inches respectively.

handkerchiefs have but little sale. Calico, rep and satin sell badly. Casinette (?) has to be sold for half its value. Ticking has a good market. Smooth ticking of inferior quality fetches the same price as chintz. Sheremetieff's ticking sells from 2½ to 3 ducats for a piece of 40 *arshins*; but not many people will buy this kind of material as they consider its price too high.

Russian woollen goods have no sale. Cloth sells badly. A piece of *drap-de-dame*, 22 *arshins* long, costs from 8 to 13 ducats. Pure cloth sells at from 15 to 20 ducats for a piece.

Cattle.—The scarcity of cattle in Kashgaria is very great. The Kashgarian *settled* inhabitants depend for their supplies on the nomad tribes, who furnish them with horses and also with sheep. The figures in the tabulated statement on the previous page relate only to the exportation of sheep from the Tokmak and Vairnoye districts. The cattle that are driven into Kashgaria from the Karakol and Osh districts bordering thereon, and from the mountain region encircling Kashgaria on the south-west, cannot be reckoned. Cattle.

Tea.—Prior to the rebellion in Eastern Turkestan against the Chinese rule,—*i.e.*, prior to the year 1864,—the people of Kashgaria received their tea from the Chinese provinces along the great trade route, through Landjei-Foo, Hami, Koonya-Toorfan, Karashar and Aksu, and so on to Kashgar and beyond to Yarkend and Khotan. But, on the commencement of the insurrection, trade relations were broken off, and with them the transport of tea ceased. Tea.

At first the people who had become accustomed to the use of tea, indented on the large stores collected by the Chinese. They then began to turn to other sources of supply. In place of tea they began to use the leaves of the *surrogatwi*, a plant which grows in Kashgaria. The leaves thus brought into use obtained the name of the locality in which the plant was found. Thus we find the designation Khotan tea and Koocha tea. The infusion in question is drunk with milk, salt and butter. Afterwards tea was imported into Kashgaria from two quarters: (i) from the province of Semiraitchensk (and latterly from Kooldja) viâ Forts Narwin and Chakmak to the town of Kashgar; (ii) from India *viâ* Ladak to Yarkend, and so on to Kashgar.

The tea received from India is of two kinds: Chinese tea imported into India and tea grown in India itself. The latter has for us, Russians, the greater interest, since it has begun to penetrate not only into Kashgaria, but is smuggled also into our own Central Asian possessions to the great disturbance of Russian tea traders. It must be observed that, for the last fifteen years,—*i.e.*, from the time of the rebellion in Eastern Turkestan,—the tea trade in that country has been in an abnormal condition. Wholesale merchants in Tashkent have in their stores Canton tea, which, before they received it, came by way of India, through the Suez Canal, to Odessa, and was then carried to Tashkent and even to Kooldja. It is evident that teas following such a route and paying dues all the way along cannot compete with teas of Indian growth, which, though inferior in quality, are cheaper and not subjected to various dues.

We see from the tabulated statement on the previous page, that the tea imported from Semiraitchensk (*viâ* Vairnoye, Narwin and Chakmak) amounted in value to 30,800 roubles (£3,850) and formed 12 per cent of the entire imports. It may be supposed, however, that the cost of the tea consumed in Kashgaria would amount to a sum several times larger. According to the calculation (probably somewhat exaggerated) of Russian merchants[1] trading to Tashkent and Kokan, on the subject of the extension of the tea trade throughout the peoples of Central Asia, a family, consisting of father, mother, and two children, would require monthly one lb. of tea; of this the man would consume $\frac{5}{8}$ths and his wife and children $\frac{3}{8}$ths. But supposing that the mass of the population of Kashgaria was to remain satisfied with its own *surrogatwi* tea, and that only 200,000 persons were to consume tea imported in the above proportion, we should find that the annual requirements of the country would amount to 15,000 *poods* (540,000 lbs. English). Reckoning the cost of this at 30 roubles a *pood*, the value of the tea imported would amount to 450,000 roubles (£56,250), or nearly fifteen times the value of the tea which now passes across the Russian border.

---

[1] Messrs. Diyatchkoff, Fedoroff and others.—*Author*.

We found in the bazaars of Kashgaria the following sorts of tea :

Chinese Teas.	*Whence received*	*Quantity.*	*Value.*
1. Kwirma tea ...	Vairnoye ..	4 poods ...	70 ducats.
2. Koomwish tea ...	Ditto ...	1 pood ...	From 55 to 62 roubles.
3. Koomwish green tea (This kind, owing to its high price, is but little consumed.)	Ditto ...	4 poods ...	103 ducats.
4. Ak tea ...	Ditto ...	4 " ...	64 "
5. Ditto ..	Ditto ...	1 pood ...	22 "
6. Do., green (This kind most resembles tea of the same name imported from India; see No. 14, under the head of Indian teas.)	Ditto ...	4 poods ...	96 "
7. At-Bash tea (This kind is most in use. It is drunk with milk.)	Ditto ...	60 djins ...	19 "
The same kind from Kooldja.	Ditto ...	3 poods ...	20 "
8. Djainak tea ...	Ditto ...	4 " ...	36 "
9. Ak-Kooiruk (a green tea, one of the most in use).	Ditto ...	1 pood ...	16 "
10. Shoovei tea ...	Ditto ...	1 " ...	17 "
11. Goora (a green tea)	Ditto ...	1 " ...	48 roubles.
12. Alma tea ...	Ditto ...	1 " ...	9 ducats.
13. Takhta tea ...	Ditto ...	1 brick of 7½ lbs.	3½ roubles.
Indian teas.[1]			
14. Ak tea ...	Ditto ...	4 poods ...	95 ducats.
15. Ditto ...	Ditto ...	4 " ...	92 "
16. Ditto ...	Ditto ...	1 pood ...	20½ "
17. Yakhan tea (coloured).	Ditto ...	4 poods ...	80 "
18. Farengi tea (very much used).	Ditto ...	4 " ...	75 "
19. Goora tea ...	Ditto ...	4 " ...	70 "
20. Balyadoor tea ...	Ditto ...	4 " ...	70 "
21. Zira tea ...	Ditto ...	4 " ...	62 "
Surrogatwi tea—Khotan and Koocha growths. These are drunk with milk and salt, and are locally prepared.	Ditto ...	1 lb ...	1 tenga.

[1] Specimens of all these teas can be obtained in the Tashkent Museum. It is very probable that amongst them are various sorts of Chinese growths which have been brought through India.—*Author.*

With the final return of Kashgaria into the hands of the Chinese, a trade route viâ Hami has again been opened, and along this, tea, direct from the provinces of the Celestial Empire, is once more making its appearance. This tea must not only drive out that which is imported by Vairnoye and from India, but it should find its way through the Terek-Davan pass to the Province of Fergana, and by Forts Chakmak and Narwin to Semiraitchensk. Then it would, in all probability, supplant the tea procured by way of Odessa and even the Kiyakhta[1] tea, which goes to Moscow before it is distributed over Central Asia. Tea of Indian growth, however cheap it may be, is less advantageous to us than the Chinese article. At present, in exchange for tea we dispose of our manufactures, especially cloth, to China, whilst for Indian tea cash exclusively must be paid. Unfortunately of late our trade relations with China have become so bad that, if we do not adopt measures, China will disappear altogether as a market for our wares, and for China tea we shall then have to pay exclusively in hard cash.

Iron, wrought and cast, and iron wares.

Iron, wrought and cast, and iron-wares are imported in but relatively small quantities. In the local manufactories, one can never get iron of a sufficiently good quality. Russian iron is brought from Vairnoye in rods and hoops, and these are converted into various articles on the spot. Kettles and tea-pots are made of cast-iron. Articles of the same sort made in the town of Koocha compete with those obtained in the other cities of Kashgaria.

Dyeing materials.

Dyeing materials for colouring *mata*. The manufacture is very large in Kashgaria, and for dyeing silken and semi-silken materials, the following dyes are used:

Neel (indigo).—This is procured from India, and is in very general use.

Ferengi rang (fooksin) and kershes (cochineal).—These are imported from Russia. The last is used exclusively for dyeing silken webs. It is to be found in every bazaar, and its shades are varied. The price of cochineal of a dark purple colour is from 16 to 18 ducats a pood. That of a grey colour is from 14 to 16 ducats a pood.

Gallnuts are imported from Badakhshan, and are used as a corrosive. A *djin* costs 10 *tengas*.

---

[1] Kiyakhta tea is Chinese tea sent overland *viâ* Kiyakhta into Russia. Abroad it is called Russian tea to distinguish it from the Canton tea that passes into Europe by the sea route.—*Trans.*

Madder is received from Fergana. From the tabulated statement on the previous page it will be seen that, during the year 1876, 4,900 roubles worth of this dye were imported. Madder roots or powdered madder sells at the rate of 64 *pool* for 1 *djin*.

Sandal is imported from Russia. The price for 8 *poods* is from 16 to 20 ducats. It is imported in chips, which are made up in the neighbourhood of Kazan. It becomes dry during its transport and is, therefore, cheaper on reaching its destination.

It should be here stated that all the dyeing materials of local manufacture were found in the bazaars.

Kara-gool, the flower of the black mallow, is grown in the gardens of the country, and yields a black dye. 1 *djin* costs 1 *tenga* and 14 *pool*.

Sophera Japonica (Tookhmiak) is procured from Yangi-Hissar. It yields a yellow dye.

Chaimak grows in Kashgaria. It also yields a yellow dye. 1 *djin* costs 1 *tenga*.

Doya is extracted from the Tamarisk shrub. In combination with alum it yields a red dye. 1 *djin* costs 1 *tenga*.

Alum is used as a corrosive. Further on we shall see that it forms an important article of export into Russian territory.

Cotton.

Of all the articles noted in the tabulated statement on the previous page, besides those we have already referred to in detail, let us turn our attention to the *cotton*, of which 104½ horse-loads, of a value of 2,120 roubles (£262), were imported.

This import, notwithstanding its smallness, is not casual, for the Khanate of Kokan very frequently furnishes Kashgaria with cotton, because the crops of this material raised in Aksu and Koonya-Toorfan do not suffice for the extensive *mata* industries centred in the neighbourhood of Kashgar. Thus, Kashgaria appears in the light of our rival, although not at present a dangerous one, in the question of the raw material from our own Central Asian possessions which it receives in exchange for other goods, for we also are workers in *mata* as an article of dress for our Central Asian subjects.

Of the sum-total of 248,000 roubles (£31,000) under the head of imports into Kashgaria, the following is the percentage for the several districts through which these imports pass:—

The Tokmak District ...	76½ per cent.	100 per cent.
" Osh " ...	21½ "	
" Karakol " ...	2 "	

EXPORT OF GOODS FROM KASH

To Russian Turkestan and to Russia in Europe, through the Districts of Tok

Description of Goods.	Through Tokmak.			Through Karakol.		
	Quantity.	Value in Russian money.	Value in English money.	Quantity.	Value in Russian money.	Value in English money.
		Roubles.	*£ sterling.*			
Silk of the highest quality.	12 poods. 432 lbs.	1,800	225	......	......	......
Silk of medium quality.	......	......	......	......	......	......
Silk of inferior quality.	......	......	......	......	......	......
White *mata* (a cotton web, also *biaz* and *doba*).	1,606,209 pieces.[1]	861,315	107,664	87,600 pcs.[1]	31,740	3,967
Mashroop (a semi-silken and very durable material).	5,237 pieces.[1]	9,352	1,169	830 pcs.[1]	1,310	163
Robes	15,327	43,345	5,418	1,770	4,250	531
Carpets	603	10,315	1,289	46	170	21
Printed linen	1,910 pcs.[1]	2,100	262	......	......	......
Russian chintz ...	......	......	......	......	......	......
Cotton handkerchiefs ...	......	......	......	......	......	......
Indian muslin ...	......	......	......	......	......	......
Calico	......	......	......	......	......	......
Sheep-skin furs ...	......	......	......	130	910	113
White lamb-skin furs ...	1,100	330	41	400	600	75
Fox-skin furs	40	400	50	350	525	65
Cotton ...	32 poods 1,152 lbs.	224	28	16 poods 376 lbs.	96	12
Red felts	1,984	3,085	385	3	6	......
Sart boots with goloshes	350 pairs	700	87	400 pairs	400	50
Horse-skins	......	......	......	......	......	......
Sheep-skins	......	1,600	200	......	......	......
Alum	......	......	......	......	......	......
Sal ammoniac	......	......	......	......	......	......
Brimstone	......	......	......	......	......	......
Opium	......	......	......	......	......	......
Copper tea vessels ...	......	......	......	18	36	4
Yambs (silver-bars, a form of Chinese currency).	......	......	......	......	......	......
Yarmahas (Chinese copper coins).	......	......	......	......	......	......
Agate stone	......	......	......	......	500	62
Girdles (qamar-bands) ...	......	......	......	......	......	......
Chinese stuffs	......	......	......	......	......	......
Tea	......	......	......	......	......	......
Gooshna (a root used in dyeing silk).	......	......	......	......	......	......
Boozgoontch (a dye prepared from the leaves of the pistachio tree).	......	......	......	......	......	......
Silken stuffs	160 pcs.[1]	480	60	......	......	......
Counterpanes	790	1,199	149	......	......	......
Brocade	607 pcs.[1]	1,514	189	......	......	......
Khotan woollen goods	750 poods 27,000 lbs.	4,000	500	......	......	......
Total ...	......	941,759	£117,719	......	40,543	£5,067
Percentage per district...	......	85½ %	......	......	3¾ %	......

[1] Every piece is from 8 to 14 *arshins* (from yards 6-0-4 inches to yards 10-2-8

GARIA DURING THE YEAR 1876.

mak, Karakol and Osh, and the Provinces of Semiraitchensk and Fergana.

Through Osh.			Sum-total in Russian money.	Sum-total in English money.	Percentage.
Quantity.	Value in Russian money.	Value in English money.			
Horse-loads.	*Roubles.*	*£ sterling.*	*Roubles.*	*£ sterling.*	
26½	25,964	3,245	27,764	3,470	5 %
64	25,197	3,149	25,197	3,149	Ditto.
16½	1,913	239	1,913	239	Ditto.
17	1,689	211	894,744	111,843	81 %
895	1,358	169	12,020	1,502	1 %
5	20	2	47,615	5,951	4 %
114	1,644	205	12,129	1,516	1 %
......	......	......	2,100	262	......
169 pieces.[1]	977	122	977	122	......
15,280	3,598	449	3,598	449	......
210 pieces,[1]	958	119	958	119	......
6 pieces.[1]	48	6	48	6	......
30	6,079	759	6,989	873	......
......	......	......	930	116	......
......	......	......	925	115	......
......	......	......	320	40	......
231	18,312	2,289	21,404	2,675	2 %
125 pairs.	230	28	1,330	166	......
19	1,834	229	1.834	229	......
24	1,300	162	2,900	362	......
44	12,864	1,608	12,864	1,608	1 %
31	1,855	231	1,855	231	......
18	797	99	797	99	......
19½	2,660	332	2,660	332	......
582	1,040	130	1,076	134	......
17	1,436	179	1,436	179	......
38	1,732	216	1,732	216	......
......	......	......	500	62	......
11	1,170	146	1,170	146	......
8 pieces[1]	114	14	114	14	......
{ 70 poods { 2,520 lbs.	} 3,071	383	3,071	383	......
1	40	5	40	5	......
1½	20	2	20	2	......
......	......	......	480	60	......
......	......	......	1,199	149	......
......	......	......	1,514	189	......
......	......	......	4,000	500	......
......	117,920	£14,740	1,101,222	£137,652	......
......	10¾ %	......	100 %	......	......

nches) in length, with a width of about half *arshin* (1 foot 2 inches).—*Author.*

An examination of the two tabulated statements shows us how great is the disproportion between the imports into, and the exports from, Kashgaria. In fact, the exports are more than four times the amount of the imports. The export of *mata* alone is three times greater than the whole amount of imported goods, and is more than eight times the quantity of the Russian cotton manufactured materials introduced into the country.

With regard to the entire trade of Kashgaria, the difference between the imports and the exports would be much less considerable, were it not for those imported English goods in exchange for which gold and silver are taken from the country. But returns for one year cannot be altogether considered as an average for a long series of years. Let us suppose, however, that the average of Russian goods imported into Kashgaria were considerably greater than the amount shown for the year 1876. Then, even all the circumstances would but little weaken the general deductions—

1. *The export of goods from Kashgaria into Russian territory exceeds the quantity imported by a very considerable amount.*

2. *During the year* 1876, *of the quantity of goods taken from Kashgaria into Russian territory,* 90 *per cent. were local fabrics, and only* 6 *per cent. were raw products.*

3. *During the same year we imported into Kashgaria but a fraction of our raw produce and of our cattle in addition to fabrics.*

4. *During the same year we paid Kashgaria about one million roubles* (£125,000) *for her local fabrics.*

Let us not forget that the same unfavourable results for us, which were produced by the administration of Yakoob Bek in Kashgaria, greatly impeded our trade, and that, with the re-conquest of Kashgaria by the Chinese, and the introduction of quiet, the future of our trade relations with that vast country cannot but be more favourable, if we begin in time the contest against the predomination of the trade of Kashgaria over that of our Central Asian possessions.

Such a predomination, coupled with the greater development of the introduction of cotton webs into Russian territory and with the extension of the market for English goods, will, instead of adding to the demand for Russian manufactured goods, lead to its diminution, and to results of such a kind *that, for Central Asian raw produce, such as cotton and silk to be used in the manufacture of different articles, we shall have to pay the natives in hard cash.*

In support of this assertion we can bring forward the following facts:—

The majority of Russian traders have had to give Russian manufactured goods in Bokhara in exchange for raw produce *at prices below those which obtain for such goods in Moscow.* Hence, evidently, proceeds that want of conformity which is met with in the trade of Tashkent. For example, chintzes, sugar and stearine candles, taken from Bokhara to Tashkent, are sold cheaper than the same class of goods imported direct from Russia.

In like manner, Russian manufactures are sometimes sold at Kashgar at prices below those which obtain at Tashkent and at Vairnoye. Hence the cost of transport to Kashgaria, which, we may remark, is very considerable, is an item of actual loss.

Mons. Shkokoff, for example, the representative of the firm of Bwikovski in Kashgaria, having deemed it inexpedient to transport manufactured goods into Kashgaria, took there 80 horse-loads of assorted goods with his caravan. Of these 40 horses were laden with sandalwood, and the rest with *fooksin* (?) and *vwidra* (?) But the whole consignment he was obliged to sell at Tashkent prices, hoping to recoup himself for the loss by the Khotan wool, which he took in exchange for his venture.

The measures for the attainment of a more favourable balance in our trade with Kashgaria are, it appears to me, comprised in the following:—

1. The better security of our trade interests with Kashgaria.

2. The establishment of a customs line on our border, and the confiscation of contraband goods.

3. The imposition of a heavy tax on English goods, chintzes, muslins, cloths and Indian teas.

4. The imposition of a tax on Kashgarian manufactures in the shape of cotton materials.

5. The encouragement of the manufacture of *mata* in the districts of the Province of Fergana, with a view to its import into the Semiraitchensk in order to exchange it for Kashgarian *mata*. The encouragement of the cotton and silk industries.

6. The construction of a good trade route between the districts of the Fergana and Semiraitchensk provinces. For example, the making of a road from the towns of Oozgent and Namangan to Fort Narwin, from which a cart-road already passes to Tokmak and the town of Vairnoye. The erection of one or more factories near Tashkent and Kokan for the manufacture of chintzes on the spot. A market would be found for the sale of these manufactures in our Central Asian dominions, and in the Independent States of Bokhara, Kashgaria, Afghanistan, and in time, it may be, in Siberia.

The following is the percentage of the several exports enumerated in the tabular statement on pages 76, 77:—

Mata	81	per cent.
Silk	5	„
Robes	4	„
Felts (coloured)	2	„
Mashroop (a semi-silken web)	1	„
Alum	1	„
The remaining manufactures	6	„
Total ...	100	„

Kashgarian cotton-webs.—The principal of these industries, *mata*, is centred in the neighbourhood of the town of Kashgar, in the villages of Khan-Arwik and Faizabad. Other webs of a somewhat inferior description are prepared in less quantities in the town of Kashgar itself, whilst the worst kinds are manufactured in the hamlets of Artoosh and Togoozak. The latter description is used for the lining of garments.

Cotton manufactures exist also in all the other Circles of Kashgaria, but only enough web is turned out to meet local requirements. That produced in the Kashgar Circle is sufficient, not only for the demands of the population, but for about a million Kirghiz dwelling in Russian territory.

In the other Circles, the Khotan *mata* is celebrated for its closeness, whiteness and softness, though, owing to its high price, it has not a large sale. Comparatively speaking, the qualities of Khotan *mata* depend on the description of the local cotton which is employed in its manufacture.

Cotton is raised in all the Circles of Kashgaria. There are exceptionally large fields of it in the Khotan, Kashgar and Koonya-Toorfan Circles. The Djitwishar cotton is generally inferior to that of Kokan. Its meshes are smaller and its threads are shorter. The Kashgar cotton is inferior to all the other local cottons. In consequence of the relative severity of the climate, the cotton of the Kashgar Circle does not attain to full growth.

In this Circle, the raising of cotton has of late begun to diminish. The cause has been the increases made by Yakoob Bek to the land taxes.

With the diminution of the raising of cotton in the Kashgar Circle, the import of the same article from the other Circles has begun to increase, especially from Aksu and also from the Khanate of Kokan.

Mata (*daba, biaz*) is a narrow, fine, but not a durable web, which is prepared in pieces of from 8 to 14 *arshins* (6 yds. 8 ins. to 10 yds. 2 ft. 8 ins.) in length, with a width of about ½ *arshin* (1 ft. 2 ins.) *Mata* is prized for its whiteness and closeness, but, in the several centres of its manufacture, there are differences of quality, length, width and cost.

The *mata* made, for example, in the Khan-Arwik settlements is prepared in pieces, 14 *arshins* (10 yds. 2 ft. 8 ins.) long, and is of two kinds. The better and ordinary kind is called *bash-mata*. A piece of this costs from 2 *tengas* 35 *pool* to 3 *tengas* 20 *pool* (*vide* page 65). This would represent about 2 *kopaikas* (about 3 farthings) for an *arshin* (2 ft. 4 ins.) of the web. With such extraordinary cheapness it is very difficult to compete. The second sort is even yet cheaper; a piece costs from 2 *tengas* 12 *pool* to 2 *tengas* 30 *pool* (*vide* page 65).

Mata is prepared in the village of Faizabad in pieces of 14 *arshins* (10 yds. 2 ft. 8 in.) long, and it costs from 2 *tengas* 6 *pool* to 2 *tengas* 20 *pool* a piece.

Togoozak *mata* is made in pieces of 8 *arshins* (6 yds. 0 ft. 8 ins.) long at 2 *tengas* 10 *pool* a piece.

Artoosh *mata* of the same length is sold for 2 *tengas* the piece, whilst *mata*, also 8 *arshins* long, prepared in the town of Kashgar, is charged at 2 *tengas* 14 *pool* the piece.

Khotan *mata* is made up in pieces of 10 *arshins* in length, and is sold for 5 *tengas* 10 *pool* the piece.

Thus, Khotan mata is nearly double the cost of all the other kinds. An *arshin* of it costs 5 *kopaikas* (about 1½*d.*)

We have said that the best kind of *mata* in the Kashgar Circle is that of Khan-Arwik, whilst the worst kinds come from Togoozak and Artoosh, and yet these kinds are actually dearer than the Khan-Arwik web.

This fact is explained by the considerable quantity of materials which is necessary in the preparation of the coarser kinds of *mata*.

A visit which we made towards the close of November 1876 to a *mata* manufactory in the village of Faizabad, distant 61 versts (40⅔rds miles) from Kashgar, on the road to the town of Aksu, gave us the following information :—

The inhabitants of Faizabad prepare *mata*, but they at the same time carry on their husbandry, and the double occupation goes on the whole year round. The men weave, and the women prepare the thread. The workshops which we visited were in small low rooms, very like lumber-rooms. In each of these were two or three frames, and sometimes a weaver's bench[1] of primitive construction. At each frame a man sat working. The narrow and inferior kind of *mata* was being made of local cotton.

They work for five days of the week, but not on Fridays (which with Mussulmans answer to our Sundays) and on market days. A man makes each day four pieces, *i. e.*, twenty pieces a week.

On market days they sell the week's work to purchasers from the towns.

They do not use their own implements.

The weavers buy their web. For each day's work three skeins, each about ½ lb in weight, are necessary. The present price of a

[1] Which put us much in mind of the benches of our own peasants.—*Author.*

skein is about 80 *pool*, so that the day's material costs 240 *pool*, or 48 *kopaikas* (about 1*s*. 3*d*.)

On the sale of the *mata*, the workman takes for his labour 20 *pool* per piece, so that for his day's work he receives 80 *pool* or 16 *kopaikas* (about 5*d*.) If to the cost of labour we add the cost of material, 240 *pool* or 48 *kopaikas* (1*s*. 3*d*.), we shall find the market-price of each piece of *mata* to be 80 *pool* or 16 *kopaikas* (about 5*d*.); but in the Kashgar bazaar a piece of the same *mata* will cost 20 *kopaikas* (about 6*d*. in English money).

They prepare the better kind of *mata* at a less profit. During one day they can only turn out two pieces of the prepared material, and since the earnings on one piece only yield 30 *pool* (about 1½*d*.), the preparation of *mata* of the better kind gives the weaver but 60 *pool* or 12 *kopaikas* (about 3*d*.) per diem, instead of the 80 *pool* or 16 *kopaikas* (5*d*.) which he gets for preparing the coarser material. As a rule, each weaver works for himself. There are, indeed, owners of two or three frames, but not many.

When using the frame and material of another person, and working for him, a weaver, instead of receiving payment in money, is allowed to retain every tenth piece of *mata* for his own use. In other words, the hire of a weaver for 2½ days labour amounts to 16 *kopaikas*, or at the rate of 6 *kopaikas* (about 1½*d*.) per diem.

As has been said above, the thread is prepared by women. One *charik* of uncleaned material is bought for ten *tengas* (1 rouble or about 2*s*. 6*d*.) Two women will prepare in a week, in addition to attending to their domestic duties, one *charik* of raw material. This quantity represents 5 lbs. or ten skeins of thread. Selling it at 80 *pool* per skein, the women receive 800 *pool*, or after deducting 500 *pool* for the cost of the material, 300 *pool* or 60 *kopaikas* (about 1*s*. 6*d*.) Thus, the earnings for one week of a woman amounts to about 30 *kopaikas* (about 9*d*.)

In spite of such a very low rate of remuneration the Kashgarian women work most energetically, scarcely losing a moment for rest. And since the money which they earn for supplying the thread is their own property, they are able to devote it in their own way, as for example, to their dress.

The Faizabad and Khan-Arwik *mata* is exported to Russia in pretty equal quantities.

Mata is only exported with the consent of the 'Badaulet.' At first this permission was accorded on two occasions only in the year. In 1876 there were five exportations, but towards the close of the present year (1877) the export of *mata* was suddenly stopped by Yakoob Bek.

The prohibition was caused by the fact that many Kashgarian youths were leaving the country with caravans under the name of mule-drivers. They were proceeding to Vairnoye with the object of avoiding the military conscription, and with the intention of remaining altogether away from their native land. According to report the number of such youths was 4,000.

The prohibition against the export of *mata* did not merely affect Russian traders, for the Sarts, as well as Tashkent and Kokan merchants, carried on a trade in this material with the merchants of Kashgaria.

The months of September, October and November are reckoned the best time for the export of *mata*, as at that season of the year it can be prepared from fresh cotton.

The best route for the transport of *mata* goes from Kashgar to Forts Chakmak and Narwin, and so on to the towns of Tokmak and Vairnoye.

The material is carried on pack-horses or camels or mules.

The pack-horses are procured chiefly from the Province of Fergana, whilst the camels come either from Semiraitchensk or Kashgaria itself. The mules all come from Kashgaria. The camel carriage is only made use of during the summer, since these animals dislike the cold.

The Kashgarian merchants make use of mule transport on a large scale.

Between Kashgar and the town of Vairnoye horses are to be hired. One that will carry a load of from 8 to 9 *poods* (288 to 324 lbs.) will cost from 2½ to 5 ducats,[1] or from 6¼ to 12½ roubles (15*s.* 7½*d.* to £1 11*s.* 3*d.*) according to circumstances. The normal rate is 3½ ducats. The distance between Kashgar and Vairnoye is traversed in from 25 to 30 days.

[1] A ducat = 25 *tengas* = 2½ roubles.—*Author.*

The hire of a camel that would carry from 13 to 15 *poods* (468 to 540 lbs.) would be from 5 to 9 ducats. The distance would be performed in from 30 to 35 days.

A mule carrying a load of from 4 to 5 *poods* would cost from 35 to 50 *tengas* or 5 roubles (12*s*. 6*d*.), and the distance would be traversed in the same time as that taken by a horse.

The traders engaged in the transport of *mata* have no other expenses beyond the payment for the hire of the particular mode of transport.

Dyed biaz, linen, chakmen. Mata of inferior quality, chiefly that which comes from Artoosh and Togoozak, is dyed blue, red, black and green, and is then classed as dyed *biaz*.

In the dyeing, indigo, madder and sandalwood are used.

Faizabad *mata* of inferior quality is coloured blue by means of indigo and sandalwood.

Dyed *mata* not only supplies local requirements, but is an article of export.

It is used for lining garments and for bed coverings, and the poor make it up into robes, &c., &c. A piece of 7 *arshins* (5 yds. 1 ft. 4 ins.) in length costs 2½ *tengas*, whilst a piece of dyed *biaz*, 10 *arshins* (7 yds. 2 ft. 4 ins.) long, is priced at from 3 to 3½ *tengas*.

Chakmen is a very close and heavy web, which is dyed in various colours. Robes of different sorts are made of this material. A piece of *chakmen* measuring 18 *arshins* (14 yds.) in length, with a width of from 5 to 6 *vershoks* (8¾ to 10½ inches), would cost as much as 15 *tengas*.

A striped cotton fabric prepared in Kashgar, and which is also used for robes of kinds, is called *alatchi*. Pieces of this material, 8 *arshins* (6 yds. 0 ft. 8 ins.) long, cost 7 *tengas*.

All the dyeing of *mata* is confined to the town of Kashgar, and is there carried on in small workshops, having from 3 to 4 workmen in each.

Silk and silken manufactures.—Of all the Circles of Kashgaria, in the Khotan Circle alone is the working of silk developed to any great extent. In the others local requirements are only met. In the Kashgar Circle, eggs from Kokan are used, but the quality of these cocoons is not so good as those from Khotan.

Although conditions of climate do not hinder the extensive development of the silk industry in the Kashgar Circle, hitherto the amount of the various sorts of silk prepared therein has not come up to local requirements, and hence silken web has had to be imported from Fergana.

In the Yarkend Circle the production of silk covers, though in a still less degree, local demands.

In the Khotan Circle the same industry is found to be in a flourishing condition, since it is apparently developing and even now satisfies not only local wants, but is, after *mata*, the most important article of export throughout the entire country.

A sort of silk called *takhfil*[1] and *kalyav* is also made. The Khotan cocoons are coarser than those from Fergana, and they are weaker and inferior altogether.

The best workmen for unwinding silk come from Fergana.

Both the *takhfil* and *kalyav* kinds of silk are imported into Hindoostan and Fergana from Khotan.

The imports into Fergana, according to the tabular statement given on pages 76, 77, were, for 1876, about 700 *poods* (25,200 lbs.), and represented a sum exceeding 50,000 roubles (£6,250). During 1877, the quantity of the same material that, it was anticipated, would represent the exports, was 1,000 *poods* (36,000 lbs.), provided that political circumstances did not interfere.

According to the calculations of Mons. Kolesnikoff, the average export from Khotan is 4,000 *poods* (144,000 lbs.) Of this quantity, 1,000 *poods* (36,000 lbs.) go to Fergana, 1,040 *poods* to the other Circles, whilst India takes the balance of 2,000 *poods* (72,000 lbs.)

Of Kashgarian silk, *takhfil* alone finds its way to Russia, whilst *kalyav* is bought up for Afghanistan in the bazaars of Kokan and Tashkent. The price of *takhfil* in the Kashgar bazaar during 1875 was for one *charik* (of 10 lbs.) from 7¾ to 8½ ducats, and the price of *kalyav*, for a *charik* (of 6 lbs.), was 2½ ducats.

During 1876, in consequence of the increased demand, the price of *takhfil* in the Kashgar bazaar rose to 10 ducats a *charik*,

[1] In Kokan it is called *hamyak* or *khamayk*.—*Author*.

and in the Khotan bazaar 8½ ducats were demanded for the same quantity. The price of *kalyav* remained the same.

Although the manufacture of silken webs in Khotan is fairly well developed, still the quantity turned out scarcely suffices to meet local requirements. The development of the *mashroop* web is much greater. This is a semi-silken, very durable and pretty material. It was indeed at one time the only material of the kind which was exported from Kokan. During the year 1876, 12,000 roubles (£1,500) worth of it were sent to Semiraitchensk. Of late, besides *mashroop*, they have begun to manufacture *adriyas, bekasap, shai* (kanaus).

Kokan silken materials in quality are superior to those of Kashgar. They are met with in all the bazaars of the country.

Of other goods that are exported, a perceptible place is taken by articles of apparel, as for instance, *khalats* (robes). These are exported to the value of 47,000 roubles (£5,875), and are chiefly taken by the Kirghiz. They are very plain and extremely cheap. As a rule, the price of a *khalat* does not exceed 3 roubles (about 7*s.* 6*d.*)

Then come felts made from cow-hair and carpets of Khotan manufacture. The latter are very pretty, but comparatively very dear, being about 80 roubles (£10) a piece. Alum too is exported from the Aksu Circle to Fergana.

Of the remaining articles it only remains to speak of Khotan wool. Its export has only just begun, but, in the opinion of experienced persons, this wool will ere long occupy one of the chief places in Russian trade with Kashgaria.

The following is the percentage of the several Kashgarian goods received into Russian territory during the year 1876 :—

Mata	81	per cent.
Raw silk	5	,,
Khalats	4	,,
Coloured felts	2	,,
Alum	1	,,
Carpets	1	,,
Mashroop	1	,,
Miscellaneous goods	5	,,
Total ...	100	per cent.

Through the various districts of our Central Asian territory there passed goods in the following percentage :—

Through Tokmak	... ...	85½ per cent.
„ Osh	... ...	10¾ „
„ Karakol	... ...	3¾ „
Total	...	100 per cent.

Regarding the extent of Kashgarian trade with India we have scarcely any information.

According to reports, there came to Yarkend from Hindoostan, during the year 1873-74, several large caravans carrying goods amounting in value to 800,000 roubles (£100,000). But the goods brought by these caravans did not meet with a ready sale, and the greater part of them is now lying in the caravanserai of Yarkend. As we have remarked above, English chintzes, although about the same price as the Russian, sell but badly, and this because their colour quickly fades, and because they are made of a soft and perishable material. Of other goods imported from India into Kashgaria, there are quantities of yellow sugar which does not sell well, woollen webs (also a failure) and cloths (red *drap-de-dame*). The latter sells only fairly well, but muslins always find a good market.

In exchange for the imported Indian goods, silk is bought at Khotan, opium in Yarkend, and goats' wool at Kashgar and Aksu.

According to the very accurate calculations of Mons. Kolesnikoff, the value of the goods imported from Kashgaria into India was as follows :—

Silk, 2,800 *poods*, at 20 ducats	...	56,000 ducats
Goats' wool, 1,600 *poods*, at 3 ducats	...	4,800 „
Opium, 700 horse-loads, at 18 ducats	...	12,600 „
		73,400 „

or 200,279 roubles = £25,034.

Moreover, it is said that considerable quantities of silver and of gold are received into India from Kashgaria.

The trade with India lies in the hands of natives of that country, but it is stated that, during the year 1876, there was one English trader also residing at Yarkend.

CHAPTER IV.[1]

Some words relating to the history of Kashgaria, B.C. — The Uigurs — First conquest of Kashgaria by the Chinese — Arab dominion — Mongol dominion — Chingiz Khan and his heirs — Tamerlane — Sultan Said — Appearance of the Khodjas — Appak-Khodja — Djoongar dominion — Amoorsana — Conquest of Kashgaria by the Chinese in the year 1760 — Tchjao-Hoi — System of Administration adopted by the Chinese — Condition of the country from the year 1760 to the year 1825.

Earlier history of Kashgaria or Eastern Turkestan.

THE country which is at present known under the name of Eastern Turkestan was, in the opinion of contemporary writers, originally peopled by an Aryan race. Shut in on the west and south by mountain ranges of the first rank, Eastern Turkestan was open on the north-east to the inroads of the semi-barbarous Mongol hordes inhabiting the vast extent of the interior of Asia. Chinese historians speak first of all of the 'Hioung-Nou,' and these, in the opinion of the French writer, the missionary Huc,[2] and of Dr. Bellew,[3] are none other than the *Huns*. This warlike race of nomads, after steadily encroaching both on its western neighbours, also nomads, and on the confines of the Celestial Empire, occupied by degrees the western and eastern portions of Mongolia.

The Huns.

In the year 134 B.C., the *Huns*, under the leadership of Lao-Khan, marched against the *Gets* or *Yuts* (the Chinese

[1] The first pages of this Chapter were written by me at a time when I had not for reference other works than those of authors whose competency, as to the history of Asia, is open to doubt. I, therefore, regard these first pages as an introduction to the history of Kashgaria, and not as possessed of any serious scientific importance.—*Author.*

[2] "Souvenir d'un Voyage dans la Tartarie et le Thibet, pendant les années, 1844-45-46," par Mons. Huc, Paris, 1860, see page 384.—*Author.*

[3] "Kashmir and Kashgar," by Bellew, 1875.—*Author.*

12

Vouëi-Tchi), peoples of Mongol origin, who dwelt in the country that at present comprises the Chinese province of Shan-Si. After a bloody fight Lao-Khan conquered his opponents, killed their leader, and made of his skull a drinking-cup, which he constantly kept about his person by fixing it to his girdle. The

The Gets.

Gets, not wishing to become subjects of Lao-Khan, set out to

Their division into two parties.

seek for themselves a new place of abode. They then became divided into two parties, the first of which moved to the north-east, where it came into collision with the *Saks*, the inhabitants of Eastern Turkestan. These people it drove out, and it then crossed the Tian-Shan range and descended into the valley of the Ili. The other party moved in a southerly direction, crossed the snowy range, and, pouring into the valley of the Indus, laid waste the kingdom founded in India by Alexander of Macedon.[1]

The *Gets*, who poured into Eastern Turkestan, in some measure allied themselves with the *Saks* and the *Yats* or *Yuks*, but they drove the bulk of these people to the south and west.

Remnants of the Huns and their divisions.

Meanwhile the *Huns*, who remained masters of Mongolia, became divided, in consequence of internal disputes, into the Northern and Southern *Huns*. The Chinese took advantage of this division, for, during the Han dynasty, they broke up the armies of the Northern Huns, and compelled them to seek a new fatherland. The *Huns*, like their predecessors, then moved to the west, and, pouring through Eastern Turkestan, continued their movement in the same direction until at last they reached the shores of the Caspian Sea and spread over the basin of the Volga.

[1] Mons. Huc ("Souvenir d'un Voyage dans la Tartarie et le Thibet") supposes that the *Gets*, after crossing the Tian-Shan (which he calls Moossoor), settled on the banks of the Ili. This party, he says, were the *Torgots* or *Torgouts*. Now the *Torgouts*, as is known, are a Kalmuck race; the same, in fact, as that which still wanders over the valley of the Ili, but chiefly in the valleys of the Koonges and of the Yuldus. In like manner, Mons. Huc supposes that that portion of the *Gets* which moved to the valley of the Indus, there encountered a Bactrian race, and, after struggling with it for a long time, finally established itself in Bactriana. This portion of the *Gets*, in the opinion of Mons. Huc, was called by the Greeks the *Indo-Skifs*.—*Author*.

Movements of the Gets and Saks.

After the inroad of the *Huns* into Eastern Turkestan, the inhabitants of that country, the *Gets* and the remaining *Saks*, moved in advance of their conquerors, partly towards the west, and partly towards the south, in the direction of Kabul and Kashmir.[1]

Those *Huns* who mingled with the remaining *Saks* and *Gets* (*Gots*) and formed the population of Eastern Turkestan became somewhat changed in later times owing to the inroads of other peoples who came with the various Arab conquerors.

At present, according to the opinion of Russian explorers of Central Asia, it is only in the more inaccessible mountains that shut in Djitwishar on the west that a pure type of the remnants of the Aryan race are to be found.

Further progress of the Huns.

Those *Huns* who, after continuing their movement towards the west, drove from before them the various small tribes of nomads whom they came across in their progress onwards, began with their assistance to make, in the beginning of the Fourth century, inroads into the Roman Empire, and in the Fifth Century to pour into Germany.[2] In Europe, these Huns went

[1] Dr. Bellew ("Kashmir and Kashgar, 1875") draws some very learned conclusions in support of his ideas as to the movement of the *Saks*, and after them of the *Gets* (*Gots*) and *Yuts*, who were driven by the *Huns* or *Uigurs* from Eastern Turkestan, partly towards the west into Europe, and partly towards the south to Kabul, Kashmir and India. He says, that in Europe traces of these peoples are preserved under many names, such as *Saksonia*, *Yutlandia*, and *Gotlandia;* that the names of the settlements which they abandoned in Kashgaria are repeated in the south; thus, *Kazi* or *Benares* (*Kazigar*, *Kashgar*), *Hari* or *Herat* (*Hari-kend*, *Yarkend*), *Koocha* or *Koochar* (*Kachar*), *Koorlia* (*Kelya*), *Kitan* (the ruins known under the name of *Khotan*). Furthermore Bellew says, that the country known in the time of Timur and now as Kashgaria, was called *Yatta*. Lastly, he supposes that the race of *Yatts* or *Jats*, who now dwell in the Punjab, are descended from those exiles from Kashgaria who left it at the time when that country bore the name of *Yatta*.—*Author*.

[2] Mons. Huc says, that the *Huns*, who began, during the year 376, their devastating inroads into the Roman Empire, first of all subdued a nomad race that wandered over the country of the *Allani* (le pays des Alains of Klaproth: the Alano-Gothes), and these people partly sought flight in the mountains of the Caucasus, and partly settled on the Danube. In their further movements, the *Huns* or *Uigurs* drove in front of them the *Sevs*, *Gots*, *Gepids* and *Vandals* (les Suéves, les Gothes, les Gepides, les Vandales), and, together with these peoples, overran Germany in the beginning of the Fifth Century.—*Author*.

by the name of *Uigurs, Ugras, Ongras,* and their representatives, at this time, are called *Vengras* or *Hungarians.*

The Huns or Uigurs.

Thus the *Huns,* or, as we shall for the future call them, the *Uigurs,* established themselves in Eastern Turkestan in the beginning of the Christian era, and intermingled with the peoples who remained in the country after their invasion.[1] Besides this, whatever country was occupied by the Uigurs, whether mountain or plain, became in course of time civilized by them. For the first time in the remote history of Kashgaria, do the people bear the name of the towns or circles in which they dwell. Thus we hear of the Kashgarians, the Khotanese the Yarkendians, the Aksutians, the Koochians, &c. All the inhabitants of these towns, in consequence of the intermixture of collateral races, lose by degrees their primitive Mongol physiognomy.

The Uigurs, who occupied the mountain region that borders on Eastern Turkestan, *i.e.*, the Northern and Western Tian-Shan ranges, have remained nomads up to the present day. In the earlier history of Kashgaria, we find them under the name of *Djoongars* (*Kalmucks*) and *Booroots* (*Kara-Kirghiz* or *Diko-kamenni* or *Wild Stone Kirghiz*). The Mongol type of countenance is especially well preserved amongst the first of these.[2]

[1] According to Bellew, the Uigurs founded an independent kingdom in Eastern Turkestan for two centuries, B.C.—*Author.*

[2] There is a curious note by Valikhanoff in the Journal of the Russian Geographical Society, No. I, for 1861, page 194, relating to the races that dwelt in Central Asia at the beginning of the present era. He says: "Amongst the number of peoples dwelling in Central Asia during the Chinese dynasty of Han, chroniclers speak of six races distinguished for their blue eyes and for the reddish colour of their hair, and these races, both Klaproth ("Tableaux Historiques de l'Asie, page 82) and Abel Remuzat ("Recherches sur les langues Tartares," Vol. I, page 306), hold to be of Indo-Germanic origin. Klaproth says, they are "Nations Alano-Gothes." Abel Remuzat speaks of them as "Nations Gothique et Hindo-Scythique." To the number of these races belonged, amongst others, the *Khakaswi,* descendants of the *Kilikitswi, i.e.*, the *Kirghiz* and the *Oosoons*, and they were especially striking to the Chinese by reason of their foreign appearance.

According to Valikhanoff, there dwell in Djoongaria at this present time two races, the *Booroots* or modern Kirghiz (those whom we call the Kara-Kirghiz) and the *Kirghiz-Kaisaki* of the Great Horde who bear the collective name of

Kashgaria—the kingdom founded by the Uigurs in Eastern Turkestan—did not long preserve its independence. Repeated quarrels with China soon began, and these ended in the annexation of Kashgaria to the Celestial Empire in the year 94 A. D. The Chinese yoke, which apparently was not especially heavy, lasted till the Eighth Century. During this long period the inhabitants of Kashgaria, taking advantage of the internal dissensions of China, often rose in rebellion, and for a time obtained their independence; and then again the Chinese, having crushed their own foes, would again subject the Kashgarians to their rule. The struggle between the Chinese and the Kashgarians caused an alteration in the original divisions of that country, which thus became parcelled out into provinces somewhat independent the one of the other (Kashgar, Yarkend, Khotan, Aksu and others). Every time these provinces succeeded in securing their independence from China, they began to quarrel amongst themselves for the pre-eminence.

First conquest of Kashgaria by the Chinese.

Repeated rebellions against the Chinese.

Alteration in the division of Kashgaria.

Its consequences.

Up to the Eighth Century, the inhabitants of Kashgaria, Chinese writers tell us, professed Buddhism. It is difficult to say in

Religion of the inhabitants of Kashgaria up to the 8th century.

Ooisoons. These Kirghiz-Kaisaki or Ooisoons, Valikhanoff speaks of simply as *Kazaks*, and he distinguishes them from the *Booroots*, whom he calls *Kirghiz.*

The nomad population of the Tian-Shan ranges,—*i.e.*, the wanderers over the Isswik-Kool, the Aksai, the Kok-Shal and other localities, according to the testimony of Soonargooloff, who is well acquainted with the native dialects, and who, in the year 1877, visited the above localities, call themselves not *Kara-Kirghiz* but simply *Kirghiz.* The members of the Great, Middle and Lesser Hordes are, these nomads say, with Valikhanoff, *Kazaks*, and they hold them to be, as to descent, of purer blood than they are themselves. Moreover, Valikhanoff says that, amongst the Ooisoons, there is a race called the *Red Ooisoons* (*Sarwi-Ooisoon*), which considers itself the remnants of a great and powerful people.

In Huc's "Souvenir d'un Voyage dans la Tartarie et le Thibet," Chapter IV, mention is made of a race of Mongols who are called *Kalkhas* (*Khalkhas*). This fact involuntarily leads us to the thought, are they not allied to the *Khakas* of Djoongaria, from whom Valikhanoff derives the Kirghiz? It is interesting to know that Mons. Valikhanoff, who has devoted time to the collection of Kirghiz tales, myths, epic songs and legends, was struck with the resemblance of their motives with the motives of the same race of people in Europe, especially the Slavs. As regards the subjects of these tales, Mons. Valikhanoff found in Mons. Afanasieff's collection of the same kind, only six tales that were unknown to him in the Kirghiz compilation.—*Author.*

what epoch this form of religion penetrated to Eastern Turkestan. This much only is known that it existed there during the Han dynasty,—*i.e.*, in the beginning of the Second Century, A.D. The Chinese Hooen-Hang, who visited Kashgaria in the year 629 during the Tan dynasty, found everywhere the religion of Buddha in full development, and many monasteries, teachers and holy hermits.

Arrival of Mahommedanism with the Arab merchants.

Mahommedanism began to permeate through Eastern Turkestan on the arrival of the Arab merchants during the Eighth Century. The first Mahommedan teachers were unfavourably received by the inhabitants of the towns, and their first converts appeared amongst the nomad population.[1]

Arab dominion established in Kashgaria.

After the arrival of the Arab merchants in Eastern Turkestan there appeared conquerors from the same nation, and they, with the sword, compelled the Uigurs, whom they subdued, to accept Islam. Chinese chroniclers tell us of a bloody war which brought Arabs to this country during the Eighth Century. In the year 712, one of the Arab chiefs, the Caliph Walid Kootaiba, occupied Kokan, from whence he sallied forth and quickly overspread the whole country from Kashgar to Toorfan and to China. It was after this campaign that the Arabs annexed the country to their own dominions[2] and began to propagate therein the tenets of Islam. The inhabitants of Khotan showed the stoutest resistance to the introduction of Islam, for a bloody struggle lasting twenty-five years became necessary before they were

Fight for the faith.

[1] Valikhanoff: see "Proceedings of the Imperial Russian Geographical Society for 1861," Vol. III, page 33.—*Author.*

[2] Bellew says that, after the campaign of the Arab leader Kootaiba, the Arabs occupied Western Kashgaria and persecuted both the Christian religion and the teaching of the Magi. One of their first converts was a follower of Zoroaster, an inhabitant of Balkh, *Saman* by name. As the result of this his sons were made governors of the principal Arab provinces, *viz.*, Herat, Samarkand, Fergana and Tashkent, which were subject to one Caliph. Saman's grandson, Nazar, governor of Fergana, took advantage of the Caliph's weak position and brought under his own rule Bokhara and Turkestan and then laid the foundation of the *Samanidæ* dynasty. His brother and heir, Ismail, led this same dynasty to the highest state of its power. At his death the sovereignty comprised the vast stretch of country from Ispahan to Toorfan and from the Persian Gulf on the south to the desert of Gobi on the north. The sovereignty of the Samanidæ lasted for 150 years.—*Author.*

classed amongst the faithful. In this fight, says Bellew, many famous Arab heroes fell fighting for the faith and were added to the long roll of Mahommedan saints.

At this day, near the town of Khotan and between Kashgar and Yarkend, and likewise near the town of Aksu, vast burial-grounds are pointed out which are called *Shaidans*, or the resting-places of those who have fallen for the Mussulman religion.

The Arab conquerors drive out the Christian and Buddhist religions.

As with Buddhism so was it with the Christian religion. All traces of it were rooted out notwithstanding that it had in places firmly implanted itself.

Weakening of the Arab dominion over Asia. Its consequences in Eastern Turkestan.

With the weakening of the Arab dominion over Asia there was formed in Eastern Turkestan a vast kingdom of Uigurs that attained to a considerable degree of prosperity. Persian literature was established in the country, and the Mahommedan creed received a fixed status consequent on the general acceptance of the pure doctrine of the Sunnis. In the Eleventh Century the Uigur sovereignty extended from the Caspian to Gobi. In the Twelfth Century, however, internal discords were the cause of its fall. Mongol hordes of Kara-Kitais, under the leadership of their chief, Gorkhan, put an end to the independence of the Uigurs. The rule of the Kara-Kitais in Eastern Turkestan lasted about a century. During this period their dominion reached to Khiva. The same internal discords that were the cause of the fall of the Uigur sovereignty were the cause also of the collapse of the Kara-Kitai power. Fresh Mongol hordes approaching from the North-East appeared as new antagonists.

Revival of a Uigur sovereignty. Dissensions amongst the Uigurs. Appearance of the Mongols.

At the head of these hordes was the famous Chingiz-Khan. His armies poured almost instantaneously like an irresistible torrent into China, Turkestan, India, Persia, Syria, and laid waste a part of Russia and of Poland, reaching to Hungary and Austria.

Mongol dominion over Kashgaria. Annexation of that country by Chingiz-Khan.

In the year 1220, Kashgaria was annexed to the kingdom of Chingiz. This annexation was accomplished without the same devastation and bloodshed which the country underwent during the innumerable inroads on the part of the Mongols, Chinese, Arabs and Kara-Kitais.

Prosperity of Kashgaria under Mongol rule.

It was during this last and brilliant rule of Mongols that Kashgaria attained the highest degree of its prosperity—a degree which it never before reached, and to which in succeeding years it never can attain. Thanks to tolerance, the Mussulman religion lost its severity. This was seen in the great freedom that women enjoyed. The Christian religion and Buddhism again appeared in the country, and raised their churches and their pagodas alongside the mosques; many of the cities too of Kashgaria, owing to the favourable trade relations established between China and Western Turkestan, acquired an important trade celebrity.

Tolerance displayed by the Mongols. Reappearance of the Christian and Buddhist religions. Trade flourishes in Kashgaria.

After the death of Chingiz-Khan, his vast dominions became divided amongst his sons. Kashgaria fell to the inheritance of Chagatai, and afterwards passed from one son of Chingiz to another. It became, however, several times divided and was the subject of continual civil war, until in the middle of the Fourteenth Century, one of the family of Chagatai, Tooglook-Timur-Khan, not only united the whole of Kashgaria, but still further extended its limits from the river Ili to the Kooen-Loon mountains. With the wise administration of Tooglook-Timur the country quickly recovered from the devastations that it had undergone during the fights amongst the sons of Chingiz for the inheritance of their famous forerunner. The rule of Tooglook-Timur-Khan is famous in the history of Kashgaria for yet another reason. At the end of the Fourteenth Century (754 of the Hejira), this ruler embraced Mahommedanism at the hands of Said Pasheddin (Sheik Said, descendant of Mahommed), and his example was followed by many Khans of the nomad hordes. From this date the Mahommedan creed became predominant throughout Eastern Turkestan.[1]

Death of Chingiz-Khan. Quarrels amongst his sons. Union takes place in the person of Tooglook-Timur-Khan. Tooglook-Timur-Khan's rule famous in the history of Kashgaria. He embraces Mahommedanism, and that creed predominates throughout Eastern Turkestan.

Tooglook-Timur removed his capital from Aksu to Kashgar. During the summer season he resided on the shores of Isswik-Kool at a place called Yatta-Moogol. Towards the end of his reign Tooglook-Timur-Khan took advantage of the state of Bokhara and annexed this country to his dominions, making his son ruler of Samarkand. On the death of this wise potentate the usual

Removal of the capital of Kashgaria from Aksu to Kashgar. Annexation of Bokhara.

[1] According to Valikhanoff, notwithstanding the predominating position of the Mahommedan religion in Eastern Turkestan, Buddhism was only expelled from the country during the 16th century.—" Journal of the Imperial Russian Geographical Society for 1861," Vol. III, page 34.—*Author.*

scene was repeated—a scene often witnessed in the history of peoples. His children had neither the talents nor the character of their father, and so the country which had scarcely yet settled down was again thrown into disorder. At Samarkand Tooglook Khan's son was overthrown by Timur (at the instigation of the celebrated Tamerlane), and in Kashgaria the power was seized by Kamar-Eddin, who destroyed the greater portion of Tooglook's family. It may be supposed that the power of this new ruler was not exceptionally strong, for, during his reign, hordes of nomads inhabiting the Tian-Shan not only unsettled Kashgaria with their constant raids, but crossed the northern portion of the range and devastated the dominions of the then powerful Tamerlane. Four campaigns undertaken by Tamerlane in succession for the punishment of the nomads and for the overthrow of Kamar-Eddin produced no results. At last, in the year 1389, he started on a final expedition equipped on a large scale. Five armies moved on different roads with the object of extirpating the entire population of the Tian-Shan mountain system as far as lake Zaisan to the north and the town of Kashgar to the south. The valley of the Yulduz (north-west of Karashar) was the meeting place of all the armies. These armies, after a bloody fight, successfully carried out their plan of operations, and the entire country, including a portion of the plains of Kashgar, was laid waste, and its inhabitants put to the sword in considerable numbers.[1]

Death of Tooglook-Timur-Khan. Dissensions amongst his heirs.

Appearance of Tamerlane.

Conquest of the country adjacent to Kashgaria by Tamerlane.

Ritter, in the following eloquent lines which he has borrowed from the Persian historian of the particular epoch, describes Timur's triumph after the assembly of his entire army in the valley of the Yulduz:[2] "The valley of the Yulduz is remarkable

[1] *Vide* Ritter's "Eastern or Chinese Turkestan," published in 1869, page 166. —*Author*.

[2] In the Memoirs of *Mirza Shemsa-Bokhara*, published by Mons. V. V. Grigorieff in 1861, at page 33, it is stated that Makhdoom-Azem (Makhdoom-Azyam), on visiting the greater portion of Kashgar, Yarkend, Aksu and Khotan, found there a population composed of two Uzbek branches, the Ak-Taulins and the Kara-Taulins. The mistake of the respected Mirza is evident. The Ak-Taulins and the Kara-Taulins, or the *white mountaineers* and the *black mountaineers*, are the names of religious parties that exist at the present day and not of races. Mons. Wahtens falls into the same error, for, in recapitulating the

as one of the most picturesque, with its excellent pasture lands and its pure and fresh air. At the time of which we write, this beautiful mountain region was studded everywhere with pavilions, and the sumptuous canopies of the nobles and the ground in front of them was spread with carpets and brocaded webs. When the Imperial tent was pitched the universal destroyer sat on his golden throne, radiant with precious stones. All the armies and chiefs assembled around were permitted to approach and kiss the Imperial carpet. With the royal crown on his head and the sceptre in his hand, he awarded robes of honour and girdles set with precious stones to the Princes, Amirs and Sherifs and to all the State dignitaries and to the leaders of his army, bestowing on each gifts varied according to the particular service rendered. He sent the most beautiful damsels of the country to bear to his favourites precious wine in golden cups. The whole army was in enthusiasm over the condescension of their ruler, whose triumph was celebrated during several days."

Timur appoints a grandson of Tooglook-Timur to be ruler of Kashgaria and returns to Samarkand.

With regard to Kashgaria, Timur having driven out Kamar-Eddin and having made one of the grandsons of Tooglook-Timur-Khan the ruler of the country, married his protegé's daughter and then returned to his own capital, Samarkand. He, however, left Kashgaria plundered and impoverished to such an extent that it has never since recovered from the blow.

Influence severally exercised over Central Asia by Chingiz-Khan and by Tamerlane.

Thus the two most famous personages in the history of Central Asia, Chingiz-Khan and Tamerlane, had a vast, though a very different, influence on the destinies of Kashgaria. The first possessed himself of the country without bloodshed, and by introducing religious toleration, fostering trade, industries and sciences, laid the foundation of the highest prosperity of the country. The second, by permitting pillage and destruction, in a few months demolished, for a long time if not for ever, that which Chingiz-Khan and his heirs had succeeded in creating during 170 years.

---

information which he has gleaned from Mecca pilgrims, he says that the native population of Eastern Turkestan consists of Uzbeks of two branches, *viz.*, Kara-Tag and Ak-Tag (Wahtens' Memoir on Chinese Tartary and Khotan.—"Journal of the Asiatic Society of Bengal, 1835," Vol. IV, page 661).—*Author.*

In the exposition of the earlier history of Kashgaria, we shall see that, in addition to all the misfortunes that produced this ruin, the country was subjected to an invasion of various Mussulman saints and wonder-workers. These persons, with their religious fanaticism, hypocrisy and partizan spirit, were the causes of fresh misfortunes that have continued even to later times.

Ruin brought about in Kashgaria by various fanatical personages.

The history of Kashgaria, from the Fifteenth to the Eighteenth Century, affords an unbroken record of civil war between two religious parties—of a struggle of which now the Chinese and now the neighbouring nomads took advantage to seize the country for themselves. Finally, the history of the Nineteenth Century tells us of the termination of the struggle for independence between the Kashgarians on the one hand and the Chinese on the other. Several times, supported by Mussulman adventurers from Western Turkestan, the Kashgarians got the upper hand and destroyed almost to a man the Chinese garrisons and the Chinese settlers, but each time again the Chinese with unchanging patience got the best of it, and signalized their return to power by a series of executions and exactions.[1]

The history of Kashgaria from the 15th to the 18th century.

During the Fifteenth and Sixteenth Centuries, Kashgaria was ruled by the numerous descendants of Tooglook-Timur-Khan. The administrations of these successors were famous only for their constant struggles together for supremacy. Several times Kashgaria became divided into two independent States, each with its capital at Kashgar and Aksu respectively. The power of these

[1] At the present moment, as we write these lines (on the $\frac{\text{21st January}}{\text{2nd February}}$ 1877 in the town of Koorlia, 40 versts (26⅔rds) miles from Fort Karashar) at several hundreds of versts distant there stand face to face, between Togsoon and Uroomtcha, Chinese and Kashgarian armies. The former has already had several successes. The towns of Manas and Uroomtcha have been taken and their inhabitants, to the number of several tens of thousands, destroyed. In the spring the same fate awaits, in all probability, fresh towns, such as Koonya-Toorfan, Koorlia, and Koocha, since the weak forces of the 'Badaulet' can scarcely stand against the tens of thousands arrayed against them by the Celestial Empire. If Russian interference does not put an end to this bloodshed, we shall probably see again the sacrifice of tens of thousands victims in Kashgaria just as twelve years ago we witnessed the destruction of several hundreds of thousands in Choogoochak and Kooldja.—*Author.*

Khans of Mongol race was not particularly lasting, for they in fact often held vassalship to the Uzbek Khans, who at this time reigned in Bokhara, Samarkand, Kokan and Tashkent. The increase of the power of the Uzbek Khans in Western Turkestan (in Maver-El-Nagra) always betokened the decrease of the power of the Mongol Khans in Eastern Turkestan. The nomads of the Tian-Shan always seized the opportunity of the outbreak of dissensions amongst the latter to interfere in the civil war in which they would espouse the cause of one pretender or the other. Not content with plundering Kashgaria they would carry their raids as far as Kokan and Tashkent. These facts gave the Uzbeks the excuse for interfering in the affairs of Eastern Turkestan. Thus it was that, in the Fifteenth Century, under the guise of punishing the nomad Mongols, they sent an army from Samarkand and occupied Kashgar.

The Uzbek Khans of Western Turkestan and the Mongol Khans in Eastern Turkestan.

Sultan Said, son of Chingiz-Khan.

Of all the sons of Chingiz who ruled Kashgaria during the Fifteenth and Sixteenth Centuries the reign of none was more famous than that of Sultan Said. He succeeded not only in subjugating the nomads of Northern Tian-Shan, but in securing his frontier to the south and west on the side of Kashmir and of Badakhshan. Besides that, in 1531—33, he marched against Tibet with 5,000 men. The approach of winter obliged Sultan Said to halt, for he found it impossible to provision his army. He, therefore, sent his son Iskander with 4,000 men into winter quarters in Kashmir, and he himself remained with the remaining 1,000 in the neighbourhood of Balti. When summer came, Sultan Said once more joined his forces and continued his march to Lhassa, of which he took possession. On the return march to his capital he died not far from the Karakorum pass. His death was caused by the action of the rarefied atmosphere.[1] This was a *Gazavat* campaign, a war, *i. e.*, against the infidel. It served as the commencement of endless wars entered into by the Khodjas or leaders of two religious sects that appeared at this time in Kashgaria.

Appearance of the Khodjas.

Bokhara and Samarkand,

In the Fourteenth and Fifteenth Centuries Bokhara and Samar-

[1] Bellew.—During his reign Mirza Mahommed Goodar wrote the history of the Mongol Khans of Kashgaria, which he called "Tarikhi-Rashidi."—*Author.*

kand became the centres of Mussalman learning and the training places of many teachers who, by preaching the creed of Islam, obtained for themselves the halo of saints and wonder-workers. In the beginning of the Fifteenth Century, the fanaticism and hypocrisy developed in these centres reached Kashgaria.

centres of Mussulman learning.

Notwithstanding that Mahommedanism had penetrated to Eastern Turkestan in the Eighth Century, it was only of an extremely fanatical type for the short dominion of the Arabs. And in later times, especially during the rule of the Mongol Khans in Eastern Turkestan, religious tolerance in this country struck European travellers, such as Rubrukvist (1254),[1] Marco Polo (1280), Hughes (1604). The two last mentioned, who were stern and strict missionaries, even lamented the laxity of morals which they observed amongst the inhabitants of Kashgaria.

Tolerance prevailing in Eastern Turkestan up to the 17th century.

The first of these travellers visited the country to the north of lake Lob, on the borders of Karashar. According to his account there lived the Uigurs, who were then under the rule of a Mongol race. The Uigurs themselves were idol-worshippers, but in their towns there dwelt Nestorian-Christians side by side with Saratsins (Mahometans). The Nestorians used Uigur letters even in their churches.[2] Rubrukvist goes on to tell us of his visit to Nestorian villages, where, with his fellow-travellers, he entered the churches, and, with heartfelt joy, sang aloud the "Salve Regina." Marco Polo also mentions that, in this country, there were at the same time three religions in vogue,—*viz.*, Buddhism, Mahommedanism and Christianity.[3] He even assures us, that, on his visiting the town of Yarkend, he took up his residence with a Catholic Bishop.[4]

As a testimony, too, to the religious toleration which then prevailed, we find in the records of the Embassy to China, under Tamerlane's son Shah-Rok, mention made that he found in the

[1] Mons. Grigorieff (in his Notes to Ritter's "Eastern or Chinese Turkestan," page 428) calls Rubrukvist by his proper name, *viz.*, Ruisbrök.—*Author.*

[2] Ritter's "Eastern Turkestan," page 161.—*Author.*

[3] See Ritter's "Eastern Turkestan," page 164.—*Author.*

[4] Bellew.

town of Komool (Khama), in the year 1420, handsome mosques side by side with Pagan temples.[1]

Arrival of narrow-minded bigots and consequent decline of religious toleration in Eastern Turkestan.

In the Fifteenth Century, there began to arrive in Eastern Turkestan from the west famous teachers, prophets of the Mussulman school. With the advent of these luminaries of Islam, religious toleration gave place to a narrow bigotry, which engendered bloody wars and economic paralysis, which, coupled with her wars with China, brought Kashgaria to her present pitiable condition.

Khodja Mahtoom-Azyam.

In the very beginning of the Fifteenth Century, a Said and a descendant of Mahomet, the Khodja Mahtoom-Azyam, a learned theologian of Bokhara, visited the principal towns of Eastern Turkestan.[2] He obtained the patronage of the Khan of Kashgar, received from him rich estates, and succeeded, moreover, in securing popular respect and reverence. Still more important in the eyes of the Khans, as well as of the people, were the two sons of Azyam—the Imam Kalyan and the Khodja Isaak-Vali, who became the religious patrons of the Mussulmans and inaugurated the importance of the Khodjas in Eastern Turkestan.

Khodja Azyam's two sons, Imam Kalyan and Khodja Isaak-Vali.

Each of these personages was surrounded by a crowd of followers and of fanatical Sooffis (*Kaibs*), *Doovans*, of dervishes and of lay brethren. The religious teaching of these two brothers differed but little in its essentials, each, nevertheless, served to form two religious sects. The followers of the Imam Kalyan called themselves *Ishkiya*, those of the Khodja Isaak-Vali, *Isakiya*, and subsequently the former were called *Ak-Taulins* (the white mountaineers), and the latter *Kara-Taulins* (the black mountaineers). These divisions exist up to the present time, although they have not their former importance.

The sects formed by these two Khodjas.

Soon the leaders of either party, not content with spiritual power, began to search for political authority, and, in pursuit of this, they not only divided the entire country into two hostile

The leaders of these sects seek political authority as well as spiritual power.

[1] Valikhanoff.—See "Journal of the Imperial Russian Geographical Society for 1861," Vol. III, page 34.—*Author*.

[2] See the Chronicles of Mirza Shemsa-Boukhara, published by Grigorieff in 1861, page 34; also Valikhanoff's article in the "Journal of the Imperial Russian Geographical Society for 1861," No. III, page 34.—*Author*.

camps, but from personal motives, gave it first into the hands of the Djoongars and then of the Chinese.

Appak-Khodja.

The struggle of the Khodjas for political supremacy and their intrigues dated from the time when Appak-Khodja became the head of the *white-mountaineers'* party.

The great renown of Appak-Khodja, both as a teacher and as a holy personage, attracted towards him the youth, not only of Eastern but of Western Turkestan. Even certain ruling personages from Maver-El-Nagra were among his disciples. The reputation of Appak, as a religious patron, is preserved in Kashgaria up till now, for many worshippers are yearly drawn towards his tomb, which lies at some versts' distance from Kashgar.

Khan Ismail, Chingiz-Khan's youngest son.

At the time when Appak's religious reputation was greatest in Kashgaria, Khan Ismail, the last of the sons of Chingiz, was ruler of the country. He was a zealous *black-mountaineer*, and, as he could not endure the glory that attended Appak, he endeavoured to drive him from the country. The offended Appak-Khodja let slip no opportunity for taking vengeance. He went to Tibet and presented himself to the Dalai-Lama,[1] whose patronage he succeeded in obtaining, and likewise the support of this real enemy of the Mahommedan religion. Moreover, Appak-Khodja, from purely personal motives, yielded up his native land to the yoke of the Djoongars, who seized Kashgaria in the year 1678, and held it for 78 years, *i.e.*, until they gave place to the Chinese, who were likewise invited by Boorkhan-Eddin, one of the *white mountain* Khodjas and a person also prompted by personal motives. (We should here remember, that the Djoongars or Kalmucks called themselves a Mongol race, and that they dwelt in the valleys of the rivers Ili, Tekes, Koonges and the two Yulduz.)

Result of the quarrel between him and Appak-Khodja.

Betrayal, by Appak-Khodja, of Kashgaria into the hands of the Djoongars.

Haldan-Bokoshta.

Taking advantage of the fall of the Mongol dynasty of Han in China, the Djoongars, in the beginning of the Seventeenth Century, concluded an alliance, at the head of which they placed Haldan-Bokoshta, a khan of the Tchoross line. He incorporated

[1] The spiritual leader of all Asiatic Buddhists, who dwells at Lhassa, the capital of Tibet.—*Trans.*

in his dominions the Mongol branch of Olëts, and after that the Djoongars for some time called themselves *Olëts*, and their Khans, *Oirats*.

Extent of the Djoongar dominion in the time of Haldan-Bokoshta.

During the administration of the Khan Haldan-Bokoshta, the Djoongar sovereignty embraced the vast country bordered on the north by Siberia, on the east by the possessions of the Mongol Khan of the Khalkhas tribe, on the west by the Kirghiz steppes as far as Lake Balkash, and lastly, on the south by Eastern Turkestan (by the line, *i.e.*, of Koocha, Karashar and Koonya-Toorfan). The Djoongars (Kalmucks) were at this time divided into four tribes, *viz.*, the *Tchoross*, the *Torgouts*, the *Khoshots* and the *Doorbats*. This division has been preserved to the present day. Each tribe is ruled by its own Khan, subject to the authority of the Tchoross Khan, who is over all.

Divisions amongst the Djoongars.

Repeated wars between the Djoongars and the Chinese.

The period of the independent existence of the Djoongar sovereignty was taken up with endless wars with the Chinese, but these wars did not hinder the Djoongars from adding Eastern Turkestan and also Tibet[1] to their dominions.

Amoorsana treacherously hands over Djoongaria to the Chinese.

Later on, the Chinese seized the opportunity of internal dissensions in Djoongaria, and possessed themselves without bloodshed of the above countries, thanks to the treachery of the Kalmuck leader, Amoorsana.

Prosperity of Djoongaria under the Tchoross Khans.

During the rule of the Tchoross Khans in Djoongaria, and especially of Haldan-Bokoshta, the country enjoyed great prosperity. Huge herds of camels, of horses and of sheep covered the rich pastures in the valleys of the Eastern Tian-Shan. The capital of the country was at Ili, whence the Khans governed their numerous nomad subjects.[2]

Ili the capital of Djoongaria.

Appak-Khodja's intrigues.

Appak-Khodja, with the advice of the Dalai-Lama of Lhassa, turned for aid to Haldan-Bokoshta against the Khan of Kashgar, Ismail, the leader of the party opposed to his own. Khan Haldan immediately availed himself of so favorable an oppor-

[1] Goloobeff.—The Trans-Ili tract. See "Journal of the Imperial Russian Geographical Society for 1861," Vol. III, page 106.—*Author*.

[2] The nomad Kalmucks were divided into *Oolooses* or sections. The places chosen for their summer and winter abodes were called *Stoibishtshas* (nomad camps).—*Author*.

tunity for interfering, and in 1678 took possession of Kashgaria. He appointed Appak as his deputy, and returned himself to the river Ili, taking with him as prisoners the family of the Kashgar Khan.

Political tact of Haldan-Bokoshta.

In this circumstance, we observe Haldan's political tact, for he introduced no sort of changes in the internal administration of Kashgaria, and contented himself with a money tribute from the country of 400,000 *tengas* a month (about 500,000 *roubles* or £62,500 a year). Soon, however, Appak divested himself of his secular calling, and, in order to free himself from the stigma which attached to him of being the betrayer of his country, he invited Mahammed-Emil, the brother of Khan Ismail, from Ootch-Toorfan, proclaimed him Khan and persuaded him to make the attempt to free the country from the Djoongars. This last act of Appak-Khodja caused his country, it may be, misfortunes still greater than did his former treachery.

Appak-Khodja seeks to free himself from the stigma attaching to him as the betrayer of his country.

Mohammed-Emil.

Khan-Emil did, it is true, carry out a successful raid on the Djoongars, and took away with him 30,000 prisoners of either sex, and much cattle and property; but then, being afraid of Kalmuck treachery, he fled to the mountains, where he was slain by one of his own people. Kashgaria then again became the arena of bloody struggles between the Khodjas, until the Chinese, by taking possession of the country, put an end for a time (till 1825) to civil war.

Appak-Khodja, on the death of Mohammed-Emil, again assumes political power. His death.

After the death of Khan-Emil, Appak-Khodja again assumed secular power. He did not, however, rule long. At his death the power was seized by his wife Khanwim-Padsha. She surrounded herself with fanatical dervishes, with whose aid she slew Appak's eldest son, in order to secure the supreme power for her own son Mehdi. Soon, however, Khanwim-Padsha herself became the victim of her own wiles, and died under the knife of the dervishes. Upon this event Yarkend and Kashgar passed respectively under the rule of the *black-mountain* Khodja, Daniel, and of the *white-mountaineer*, Ahmet. These two entered into a bloody struggle. Daniel at first called to the aid of the Yarkend Kirghiz bands, whose leader, Sultan Ashem, was made for a time Khan of Yarkend, but later on, learning that the Djoongars were collecting their forces to

Yarkend and Kashgar pass respectively under the rule of the *white* and *black* mountain Khodjas.

Struggle between the *white* and *black* mountain Khodjas.

Daniel's treachery.

avenge themselves for Emil's raid, he, in order to gain the favour of the enemies of his country, went over with his Yarkendians to the Kalmuck army, which marched on Kashgar. With his new allies Daniel now entered into several engagements with the Kashgarians, who were defeated and obliged to surrender their city. On this occasion likewise, the Djoongars proved themselves to be very mild conquerors. There is no mention made anywhere of their plundering or killing their enemies. After capturing the town of Kashgar they put up a ruler chosen by the people, and then returned to their own country, taking with them the Khodja Ahmet and his family, together with his most influential adherents, and likewise the Khodja Daniel.

Clemency of the Djoongars.

Haldan-Bokoshta's death. Tsapan-Raptan.

On the death of Haldan-Bokoshta in the year 1720, Tsapan-Raptan ascended the Djoongar throne. This ruler assigned the administration of six towns of Kashgaria to Daniel Khodja, who, after returning to Yarkend, there founded his capital and appointed Hakims of his own choice in each town. It is probable that to this time belongs the affixing of the title Altwi-Shar (six cities) by which Kashgaria came to be known. The six cities were Kashgar, Yangi-Hissar, Yarkend, Khotan, Aksu and Koocha.[1] Daniel Khodja's eldest son was retained as a hostage at the Djoongarian Court.

Altwi-Shar.

Haldan-Shirin.

On the accession of Haldan-Shirin to the Djoongar throne, Daniel's rights were continued, and thus the power of the *black-mountain* Khodjas in Kashgaria came to be established. On Daniel Khodja's death, Haldan-Shirin sent to his four sons his royal decree, conferring on the eldest Yarkend, on the second Kashgar, on the third Aksu, on the fourth, Yunus Khodja, Khotan. In this way, by dividing Kashgaria, he made it less dangerous for himself.

Partition of Kashgaria.

Yunus Khodja.

Yunus Khodja was by far the most energetic and ambitious of all the four brothers. He, being aware of the weakness of Djoongaria, determined to secure independence for Kashgaria, and he at once began to actively prepare means to attain this end. The reports of the Hakims of Aksu and of Ootch-

[1] Later on Yakoob Bek added to these six cities another—Karashar. Kashgaria then became known as *Djitwi-Shar*, which means the seven cities.—*Author.*

Toorfan acquainted the Djoongar authorities with the preparations that were being made by Yunus; but, since they were too much taken up with internal dissensions, they were not in a position to defeat the designs of Yunus in their very conception.

Death of Haldan-Shirin.

On the death of Haldan-Shirin a struggle arose in his family for the pre-eminence, and this struggle ended in the mutual overthrow of the direct heirs.[1] Amoorsana, a distant relation of Haldan's and a chief of one of the Kalmuck tribes, thought that he would take the opportunity of these dissensions to possess himself of the Djoongar throne. Accordingly, with the aid of those devoted to his cause, he made the attempt. Being unsuccessful, he and his tribe declared themselves, in the year 1774, to be subjects of China. The sons of the Celestial Empire did not let slip the favourable opportunity afforded to them of gaining possession of Djoongaria. Accordingly, a Chinese army was immediately advanced towards that country. Amoorsana, who accompanied the Chinese forces, succeeded in persuading the chiefs of the Kalmuck tribe to come over to the Chinese without fighting, and soon the entire country passed into their hands. The last Djoongar Khan, the weak Tavatsi, made no opposition and fled to Ootch-Toorfan, where he hoped to find a refuge with

Amoorsana declares himself a subject of China.

Conquest of Djoongaria by the Chinese.

[1] As a specimen of the evil deeds that were perpetrated by members of the house of Haldan in order to secure the supreme power, we will produce the following extract from an article by Mons. Abramoff (" Proceedings of the Imperial Russian Geographical Society for 1861," page 160), compiled from a translation of the Chinese work entitled *Su-Yuivwin-Dziyan-Loo* (chronicles of the countries lying near the western borders of China): " In September 1745, Khan Haldan-Shirin died. In accordance with the terms of his will, his second son, Tsavan-Dorizi-Atchja-Namiyal, succeeded to the Khanship, and he at once slew his youngest brother Tsavan-Djail. Haldan-Shirin's eldest son, Lama-Dardja, fearing a like fate, killed the successor to the throne, and assumed the reins of government; Lama-Dardja's sister Oolan-Bayar and her husband, having rebelled against him, were also killed. We must observe that all these murders were accomplished in the course of several years. In the year 1754, the Khan's two kinsmen, Tavatsi and Amoorsana, rose against him. Amoorsana with 1,500 men came by night to Ili and killed Lama-Dardja in his palace. The Djoongars then chose for a Khan Tavatsi (he being the nearest relative of the deceased) and not Amoorsana as he himself expected. Amoorsana being offended at this, as we shall see further on, acknowledged himself a subject of the Chinese and betrayed his own country to them."—*Author.*

the Hakim of the city. Indeed he had himself not long beforehand appointed this very man to that post. But gratitude and nobility of character were not virtues frequent among the political actors of the epoch of which we write. The Hakim, therefore, made Tavatsi dead drunk, and, whilst in that state, seized him and made him over to the Chief of the Chinese army. Amoorsana, who was now serving with the Chinese forces in Djoongaria, devised a plan for the conquest of Kashgaria. Without the display of force, and in order to attain his object, he decided to take advantage of the conflict between the Khodjas of the *white-mountaineer* and *black-mountaineer* party respectively.

Amoorsana's intrigues for the conquest of Kashgaria.

We have said above that the last Djoongar Khan had established the power of the *black-mountaineer* Khodjas. At the time, therefore, that Amoorsana made his attempt, Khodjas of this party were ruling in Yarkend and in Kashgar. The two Khodjas were Padsha Khan and Djagan Khodja, sons of Yunus. Knowing the attachment of the Kashgarians to Khodjas of the *white-mountaineer* party, Amoorsana sought out a person of that party with whose aid he hoped to easily take possession of the country. With this object, and with the consent of the leader of the Chinese forces, he invited to the river Ili Boorkhan-Eddin (Booranidoo) and Khodja Khan, sons of Khodja Ahmet, who had been a former ruler of Kashgaria.

Padsha Khan and Djagan Khodja, sons of Yunus.

Boorkhan-Eddin (Booranidoo) and Khodja Khan, sons of Khodja Ahmet.

Boorkhan-Eddin, having received a small force composed of Kalmucks, a few Chinese and fugitives from Eastern Turkestan, moved on Aksu, leaving as a hostage at Ili his brother Khodja Khan. The inhabitants of Aksu surrendered to him without opposition. After increasing his forces in this town, Boorkhan-Eddin marched on Ootch-Toorfan, the inhabitants of which place received him with joy. From Ili to the town of Aksu there are two roads, the one direct, through the Moozart pass, the other more circuitous and leading to the north-eastern portion of Lake Isswik-Kool, and so by the town of Ootch-Toorfan to Aksu.[1] It must be supposed that Boorkhan-Eddin reached Aksu by the

Roads leading from Ili to Aksu.

[1] At present the Moozart pass is shut by order of the 'Badaulet,' and the trade between Aksu and Kuldja is carried on by the alternative route.—*Author.*

former route, *i.e.* by the Moozart pass. Unfortunately there is nothing to show us at what time of the year this movement took place. Meanwhile the Khodjas of Yarkend and Khotan, hearing of the occupation of the town of Aksu by a hated Khodja of the *white-mountaineer* party, equipped a considerable force, which they moved against the town of Aksu. Along the road this force was joined by bands from the town of Kashgar and by crowds of Kara-Kirghiz, who were invited to take part in the fight against Boorkhan-Eddin. The latter, hearing of the preparations of the *black-mountain* Khodjas, shut himself up in Ootch-Toorfan and refused to advance further. His forces were indeed far from being sufficient to cope with the united bands of Yarkend, Kashgar, Khotan and of the Kara-Kirghiz. They consisted of 5,000 Mussulmans from Koocha, Aksu, Toorfan, of Doolans, of 1,000 Kalmucks and of 400 Chinese.[1] The army of the *black-mountain* Khodjas having reached the town of Ootch-Toorfan, prepared to lay siege to it.[2] Before opening military operations the *black-mountain* Khodjas sent emissaries to Boorkhan-Eddin in order to settle the affair by agreement. They offered to give him the towns of Aksu, Koocha and Kashgar, retaining for themselves Yarkend and Khotan. Their idea was, instead of having a civil war with Boorkhan-Eddin, to unite their forces with his for an attack on Ili. The negotiations, however, came to nothing and military operations began.

Action of the Khodjas of Yarkend and Khotan.

Halt of Boorkhan-Eddin.

Strength of his forces.

Terms offered to Boorkhan-Eddin.

It soon appeared that in the camp of the besiegers there were many in favour of the return of the *white-mountain* Khodjas to Kashgaria. The Kirghiz, who were always ready to serve whosoever offered them the best terms, were probably bought over by Boorkhan-Eddin. In the first fight, therefore, the

Treachery in the camp of the besiegers.

[1] Valikhanoff.—See Vol. III, page 41. We here meet for the first time with Dolons or Doolans, a people who now inhabit the country about Fort Maral-Bashi.—*Author.*

[2] In Valikhanoff's work there is an indication to the effect that these forces moved from Kashgar on Ootch-Toorfan *viâ* Aksu and Kokshal. This is very unlikely, for we may suppose that the route chosen by them was the mountain road from Kokshar *viâ* Artoosh and Kalpin. A little before Mons. Valikhanoff himself says, I suppose when thinking of this road, that the Khotan and Yarkend forces moved on Yangi-Hissar, and after uniting with the bands from this city went *viâ* Artoosh along the Ootch road.—*Author.*

Kirghiz, and with them the greater portion of the Beks and their forces, went over to the side of the besieged. The leaders of the *black-mountain* party scarcely managed to fly with the remnants of their army. Encouraged by a so easily-attained success, Boorkhan-Eddin marched on the town of Kashgar and took it without opposition.[1] The *black-mountain* Khodjas fled. Having stayed for a short time at Kashgar, Boorkhan-Eddin appointed the Kirghiz Kabid ruler of the city, and then moved against the town of Yarkend. Of the Kalmucks and Chinese sent with him by Amoorsana, there remained with Boorkhan-Eddin, of the first 600, and of the second 200 men. As we have said above, at this time the ruler of Yarkend was a Khodja of the *black-mountain* party. This was Djagan, a person very much beloved by his subjects for his kindness and nobleness of character.[2] The inhabitants of Yarkend, probably more from a feeling of devotion to their ruler than from any religious convictions, resolved to make a brave resistance.

Boorkhan-Eddin captures Kashgar.

Djagan, the reigning Khodja at Yarkend.

Boorkhan-Eddin lays siege to Yarkend,

Boorkhan-Eddin, having sent forward a deputation to Djagan, with proposals in the name of Amoorsana and of the *Bogdwi Khan*,[3] that he should surrender and acknowledge himself a subject of China, approached Yarkend. Before the emissaries were presented to Djagan, they were obliged to prostrate themselves at the threshold of his courthouse. The Khodja replied to the propositions brought to him to the effect, that he, as a Mussulman ruler, could have no relations with the unfaithful other than a *Gazavat*.[4] The military operations, which were

[1] Valikhanoff says, that the *white-mountain* Khodja was received in Kashgar not merely without opposition, but with shouts of joy, and that the people stood at the city gates beating tambourines and playing on reed instruments.—*Author*.

[2] A native writer, living at the time of Djagan, describes him as a man who encouraged the sciences, and compares his rule with that of the time of Mirza Hoossein.—*Author*.

[3] A title given to the Chinese Emperor.—*Trans*.

[4] Or war against an infidel. "Ghazi is a title (signifying 'ravager') assumed only by those engaged in war with infidels."—Journal of Royal Geographical Society, Vol. XL, 1870, p. 73, *note*. The substantive *Ghazavat*, meaning a *ravaging* crusade, is in use amongst the Central Asiatics north of the Oxus or of the country of the Tian-Shan range. *Vide* Notes on Eastern Turkistan, by Major J. M. Trotter, B. S. Corps.—*Trans*.

then begun, were not decided enough, and success inclined to the side of the besieged. Boorkhan-Eddin hereupon resorted again to the means which he had employed at Ootch-Toorfan,—*viz.*, to a bribe. Two persons occupying high posts amongst the court priesthood,—*viz.*, Ishik-Aga-Niaz and Ashoor-Kazi-Bek, having been gained over by promises, entered into a plot in favour of Boorkhan-Eddin. During a general sortie from the town made by 40,000 men, the besiegers were driven back, and success could not have been otherwise than complete, when all at once the conspirators threw down their standards and fled back, causing at first disorder and then flight in the ranks of the Yarkendians. The Kirghiz, who had as yet taken no part in the affair, now rushed on the fugitives. The panic became general. The whole mass rushed in through the city gates, and the majority of the besieged were slain. Khodja Djagan, after this engagement, fled by night from the city, and the inhabitants next day opened the gates to Boorkhan-Eddin. Those of the besieged who had taken to flight were pursued, and on being overtaken were, after a stout resistance, captured and brought back to Yarkend, where they were executed.

and bribes certain personages attached to Djagan's court,

and so captures Yarkend.

Djagan's flight and the massacre of the garrison.

By such a bloody war was the sovereignty of those *white-mountain* Khodjas, who had acknowledged their fealty to China, re-established in Kashgaria. As a result, the Chinese were enabled in a few years to obtain, with very insignificant means, dominion over two vast States, Djoongaria and Kashgaria.

Chinese sovereignty established over Djoongaria and Kashgaria.

Nevertheless, the Chinese authorities, by not maintaining a proper army in those countries, held very insecure tenure in both Djoongaria and Kashgaria. During 1757, Amoorsana in the former country, and Boorkhan-Eddin in the latter, rose up against them.

Rebellion of Amoorsana in the one country and of Boorkhan-Eddin in the other.

Amoorsana, who had betrayed his country to the Chinese, soon became convinced that his doing so was but the means to enable him to take possession of the country for himself, and accordingly he was ready at the first opportunity to free it from their yoke. Taking advantage of the withdrawal to China of the greater portion of the Chinese army, Amoorsana determined to rise against the enemies introduced by himself and to declare himself Khan. His plan succeeded, for, 500 Chinese with their leaders having been overthrown, the Kalmucks acknowledged him as their Khan. But the new Khan, having heard during the year following of a march against him of a fresh Chinese army, did not consider himself strong enough to defend his kingdom, and so he fled across the Kirghiz steppes into Siberia, where he died of small-pox within a year.[1] A Chinese army occupied Djoongaria for the second time without opposition. Perhaps, they considered their power to be but insecurely established in Djoongaria, because this country had come into their possession without any bloodshed. It was therefore that in the year 1758, that the Bogdwi Khan made the excuse of some insignificant and partial risings to send three armies under the leadership of Tchjao-Hoi and Foo-De with orders to root out the Djoongars. Thus began that terrible slaughter of Kalmucks without respect of age or sex. About 1,000,000 persons perished in this inhuman slaughter.[2] (One hundred years after in this very country there were slain during the Doongan insurrection about half a million Chinese, Solons, Sibs and Kalmucks.)

Flight and death of Amoorsana.

Severity of the Chinese.

Termination of the Djoongar sovereignty.

The Djoongar sovereignty had now ceased to exist. Only a small number of the Kalmuck tribe of Doorbats were spared, the remaining inhabitants of this once rich country were killed. A few, indeed, escaped to the Kirghiz steppes, and, perhaps, as many as 10,000 *Kibitkas*, under the leadership of Sultan Taish-Seren, succeeded in avoiding destruction, and fled to join the Russian Kalmucks on the Volga. Djoongaria now became parcelled out into seven Circles. Of these Ili, Tarbagatai and Koor-Kara-Oosoo formed the province of Ili. Barkool and Ooroomtchi were added to the province of Han-Su, and the other two Circles, Kobdo and Oolya-Sootai, received a separate

Partition of Djoongaria.

[1] Mons. Goloobeff relates (Sketch of the Trans-Ili tract, 1861, Vol. III) that many Torgout Kalmucks asked him, "Will our Amoorsana soon return? He went long since to ask the White Tsar for aid against the Chinese." Thus Amoorsana, who had betrayed his country, and who had been the main cause of the destruction of hundreds of thousands of his kinsmen, continues to live in the memory of the people as a hero who would come again to free them. A fact which shows that the simple faith of a primitive people in its would-be benefactors partakes of the nature of child-like confidence.—*Author*.

[2] Abramoff.—Proceedings of the Imperial Russian Geographical Society for 1861, Vol. I, page 112.—*Author*.

administration.[1] On the site of the Djoongar Khan's place of abode, the Chinese built the town of Kooldja, and introduced into the country military settlers of Mongol races, soldiers of the green standard, from the frontiers of Mandjooria, Sibs, Solons and Daurs. Criminals and vagabonds, who possessed no lands in China, also emigrated to the same place. To this period, in all probability, belongs the deportation by the Chinese of Mussulmans, known under the name of Doongans,[2] from their western provinces, Han-Su and Shan-Si, into Djoongaria. Besides this, during the year 1771, the greater portion of those Kalmucks who had gone to Russia in the beginning of the Seventeenth

The Chinese build the town of Kooldja.

The Chinese Mussulmans or Doongans.

[1] Goloobeff.—"The Trans-Ili tract." Proceedings of the Imperial Russian Geographical Society, 1861, Vol. III, page 107.—*Author.*

[2] In the "Turkestan Compendium" for 1867, Vol. V, there occurs a very interesting article by Mons. Heins, on the subject of "The rising of the Doongans in Western China." The author supposes that Eastern Turkestan was originally peopled by a race of Turkish origin, the *Uigurs* or *Oikhars*, and he identifies these as the Doongans, the number of whom he puts down at 30,000,000. Their capital was established at Karashar, which before that time was called Hao-Tan. The Chinese began the war against the Uigurs in the Seventh Century during the Tan dynasty. In the Eighth Century they subdued and overthrew Hao-Tan. Afterwards, *i.e.*, during the Eighth and Ninth Centuries, *families of Uigurs to the number of* 1,000,000 *were deported to Djoongaria from the provinces of Han-Su and Shan-Si.* At first zealous Buddhists, the Uigurs, in the Fourteenth Century by degrees accepted the Mussulman faith which came to them from Eastern Turkestan.

The supposition of Mons. Heins that the Doongans and the Uigurs are one and the same race, has evidently no foundation. Apart from the fact that this question has already been settled by modern explorers, I, whilst admitting that the Chinese did deport a portion of the Uigurs into their western provinces, allow myself to suppose that the name *Doongans* referred only to those exiled Uigurs who were largely mixed with Chinese. To the Uigurs who remained in Eastern Turkestan the name *Doongans* can in no way be applied. At present in all the towns of Kashgaria, one general and very similar type of countenance prevails. This proceeds from a mixture of a Mongol race with a Turkish or, perhaps, with an Indo-Germanic, in which Turkish predominates. The inhabitants of Kashgar cannot be distinguished from the inhabitants of Khotan, and the inhabitants of Khotan from those of Aksu. In the latter city the prominent type of a Mongol race is more noticeable. The Doongans form a marked contrast to the original inhabitants, for the Doongans only came into Kashgaria with the Chinese in the middle of the past century. Amongst the Doongans the Chinese admixture is so apparent as to be recognizable without mistake amongst hundreds of natives.—*Author.*

Century with Khan Ho-Oorlook[1] returned to Kashgaria. Finally, the Chinese, during the last collisions with Eastern Turkestan, deported a portion of the population of that country to Djoongaria, where they became known under the name of Tarantchis.[2]

The Tarantchis.

After the subjugation of Djoongaria, the Chinese at once turned their arms against Kashgaria with the object of putting down the rebellions that were taking place therein, or, to speak more correctly, with the object of conquering the country, since the campaign of Boorkhan-Eddin, with a few hundred Chinese and Kalmucks, had not yet obliged the population to acknowledge for all time the hated Chinese supremacy.

The Chinese again march against Kashgaria.

On receipt of the first news relating to a rising in Kashgaria, Tchjao-Hoi, ruler of the province of Ili, moved from the town of the same name with a detachment of 2,000 Kalmucks and a small number of Mandjoor and Turkestanese, over the Moozart pass, to the town of Koocha. This town was prepared to make a stout resistance, so that the small force that had been sent from Ili had to return without success. Tchjao-Hoi now despatched a fresh force, numbering 10,000 men, composed of Mandjoors and Chinese, by the route *viâ* Koonya-Toorfan to Koocha. On

Siege of Koocha by a Chinese force.

[1] During the Seventeenth Century, a portion of the Kalmucks of the Toorgout tribe, together with their Khan Ho-Oorlook, decamped to Russia and took up their abode between the Ural and the Volga. (Goloobeff.—"Trans-Ili tract.") They became subjects of Russia and took part with her armies in the war against the Crimean Tatars. These Kalmucks maintained a connection with their kinsmen in Djoongaria, and bearing in mind the abundant and rich pastures of their native land, probably thought very frequently of returning to Djoongaria. At last a princeling, who had succeeded in escaping from the massacre of Kalmucks by the Chinese, persuaded them to fly from Russia. Accordingly, in the year 1771, the greater portion of the Volga Kalmucks under the leadership of the Khan Oobashi began their march. The Russian Government directed that they should be pursued, but since the pursuit was not a vigorous one, the Kalmucks were not brought back. They had, however, to face another enemy. The Kirghiz, who followed them step by step, came up with them at lake Balkhash, and utterly routed them. Only a third of their number reached Djoongaria, for two-thirds perished on the way. Nor did the freedom, for which they sought, come to them after all. Having arrived within the borders of their native lands, they were obliged to acknowledge Chinese supremacy.—*Author.*

[2] According to Valikhanoff the Chinese enrolled 7,000 Mussulmans for the purpose of cultivating the State domains (*taran*).—*Author.*

the other hand, the Yarkend Khodja sent a reinforcement to the people of Koocha composed of 10,000 selected troops.[1] The Chinese having driven off the reinforcement laid siege to the town. They carried their saps to within a *li* (about 200 *sajens*, or about 460 yards English) of the town, and had arrived sufficiently near to make an assault, when all at once the besieged let out some water, drowning 10 officers and 600 soldiers of the Chinese forces. The position of the besiegers was not indeed especially favourable, and they had thought of raising the siege, but the flight of the Khodja from Koocha aided them. The inhabitants of the town after the Khodja's flight, not wishing to make any further resistance, opened the gates. Notwithstanding this spontaneous surrender, about a thousand of the Koocha troops were slain by the conquerors on their entry into the town. The Chinese Emperor Tsian Loon, on receiving the report that the Chinese leader had allowed the offending Khodja to escape, and that he had slaughtered some of those who had surrendered, ordered him to be executed, and he at the same time ordered Tchjao-Hoi, the Governor of Ili, and his colleague, Foo-De, to move against Kashgaria with fresh forces. The movements of the Chinese were carried out very rapidly, though their forces were insufficient, and their plan of operations was badly conceived. Having reached Aksu, Tchjao-Hoi took possession of this town, and then with 2,000 selected cavalry, composed of

The inhabitants surrender and are put to the sword.

Disapproval on the part of the Chinese Emperor of the circumstances attending the capture of Koocha.

Aksu is captured by a Chinese force.

[1] Ritter (in his "Eastern Turkestan," page 25) says, that the Yarkend Khodja (Boorkhan-Eddin) sent to the aid of the town of Koocha 10,000 picked troops, and that these went from Yarkend by the shortest route over the Aksu steppe. In the remarks of Mons. Grigorieff (see page 516 of the same compilation) it is stated that there are two roads between Koocha and Aksu. The shorter of these two is that by the village of Egul-Aman, where there is but one ford; this lies across the road. The other is the main road across the sandy steppe of Kwizwil (see Klaproth's Khechel-Gobi). By this the passage across the "Northern Mountain" cannot be avoided.

Regarding the first of these two roads we have not succeeded in procuring fully accurate information. They told us that one cannot ride direct to Yarkend from Koocha, and that one would have to go to Maral-Bashi *viâ* Aksu; that from Maral-Bashi there are two roads leading direct to Yarkend and to Khotan. According to our information the existence of the second road above spoken of does not admit of a doubt.—*Author.*

Solons and Mandjoors, he moved on to Yarkend,[1] directing his colleague, Foo-De, to follow with the infantry. The Khodja marched out from Yarkend with 10,000 men, defeated the Chinese, and compelled them to hurriedly return to Aksu, where they passed the winter. Having received additional reinforcements from China, Tchjao-Hoi advanced for the second time against the town of Yarkend, of which he took possession this time without any fighting. The Khodja, accompanied by his adherents, fled to the town of Khotan. In his despatch to the *Bogdwi Khan*, Tchjao-Hoi said that the inhabitants of Yarkend received the Chinese with joy, and that they came out with refreshments. "All the streets along which I passed," continues the Chinese Commander, "were filled with people who knelt down during my progress. From time to time I turned towards the populace with encouraging words and endeavoured to explain to them what great happiness would be their lot if henceforth they would remain faithful to the sceptre of your Majesty. I at the same time promised them that their customs and their religion would not be interfered with." (The joy of the inhabitants on the entry of the Chinese troops, of which Tchjao-Hoi speaks, was very suspicious, seeing that it was coupled with the fact that the inhabitants met the Chinese in a kneeling posture. It would have been truer to say that the people felt very uncomfortable, fearing that the fate of the Djoongar or Koocha population would be theirs also. The kneeling posture was chosen, because they wished to conciliate their conquerors, who would for this reason, perhaps, turn to them from time to time with encouraging words.)

Defeat of the Chinese force.

The Chinese capture Yarkend.

From Yarkend Tchjao-Hoi moved on Khotan. Khan Khodja (Boorkhan-Eddin's brother) advanced to meet him, but was defeated and had to fly. The town surrendered without a blow. Sending his colleague, Foo-De, from Khotan towards Badakhshan to follow after the Khodjas, Tchjao-Hoi moved on Kashgar, which he also took without opposition. Foo-De overtook the Khodjas and utterly routed their band of adherents. Four Khodjas were slain in the fight and two were taken prisoners. Boorkhan-Eddin's son, Sarwim-Sak or Saali-Khodja, alone escaped.

The Chinese march against Khotan.

Surrender of the towns of Khotan and Kashgar.

Flight and slaughter of the Khodjas.

[1] Probably by way of Fort Maral-Bashi.—*Author*.

Thus during the year 1758, Kashgaria was conquered by the Chinese. The weak opposition made to them shows how meagre was the patriotism and bravery of its population, and also how dissatisfied that population was with the rule of the Khodjas. It may be supposed that the people, who surrendered large towns to their enemies without a fight, counted on the attainment of quiet in exchange for subjection to a foreign and hated dominion—a quiet such as the inhabitants of Kashgaria had been long without.

Moderation of the Chinese Commander Tchjao-Hoi.

Fortunately for this unhappy country, the Chinese Commander Tchjao-Hoi was able by his moderation and wise arrangements to lighten the burden of the foreign yoke that was placed on its people. His despatch to the Emperor Tsian Loon, sent from camp near Kashgar on the 13th September 1759, served as a model, and a copy of it was distributed to all the Chinese officials for their guidance. This curious document depicts very exactly the condition in which the Chinese found Kashgaria. We therefore produce from it certain extracts.[1]

From the despatch it is apparent that, besides the six cities of Kashgar, Yarkend, Khotan, Yangi-Hissar, Aksu and Koocha, the Chinese reckoned that there were thirteen other small towns and also 16,000 villages and farm-houses.

Census of Kashgaria taken by the Chinese.

A census of Kashgaria, verified by Chinese officials, showed that there were in it from 50 to 60,000 families besides those of the persons who had taken flight with the Khodjas, and besides 12,000 political offenders condemned to exile at Ili and who were employed in agricultural operations.[2]

---

[1] Ritter's "Eastern Turkestan," pages 263-269 and 521-525.—*Author.*

[2] In Ritter's work on "Eastern Turkestan" and in Mons. Grigorieff's notes to the same, we find the following figures given, which do much to enable us to arrive approximately at the amount of the population in Kashgaria and at the number of those who pay taxes:—

(i.) According to the Geography of Si-Yui-Dziyan-Loo, published in 1778 (Timkovski's translation), in the Kashgar Circle taxes were paid by 16,000 persons, in the Yarkend Circle, by 32,000 persons,—*i. e.*, 48,000 persons out of a total of 80,000 families, or 400,000 *souls.*

The taxes in the Kashgar Circle yielded 36,000 *lans* of silver, 14,000 sacks of corn, and 10,000 pieces of *mata.* Those in the Yarkend Circle produced 35,370 ounces of silver, 30 ounces of gold, 1,649 ounces of silver by taxes on goods,

In the Kashgar Circle there were only about 16,000 families comprising 100,000 souls (*rwils*), and the population of the whole of Kashgaria amounted to 375,000 *rwils*. The town of Kashgar had a circumference of not more than 10 *li* (about 4 versts or 3⅔rds miles). It was very poor and deserted, and only contained 2,500 families. To the east of Kashgar and in the direction of Aksu and of Ootch-Toorfan lay three cities, Faizabad, Poinike (?) and Artoosh, and two settlements called Perser-

---

57,569 pieces of *mata*, 15,000 *djins* of corn amounting to 1.432 sacks, 1,297 pieces of cord, 3,000 *djins* of copper. (In Mons. Timkovski's opinion the money exactions in the Kashgar and Yarkend Circles went to maintain the army.)

(ii.) According to Timkovski, the garrison of Kashgar consisted of 10,000 men and that of Aksu, of 3,000 men.

According to the work of Mir-Oozet-Oollah, who visited the country in the year 1812, there were 40,000 tax-paying people in Yarkend. The taxes paid by the town of Kashgar amounted to 6,000 *tengas* (about 600 roubles, or £75) a month. The same work tells us that the garrison of Kashgar consisted of from 5,000 to 6,000 men, that of Yarkend, 2,000 men.

(iii.) According to information collected (in 1835) from pilgrims to Mecca (this kind of information should be received with great caution), in the town of Kashgar there were 16,000 souls, in the town of Yarkend, 30,000 families numbering 200,000 souls, in the town of Khotan there were 700,000 souls. The population of the whole country was 2½ millions. The garrison of Kashgar had, on account of the unfavourable relations existing with Kokan, been increased to 8,000 men. In Yarkend there were 2,000 men. On market days as many as 20,000 people crowded to the towns. The Khotan Circle yielded a greater revenue than did the Yarkend Circle.

(iv.) According to ancient Chinese information, the population for thirty years before the Birth of Christ was 1,510 families or 18,647 *rwils* (according to other information it numbered as many as 100,000 *rwils*). Kashgar was at that time known under the name of Soo-Le.

In the town of Khotan, in the First Century B. C., there were 3,300 families or 19,300 *rwils* (according to other information, 3,200 families or 83,000 *rwils*). The garrison of the town of Khotan was 2,400 men (according to other information, it comprised 30,000 soldiers). The garrison of Kashgar was 2,000.

(v.) According to other information, the population of Aksu comprised 20,000 families; that of Ootch-Toorfan, 10,000 families; that of Koonya-Toorfan, 3,000 families or 20,000 *rwils*; that of Boogoor, was at first 2,000 families, but in the year 1778 it decreased to 500 families; that of Koocha, 1,000 families; that of Sha-Yar, 700 families; that of the town of Bai, 500 families. According to the same information the inhabitants of the town of Koocha paid taxes as follows: 200 sacks of corn, 1,080 *djins* of copper, 200 *djins* of saltpetre and 300 *djins* of brimstone.—*Author*.

gooep (?) and Yangabad. The united population of all these points amounted to 6,000 families.

To the west of Kashgar lived the Andijan Booroots (the wild Kirghiz). Close to Andijan there were the villages of Western Artoosh, Oopal, Tashmalwik, Sairam and Togoozak. To the south of Kashgar and on the road to Yarkend there lay two towns, Yangi-Hissar and Kalik (?), and two settlements, Togsoon and Kapalskar (?) In all these places there were from 4,000 to 4,100 families.

To the north of Kashgar dwelt the Booroots. Before coming to their settlements it was necessary to pass through the town of Argoo (?) and the village of Koorgan, which had a population of 800 families.

Tchjao-Hoi's opinion as to the state of Kashgaria.

In the opinion of Tchjao-Hoi, the constant civil wars had brought Kashgaria to such a state of poverty that during the reign of the last Khodja, it payed as tribute to the Djoongars but 20,000 ounces of silver and 2,564 *batmans* [1] of bread.[2] Tchjao-Hoi found that the soil of Kashgaria was not a fruitful one. An average harvest amounted to a $\frac{1}{4}$th or $\frac{1}{5}$th: $\frac{1}{2}$ was considered a good crop and $\frac{1}{8}$th or $\frac{1}{6}$th a bad one.

The Emperor Tsian Loon, on receiving a despatch regarding the happy termination of the war, himself composed some valedictory verses on the event, and these he directed to be circulated in all the official departments. The Khodja's head was sent for to Pekin, and exhibited to the people through the bars of an iron cage.

Chinese rewards to the participators in the war against Kashgaria.

Those who took part in the war were liberally rewarded. Tchjao-Hoi was raised to the title of a Hoon-A, or prince of the fifth class, and it was ordained that he should be shown all the respect accorded to princes of the Imperial house. Foo-De received other rewards; amongst these he obtained permission to *ride* into the courtyard of the Imperial palace. The bestowal of these rewards took place in the year 1760. From this year the Chinese peacefully administered the country until the year

---

[1] A *batman* = 10 Russian lbs., or about the same amount of English.—*Trans.*

[2] The cause of the decrease in the tribute paid to the Djoongars must be sought in the weakening of the Djoongar rule over Kashgaria.—*Author.*

1765, when there broke out a partial rebellion in the town of Ootch-Toorfan, *i.e.*, five years after the occupation of the country. The cause of the rising in this town was the severity and looseness of the officials placed there by the Chinese. The Hakim of the town, a Mussulman from the town of Hami, and the commandant of the Chinese forces were the individuals against whom the movement was directed, against the first because of his severity and extortions, against the second on account of his loose conduct.

Rebellion against the Chinese in the town of Ootch-Toorfan.

The inhabitants of the town, having at length lost all patience, rushed to arms, killed their Hakim, and slew the whole of the small Chinese garrison.

Partial successes of the insurgents.

The leader of the Chinese forces at Aksu, the point nearest to Ootch-Toorfan, one Banshaga, marched against the insurgents, who came out to meet him and drove him off. Such, too, was the fate of the Chinese leader from the town of Koocha who had hastened to assist the Aksu garrison.

Nashitoon, the commandant of the Chinese forces in the town of Kashgar, having received news of the insurrection, set out for the town of Ili, whence he moved forward two columns composed of 10,000 Mandjoorians and Chinese. These troops having crossed the Moozart pass, reached Ootch-Toorfan and laid siege to it.

Defeat and massacre of the insurgents.

The inhabitants defended themselves desperately, and it was only after a three months' blockade that the town was taken by assault. The whole of its inhabitants were slaughtered agreeably to orders received from Pekin, and people from other places were settled in the deserted city.

Energetic measures attended with severity adopted by the Chinese.

The energetic measures adopted by the Chinese for the putting down of the rebellion prevented its spreading to other towns, and the severity with which the inhabitants of Ootch-Toorfan were treated, whether innocent or guilty, frustrated the desire on the part of others to make a similar attempt, but it nevertheless increased the hatred to their conquerors—a hatred which the conquered had to hide for a long time.

Commencement of a new and successful rebellion against the Chinese.

It is true that after the Ootch-Toorfan rising the Chinese peacefully ruled the country for sixty years, so much so that they held their position in Kashgaria to be durable. But in the year 1825, there appeared in Kashgar a Khodja named Djengir, who, with a handful of men, destroyed in a few months all that had been accomplished by the Chinese in the course of sixty years. This man revealed in their true colours both the rottenness of the system adopted by the Chinese for the administration of the country which they had conquered and also the hatred of the people for their conquerors.

Chinese system of administration.

With regard to the peculiar interest presented by the question relating to an organized system of administration in a conquered tract of Asia, let us examine in all possible detail how far the Chinese solved this question in the case of Kashgaria.

We repeat that the measures adopted by Tchjao-Hoi in subjugated Kashgaria must be acknowledged as fair specimens. These measures were as follows:—First of all the people had been promised non-interference in their religion and customs. Then followed the punishment of offenders. The Khodjas who were taken prisoners were triumphantly executed. Of the principal participators in the last rising there were taken 12,500 [1] persons, who were banished as political offenders to Ili, where they were turned into tillers of the State lands. The considerable possessions of the Khodjas and of these 12,500 persons were confiscated to the State.

By the two last measures the Chinese effected at the same time a twofold object: (1) they banished from the country the most restless portion of the population; and (2) they became the possessors of a considerable amount of landed property which would serve for their colonizing projects. At first this description of land was leased out to private persons who were obliged to furnish the State with half of their produce.

In order to hold the conquered country in continual subjection Tchjao-Hoi distributed garrisons in every direction, but these garrisons were at first very small. For example, in the Kashgar Circle there were only 450 Mandjoors and 900 Chinese, and in places less important there would be but 100 Chinese. On the arrival of fresh reinforcements from China, the strength of the garrisons was greatly increased. The inhabitants were obliged

[1] In a population of 375,000 souls the number of exiled would amount to about 15 per cent. of the entire adult male population.—*Author.*

to furnish provisions for the troops, and they were paid for such supplies by the State at the market-price.

For purposes of administration the country was divided into Circles. In each of these were at first retained the same officials that existed in the time of the Khodjas. The higher officials were appointed from among natives of the country by Tchjao-Hoi, but the Hakims of the towns were nominated from Pekin.

Both the amount of the taxes and the method of their collection remained just as in the time of the Khodjas. But the Chinese Commander-in-Chief, when making his report as to the method of collecting taxes which obtained in the country, petitioned the Emperor to exact less from the inhabitants of Kashgaria for the future on account of the great decrease of the population of the country and their comparative poverty.

In order to restore trade which had begun to decline to a considerable extent, Tchjao-Hoi adopted certain measures; amongst these was the alteration of the monetary system of the country. In Kashgaria the currency was that of the Khodjas'. It consisted of a copper *pool* equal to two Chinese *kash.* During the reign of Haldan-Tseren (Shirin), on one side of this piece was stamped the figure of the ruler, and on the other a sentence from the Koran. Tchjao-Hoi made arrangements for melting down the useless guns which he found in Kashgar, and thus procured 7,000 lbs. of metal, from which were struck 500,000 pieces of small money with the words *Tsian-Loon-Doon-Bao* (Tsian-Loon's *copper money*) on one side and *town of Kashgar* in Arabic and Mandjoor letters on the other. Tchjao-Hoi's plan was adopted in Pekin as a model which served for the system which was put in force throughout the whole of Kashgaria.

The following were the principal features of the Chinese administration of the country :—

(1) Non-interference in religion and customs; (2) the employment of natives of the country in the distribution and collection of taxes and in the trial of natives. Such officials were of course subject to the control (in practice very weak) of higher officials amongst the body of the Chinese; (3) the maintenance of the same scale of taxation as that which obtained

during the Djoongar rule; (4) the devoting of the taxes taken from the country to the maintenance of the army and of the local administration only.

Let us now see how the Chinese carried out this programme.

Of Eastern Turkestan there were made two provinces of China, Djoongaria and Kashgaria, and these formed one lord-lieutenancy. At the head of the united province was placed a *Dzian-Dzun* as lord-lieutenant. Kashgaria was divided into six Circles or governorships (Yarkend, Kashgar, Yangi-Hissar, Aksu, Ootch-Toorfan and Koocha). These formed one governor-generalship, at the head of which was a *Khova-Amban*, and he was subordinate to the *Dzian-Dzun*.

At the head of each Circle were *Ambans* who were subordinate to the *Khova-Amban*.

Both the civil population and the garrisons were subject to the *Ambans*. A *Djintai-Amban* directly commanded the troops, and he was in fact the military adviser of the *Amban*.

The actual administration of each governorship was conducted by a Hakim-Bek, who was chosen from amongst the natives by the *Khova-Amban*. The confirming of the Hakim-Bek in his position required a great amount of red tapeism. The *Khova-Amban* only selected a person for the office in question. The *Dzian-Dzun* then presented the selection for the consideration first of the *Dzun-Tan* at Pekin, then of the *Zoon-Dwi*, finally it was put before a council composed of twelve members of the *Lipayakoo*, who ratified the choice or not as the case might be.

Each *Hakim-Bek* had an assistant in the person of an *Ishik-Aga-Bek*. Each Circle was subdivided into sections, at the head of each of which was a *Mirab-Bek*. This official was appointed by the *Khova-Amban* on the recommendation of the Hakim-Bek, but the appointment was subject to the orders of the *Dzian-Dzun*.

For the collection of taxes each *Mirab-Bek* had a *Min-Bek* as an assistant. In the Kashgar Circle there were 16 sections, each with its *Mirab-Bek*. Each Circle was comprised of one or more hamlets with all the cultivated land adjoining.

These sections were :—Moosh, Sarman, Koorgan, Kara-Kir, Togoozak, Tazgoon, Khan-Arwik, Kwizwil-Booi, Faizabad, Yango-

Bad, Oopal, Tash-Balwik, Argoon, Oostoon-Artoosh, Altwin-Artoosh, Bish-Karan.

In each section according to its size were one or several *Yuz-Bashis,* answering to the *Aksakals* in Russian Turkestan. The number of these Yuz-Bashis in the larger sections amounted to 50. The Yuz-Bashi was selected by the *Mirab-Bek* and approved by the Hakim-Bek. The assistants of the Yuz-Bashi were the *Oon-Bashi* (or tithing man). They had also to be approved by the Hakim-Bek. Last of all, in the lowest grade of the official world, were the *Agalagtchis,* a kind of messenger.

All the above personages were chosen from among the natives. Besides the above designated dignitaries there were in each Circle the following offices that were likewise held by Mussulmans.

The *Naib-Bek* and the *Divan-Begi-Bek*—officials in the suite of the Hakim-Bek. The calling of these personages was considered above that of a *pansat,*[1] and they were held as eligible candidates for the office of *Ishik-Aga-Bek.*

The *Kazis,* the judges, and the *Mufti* or the interpreter of the *Shariat* or holy law.

Besides these, in the suite of each *Mirab-Bek* there was either a *Kazi* or a *Mufti,* or a *Rais* or a *Mookhta-Saib* or some *Moodarisses.* The last were teachers in the schools.

The *Padsha-Shab* (king of the night) or chief of the night-police.[2]

The *Mookhta-Saib* or *Rais,*[3] the supervisor of temples, schools and of the public morals. His badge of office was a leathern thong with which he had the right to beat all offenders, irrespective of age or sex.

The *Mootavalli-Bek,* or the person who administered the properties of the mosques or schools and pious institutions.

The *Badaulir-Bek,* or collector of the dues levied on goods of all kinds.[4]

---

[1] The *pansat* is a military rank which corresponds to the captain of 500.—*Author.*

[2] In the Khanate of Kokan this official bore the title of *Mir-Shab.*—*Author.*

[3] The same as the *Rais* of Bokhara.—*Author.*

[4] In other words the *ziakat* tax.—*Author.*

The *Kereyyarakh-Bek*, or inspector of foreign wares.[1]

The *Arbab-Bek*, whose duty it was to furnish *arbas*,[2] horses and transport generally for the use of troops or official personages. It was his business to procure what was necessary from the inhabitants, and to see that they got their property back again. The same duties pertained also to the *Ishkaul-Bek*, who was considered superior to the *Arbab-Bek*.

The *Bag-Mehter*, or inspector of the State gardens or vineyards.

The *Kook-Bashis*[3] and their assistants the *Dakalchis*, who managed the irrigation.

Later on, the Chinese created two more offices—that of the *Shan-Begi*, or second assistant to the *Hakim-Bek*, and the *Sun-Begi*,[4] or collector of grain from the people.

The Chinese kept up the same taxes as those which the Kashgarians paid to the Djoongars; they themselves, however, took no part in the preparation of the *dafters* or tax lists, but merely reserved the right of verifying them.

The preparation of these *dafters*, the collection of the taxes, and their payment into the treasury, formed the duty of the *Mirab-Beks*, and their assistants, the *Ming-Beks* and the *Yuz-Bashis*. The nomad population of the several Circles were not subject to the Hakim-Beks, but were governed by the *Biis*, who collected their tribute and paid it direct to the Ambans.

The number of the population of Kashgaria on the arrival of the Chinese, and the amount of the taxes paid by the inhabitants to them.

From such information as we possess of Chinese rule in Eastern Turkestan at this particular period, it is very difficult to form an exact idea as to the actual number of the population found by the Chinese in Kashgaria, or as to the amount of the taxes which were paid to them.

Nevertheless, having regard to the interest raised by these questions, we will make an attempt to give, from the scattered details that have been published, figures which we will

---

[1] During my stay in Kashgar it was naively explained to me that the chief duty of the *Kereyyarakh-Bek* was to select from the imported wares all those that it would be pleasing for the *Amban* to accept without payment.—*Author*.

[2] Or tilted carts.—*Trans*.

[3] These correspond to the *Mirabis* in Tashkent.—*Author*.

[4] Called *Ambar-Beki* in the Khanate of Kokan.—*Author*.

supplement by information collected on the spot—figures that will perhaps determine the amount of the population in the several Circles, and the sum-total of their taxes. These figures are of course only approximate, and in every case are below the real amounts. The population of Kashgaria for the period from 1760 to 1825 was—

In the Kashgar Circle, from	...	100,000	to	150,000	souls.
" Yarkend " "	...	200,000	to	400,000	"
" Khotan " "	...	100,000	to	700,000	"
" Aksu " "	...	150,000	to	200,000	"
" Koocha " "	...	25,000	to	50,000	"
Total from	...	575,000	to	1,500,000	souls.

The amount of the taxes paid yearly by the inhabitants between the dates above given was as follows:—Kashgar Circle, 72,000 roubles (£9,000); 170,000 *poods* (6,120,600 lbs.) of grain; 10,000 pieces of *mata*. Yarkend Circle, 80,000 roubles (£10,000); 60,000 pieces of *mata;* 1,400 woollen bags; 1,300 hanks of rope; 3,000 *djins* (110 *poods* or 3,960 lbs.) of copper and 15,000 *djins* of cotton. Koocha Circle, 24,000 *poods* of grain; 1,080 *djins* (27 *poods* or 972 lbs.) of copper; 200 *djins* (7½ *poods* or 270 lbs.) of saltpetre; and 300 *djins* (11 *poods* or 396 lbs.) of brimstone.

On turning the value of these products into money[1] we shall find that the taxes of the Kashgar and Yarkend Circles together amounted to 190,000 roubles (£27,250), and taking the taxes of the Aksu, Khotan and Koocha Circles at the approximate value of 210,000 roubles (£26,250), we shall arrive at an average of 400,000 roubles (£50,000), or 300,000 roubles (£37,500) in money and 100,000 roubles (£12,500) in products.

Strength of the Chinese forces in Kashgaria.

The Chinese devoted the whole of the taxes which they raised in Kashgaria to the maintenance of their garrisons, and to the general administration of that country.

[1] I take the value of a piece of *mata* (of from 6 to 8 *arshins* or 4⅔rds yards to yards 6-0-8 in length) to be 30 *kopaikas* (about 9*d*. in English money), that of a *pood* (36 lbs.) of grain to be 10 *kopaikas* (about 3*d*.), that of a *djin* (about ¾ lb) of cotton, 10 *kopaikas*, that of a *djin* of copper, 30 *kopaikas*.—*Author.*

They exported from Kashgaria to Kuldja only *mata,* copper, brimstone and saltpetre.[1]

The total strength of the forces which the Chinese kept up in Kashgaria can only be approximately given. The strength of the garrisons of the several towns was as follows :—

In Kashgar	from	...	6,000 to 10,000 men.
,, Yarkend	,,	...	2,000 to 3,000 ,,
,, Khotan	,,	...	2,000 to 3,000 ,,
,, Aksu	,,	...	3,000 to 4,000 ,,
,, other places	,,	...	4,000 to 5,000 ,,
Total from		...	17,000 to 25,000 men.

To these troops, composed of Chinese and Maudjoors, must be added the regiments recruited from the Doongans. The number of these was from 10,000 to 15,000. Therefore the total number of Chinese troops in the country amounted to from 27,000 to 40,000 men.

The principal part of the Chinese forces consisted of infantry armed with bows or with flint muskets.

Stipends of the Chinese administrative staff.

With regard to the stipends of the persons composing the administrative staff of the country, the charge under this head had only to do with the Chinese officials. The salaries of the native officials were arranged for by the Hakim-Beks. Many of these, instead of receiving a money wage, were recompensed by a temporary enjoyment of the proceeds derived from confiscated lands, or had their holdings cultivated for them free of charge.

Religious tolerance of the Chinese.

On the question of religious tolerance the Chinese proved themselves to be very humane. In the towns which they occupied mosques might be seen to exist side by side with Buddhist pagodas. They did not interfere in the choice of Moollahs, nay they even reserved to such certain exclusive rights.

In like manner the Chinese abstained from interfering with the manner and customs of the people. They left to the Kash-

[1] According to other information they exported from Kashgaria gold and jade stone also.—*Author.*

garians their Mahommedan tribunals and took no part in the choice of Kazis and Mooftis. They nevertheless maintained for themselves the right to send to the Mahommedan sessions their own interpreters of the law so as not to admit of the interests of their own countrymen being interfered with.

The people were allowed to retain their national costume, excepting those officials who were obliged to wear long hair and the Chinese style of dress. An exemption, however, to this rule was made in favour of the Moollahs and Kazis, who wore their national dress.

As a reward for devoted service, the Chinese raised the superior Mussulman officials to the grade of *Vin-a* and *Baitszwi*. The former wore in their headdress a peacock's feather and three flowers fastened by a button set with precious stones. All officials wore a button in their headdresses, but each button differed according to the rank of the wearer. There were seven kinds of such badges. The first was set with rubies, the second was of coral, the third of lapis-lazuli, the fourth of blue glass, the fifth of green glass, the sixth of a white stone, the seventh of silver.

Marks of respect required by Chinese officials.

All Mussulmans had to dismount from their horses on meeting a Chinese official in the streets.

During the *Amban's* tour round the city, the people were obliged to remain in a kneeling posture in the streets until he passed.

If the *Amban* went to a pagoda, all the Mussulman officials, not excepting the *Hakim-Bek*, had to kneel at the entrance with their arms folded behind the back. Casuistical Chinese would tell the officials that they knelt not before the *Amban*, but before the representative of the *Bogdwi Khan*, who had entered the pagoda. This consolation was scarcely sufficient, and it may be supposed that the degrading conditions, which the Chinese imposed on the Mussulmans little by little, neutralized the good done by them in their system of administration.

Capital punishment.

With regard to capital punishment, it is evident that the Chinese were in times of peace far from being as severe as has been described by various writers more than once. Punishment by death was resorted to very seldom, and sentences were carried out only after careful consideration. The *Khova-Amban* had the power of punishing all the people excepting official personages. The *Amban* could pass sentence of death for political offences only. In the case of officials who by the law were guilty of death, the *Amban* had to report to the *Khova-Amban*, and he again to the *Dzian-Dzun*, who alone could direct the sentence to be carried out.

But the crafty Chinese found a way of avoiding the legal procedure. On the *Khova-Ambans* and the *Ambans* was conferred the right of degrading all officials except those of superior rank, so that when the holder of an office offended, he was first of all degraded and then executed in the usual way.

Executions.

Executions were carried out with great ceremony.

The convicted one—no matter whether he had been sentenced by the *Shariat* or by order of the *Khova-Amban*—was led forth to the market-place of the town attended by soldiers and crowds of people. With his hands fastened behind him he was then placed before the throng. The executioner now approached, and before his very eyes began to sharpen a knife. Whilst the criminal could not take his eyes off the knife, which apparently figured in all capital sentences, another executioner would stealthily creep up behind him and with one stroke of an axe would cut off his head.

Civil death.

Besides this, for certain offences the Chinese imposed civil death as it was called. The offender was taken out with various ceremonies on a sunny day and placed against a tree. His shadow on that tree was then marked out. The offender was then taken back to his house, whence from that day forth he would not emerge again. After the award of this kind of punishment, the kinsmen of the condemned, in answer to questions put to them concerning the personality of the offender, were obliged to answer, that he died on such and such a date.

Social life of the people of Kashgaria.

We have but very little information on the important question of the social life of the Mussulman population during the Chinese dominion. A Mussulman traveller, during the year 1812, Mir Izet-Oollah,[1] bears the following testimony :—

"The inhabitants of Yarkend are very industrious, and con-

[1] Ritter's "Eastern Turkestan," page 101.—*Author.*

sist principally of traders, shop-keepers and pedlars. Slaves are very rare amongst them. Goitrous people are very frequently met with. This disease is ascribed to the water which they usually drink from gourds. The women, whether of the upper or lower classes, do not hide their faces with a veil according to the generally received custom of the East."

Regarding the greater freedom of the women in Kashgaria as compared with that in other Mussulman countries, there are other indications of the same kind. Thus it is stated in ancient chronicles that the women of Khotan, during the Fifth and Sixth Centuries, were allowed into the society of men, and that they even remained there after the arrival of some person or persons whom they did not know. The same chronicles tell us that the inhabitants of Khotan were very polite, and that they always knelt down on meeting one another.

The following interesting extract from Si-Yue-Vwin-Tszian-Loo's Chinese geography, published at Pekin in the year 1778, depicts the character of the native population as it appeared to a Chinese observer:[1]—

"The natives are peaceful; they respect the Chinese and are devoted to their chiefs. They are simple-minded, and are fond of lights and feasting. Their women sing and dance beautifully, and are skilled in various kinds of jugglery. It is worth seeing them take somersaults, walk on a stretched copper wire, &c. In this country the strong drive out the weak. The Beks are extremely avaricious. If a poor man succeeds in scraping together a little money, the Beks at once endeavour to pilfer it. On this account, notwithstanding the populousness of the town, there are but few wealthy families in it. The inhabitants are generally given to sensuality and even to sodomy. Their morals are in fact like those of the inhabitants of Foo-Tszian-I and of both the Hoo-Ans."

The respected Chinese geographer, without himself knowing it, passes sentence against the system of administration in the land occupied by the Chinese—a system which admitted of such wide extortion on the part of officials.

In our further exposition we will endeavour to show how

[1] Ritter's "Eastern Turkestan," pages 61 to 116.—*Author.*

much this extortion, in conjunction with other causes, rendered the rule of the Chinese over the country unstable.

According to another Chinese authority "the inhabitants of the town of Sha-Yar (to the south of the town of Koocha) were extremely churlish, stupid and quarrelsome. The women were famous for their beauty, and especially for the beautiful colour of their complexion." [1]

Advantages attained by the Chinese in the conquest of Kashgaria.

The advantages attained by the Chinese in the conquest of Kashgaria and of Djoongaria consisted in the better security of the western frontiers of China, but, above all, in the opening out of vast markets for the sale of Chinese products and especially of tea.

Chinese tea not only began to come more generally into use in the conquered towns, but to be exported in considerable quantities through the town of Kashgar into Kokan, Bokhara and even Afghanistan.

Moreover, the Chinese kept to themselves the monopoly of the working of precious metals in Kashgaria. Thus, for example, in Keria (to the east of the town of Khotan) there were 300 men in daily employment in the State mines.

The pacification of the country could not but tend to the increasing of its trade and of its industries. The Chinese geographer, from whose work we have abready quoted, speaks with enthusiasm of the bazaar at Yarkend: "The wares in it are piled up like the clouds in the heavens, and the people in it swarm like bees in a hive." According to the declaration of a Mussulman merchant, during the twenty years of the present century, thanks to Chinese rule there was a safety in the country that was favourable to the development of trade such as had never existed before in consequence of the ceaseless robberies and internecine wars. The trade of Yarkend extended in a special degree so that its dimensions far exceeded that of Kashgar. In the vast bazaar of the city there were erected some exceedingly well-built shops, and these were principally held by Chinese merchants. For the accommodation too of travellers, many caravan-serais were likewise built.

[1] Ritter's "Eastern Turkestan," page 173.—*Author.*

In the town there were more than ten Mussulman superior schools, to which large properties were attached. Besides the regular inhabitants, there also resided in the town a number of Arabs who were engaged in trade with Kafiristan and Badakhshan.

The Chinese, who were well aware of the advantages to be derived from a trade with the adjoining Asiatic States, departed from their customary close system, and opened out Kashgaria to trade with her neighbours. Moreover, the insufficiency of cattle in their new province induced them to encourage the Kara-Kirghiz, who were independent of their rule, to bring their cattle into Chinese territory.

All foreigners, even if they constantly resided in the towns of Kashgaria, and had brought their families with them, were considered as guests and as travellers, and were not asked to pay any taxes.

On goods intended as offerings or imported in small quantities no taxes were levied.

On cattle driven in by foreigners (counting amongst these the cattle of the independent Kara-Kirghiz) they imposed a levy of $\frac{1}{30}$th of their value, whilst on cattle belonging to Chinese subjects, a tax of $\frac{1}{20}$th was charged. No charges were made on inland trade.

Disputes amongst traders.

Disputes amongst traders were settled by a jury composed of the traders themselves.

Kirghiz Divisions.

The Kirghiz were divided into tribes, and each tribe had its own *aksakal* or elder, who was appointed by the Hakim-Bek.

Monetary system of Kashgaria.

The monetary system, which was in use at that time in Kashgaria, was borrowed from China.

A *yarmak* or *tchokh* was the smallest piece of copper that was in circulation. Five *tchokhs* were equal to one *pool* or one *kara-pool*, or one *khotchan*.[1] Two *khotchan* were equal to one *dolchan*.

[1] Of late, Yakoob Bek had begun to coin silver *tengas*. These were worth 50 copper *pool* or 25 *dolchans*. Two Kashgar *tengas* were equal to one Kokan *tenga*, a piece of money that was current in Bokhara, Khiva and the Russian Central Asian possessions. A Kashgar *tenga* was equal also to 20 Kokan or 30 Tashkent *tchokhs*. *Yambas* of 4¾ lbs. weight are now worth from 1,000 to 1,100 *tengas*.—*Author*.

Fifty *pool* made one *tenga*, a piece of money that does not really exist. One *pool* or one *khotchan* was equal to $\frac{1}{5}$th of a *kopaika*. One *tenga* equalled 10 *kopaikas* (about 3*d.*) The Chinese calculated their taxes in *pool* or in *lans* and *yambas* if they had a great amount to reckon up.

A *lan* equalled one ounce of silver. A *yamba* was a bar of silver of variable size. The largest *yamba* weighed as nearly as possible 4¾ ℔s.

The exchange on silver fluctuated very much. At the beginning of the present century Chinese silver fell very much in price. Gold was reckoned in *lans* or in *zolotniks* (about 2 drams).

The Chinese took as their unit of weight the *djin* which equalled 1½ Russian ℔s. Grain was weighed by sacks or by *batmans* (= 12 *poods* = 432 ℔s.) or by *halbirs* (*rayshets*). Whether al lthese units of measurement are now in use or not I have not succeeded in ascertaining with certainty. The approximate weight of a *batman* or sack of corn was equal to about 12 *poods*, that of a *halbir* to about 1½ *poods* [1] (54 ℔s.)

Cotton, copper, brimstone and saltpetre were reckoned in *djins*.

The *li* was the standard used in long measure. One *li* was equal to about 200 *sajens*, and an *alchin* was about the same as a Russian *arshin* (28 inches).

[1] At present for weighing dry goods the *charik* is the standard in Kashgaria. One *charik* of wheat = 24 ℔s., one *charik* of maize = 26 ℔s., one *charik* of barley = 25 ℔s. For goods that are not dry the *djin* is the standard of weight. In long measure *tash* are used: one *tash* = 12,000 paces. But *tash* vary according to the height and idea of the measurer, and hence a *tash* may be equal to either 7 or 9 *versts*; but their normal length is 8 *versts*.—*Author*.

CHAPTER V.

Rebellion against the Chinese in the year 1825 — Djengir-Turya — Insurrection of the Kokanese in the year 1830 — Khodja Med-Yusoof — Rebellion of the seven Khodjas (Katta-Turya) — Rebellion of 1857 — Valikhan-Turya.

Further progress of the Chinese.

HAVING conquered Djoongaria and Kashgaria with such ease, the Chinese now became bellicose. During the years 1756, 1758 and 1760, their forces penetrated to the steppes of the Middle Horde and compelled the Khans of that horde to acknowledge Chinese sovereignty. After that both the Khans of the Lesser Horde and the Elders of the Booroot Section of the Kara-Kirghiz, following the example of the Middle Horde, acknowledged the same supremacy, and were then obliged to pay a yearly tribute of one horse and one ox in every hundred and one sheep in every thousand. In order to collect this tax, the Chinese despatched yearly four detachments, whose duty it was also to uphold Chinese influence in the Kirghiz country.

Routes taken by the Chinese detachments.

Two detachments were sent from Ili, one from Tarbagatai and one from Kashgar. The Tarbagatai detachment united with one of the two from Ili in the valley of the Ayagooz (between Kopal and Sergiopol). The second detachment from Ili then united with the detachment from Kashgar in the valley of the Narwin.

These detachments, having exchanged the tribute collected, returned homewards.[1] Chinese merchants generally accompanied these forces in order to barter their wares for cattle, taking care of course to profit by the exchange with the semi-barbarous Kirghiz.

---

[1] The Kashgar detachment reached the valley of the Narwin after having crossed the Terek pass, and having come out on to the Aksai plateau, and so into the valley of the At-pash.—*Author.*

The Kirghiz Khans acknowledge the sovereignty of the Chinese.

After the Kirghiz Khans, the Kokan rulers, Erdenya Biï and his heir, Narboota Biï, declared themselves under the protectorate of the *Bogdwi Khan*. Such swift successes caused the Chinese to be regarded as invincible, and made their name terrible throughout Central Asia.

The Chinese contemplate the conquest of Bokhara, Samarkand and Tashkent.

It may be supposed too that amongst the Chinese themselves there arose such an amount of self-confidence that they seriously began to think of the conquest of Bokhara, Samarkand and Tashkent. Tidings of the preparations for this campaign quickly reached the Central Asian Khans and made them, in regard to the threatening position assumed by a common enemy, forget their own quarrels. They formed, therefore, an alliance, which was joined also by Ahmet Shah, the ruler of Afghanistan. To all Mussulman potentates a summons went forth inviting them to participate in the *gazavat*,[1] or holy war, *i.e.*, a war for the faith against the infidel. An alliance was thus concluded in the year 1763, and in the same year the Afghan forces reached Khodjent.

An alliance is formed between the rulers of these places and the ruler of Afghanistan against the Chinese.

This league is broken up.

But the league which had been formed soon broke up. The Afghans were obliged to return to their own country, and the remaining chiefs considered themselves too weak to enter upon a struggle with such a powerful foe. The towns of Ootch-Toorfan and Badakhshan alone held out.

Massacre by the Chinese of the inhabitants of Ootch-Toorfan and devastation of Badakhshan by the Afghan forces.

The first, having trusted in the promised aid, rebelled, and its inhabitants were slain, as we have already related, by the Chinese forces. With regard to Badakhshan, that beautiful country was devastated by the Afghan forces, and its ruler, Sultan Shah, was executed, because he not only refused to give refuge to those Khodjas who fled from Kashgaria during the siege of the town of Khotan by the Chinese (in the year 1758), but because he also killed two of the Khodjas who were taken prisoners and sent their heads to Pekin.

Mistakes committed by the Chinese in the administration of Kashgaria.

The Chinese perceiving the weakness of the Central Asian rulers raised their heads still higher. The wise policy adopted towards the conquered people and the administration of the country on the system founded by Tchjao-Hoi ceased by degrees

[1] See note at foot of p. 100.—*Trans.*

to be considered indispensable. Amongst mistakes too that were committed must be classed the appointment to the town of Kashgaria of a Hakim-Bek and other officials from the western provinces, and the compelling the people to erect without payment vast fortifications called *Goolbaghs*[1] for the occupancy of the Chinese garrisons.

The officials, introduced from the western provinces of China, from the towns of Hami and Koonya-Toorfan, came with the intention of gaining a lucrative livelihood, and they did not shrink from employing every means to attain this object. From the Hakim-Bek down to the lowest official, all looked upon the people as on a milch-cow, and they behaved like bad owners who desired their cow to give more milk than was in its power to give. The flagrant plundering on the part of the Hakim-Bek was known to the Chinese authorities, and since they permitted him to continue it, they in all probability themselves benefited by his actions. The extremely luxurious style of living in vogue amongst Chinese officials also gives us the right to think that the plundering of the people which they carried on brought to each one of them considerable material gains. Every protest and every act of disobedience was punishable by death, and so the people became still more exasperated. The more energetic amongst the population began to emigrate to Kokan, Bokhara and Tashkent, where, by their stories of the excesses of the Chinese, they everywhere excited a sympathy for their native land.

Action of the Khodja of the *white-mountain* party, Sarwim-Sak.

In expounding the circumstances which led to the conquest of Kashgaria, we mentioned that, after the capture of the town of Khotan, one Khodja only of the *white-mountain* party, Sarwim-Sak, saved himself. This Khodja, after long wanderings, settled in Kokan, where, having collected around him the Kashgarian emigrants, he explained his plan of operations for the

[1] Literally a *goolbagh* is a rose garden, but the name came to be applied to the citadel which the Chinese built not far from the native city for the occupancy of their officials and for their garrisons. These *goolbaghs* were very substantially built by the inhabitants of the town to which they were attached. Furnished with provisions, they could withstand a lengthened siege pending the arrival of reinforcements.—*Author.*

deliverance of their native land from the Chinese yoke. His agents too, who were traversing the towns of Western Turkestan, collected offerings in furtherance of the same object, and made their hearers fanatical by descriptions of the sufferings of their co-religionists. The Kashgarian people, on hearing the news brought to them by merchants from Kokan, began to look upon Sarwim-Sak as their deliverer, and awaited only an opportunity to openly show him their sympathy. However, it was not from the side of Kokan that the Chinese received the first warning. In the year 1816, after a peaceful administration of fifty years' duration, one of the members of the *black-mountain* party, Ziaveddin, escaped to the mountains, and collecting around him bands of Kirghiz, began to make inroads, hoping thereby to rise the population. Ziaveddin's plan did not succeed. His bands were broken up, and he himself was slain, whilst his infant son was taken off to Pekin, where, on attaining manhood, he was executed.

Failure of the Khodja of the *black-mountain* party, Ziaveddin.

After this experience, the Chinese began to perceive more clearly the danger which threatened them from the side of Kokan, from Sarwim-Sak, who considered himself to be the lawful ruler of Kashgaria. They, therefore, entered into an arrangement with the Khan of Kokan, Omar, by which they undertook to pay him yearly 200 *yambas* (about 20,000 roubles or £2,500) if he would exercise strict supervision over the Khodjas.

The Chinese enter into an arrangement with the Khan of Kokan for the supervision of all the Khodjas in his territory.

Now Khodja Sarwim-Sak had three sons, Med Yusoof Khodja, Pakhavveddin Khodja and Djengir Khodja. The last of these was destined to soon play a great part in the history of Kashgaria and to introduce into that history yet another bloody page.

Sarwim-Sak's three sons.

In the year 1820, Omar, the Khan of Kokan, died. Sarwim-Sak also died about the same time. Djengir Khodja, who was much the most energetic of his sons, now resolved to act. He fled from Kokan to the Tian-Shan and there induced the Kara-Kirghiz to attack the Chinese. His first attempt was not successful, but Djengir did not lose heart. Transferring his scene of action from the Fergana portion of the Tian-Shan to the highlands of the Narwin, he sent his agents in every direction to enlist volunteers and all who were ready to serve under the

Action of Djengir Khodja.

standard of the Appaks in a war for the faith against the Chinese. Circumstances now aided Djengir. The Chinese, thinking to seize him unawares and thus put an end to an agitation that was hostile to themselves, sent a force of 500 men to the Narwin. Warned in time, Djengir made his escape, and then, having collected his adherents, he availed himself of his knowledge of the country to cut off the retreat of the Chinese, all of whom were slain. In consequence of this success, exaggerated as it was according to Asiatic custom to a vast extent, crowds of volunteers now flocked towards Djengir's standard from all sides.

He destroys a Chinese force of 500 men.

He marches against Kashgar.

In the spring of 1826, Djengir, with a considerable force composed of Kashgarian emigrants, Kokan *sipahis,* Oozbeks, Kipchaks, Kara-Kirghiz, mountain Tadjiks from Karategin, under the leadership of Isa-Datkha (formerly commandant of the town of Andijan) marched against Kashgar. The Chinese forces under the personal leadership of the *Dzian-Dzun* of Ili, went out to meet him and were defeated. After evacuating the town of Kashgar, the Chinese shut themselves up in the citadel (or *Goolbagh,* see foot-note on page 136).

He defeats the Chinese forces and occupies the town of Kashgar.

The people receive him with joy.

Djengir now entered the town of Kashgar amid cries of joy from the people and assumed the title of Said Djengir-Sultan.

All the Beks were confirmed in their positions with the exception of the Kashgar Bek, a native of the town of Komul, and he, in return for his extortions from the people, was sentenced by a council of *Akhoons* [1] to capital punishment.

Moderation of Djengir and its effects.

Through his moderation, Djengir drew towards his side even persons who belonged to the Chinese party, and he succeeded too in gaining the sympathy of the people.

Aid afforded to Djengir by the inhabitants of Yangi-Hissar, Yarkend and Khotan.

The inhabitants of the towns of Yangi-Hissar, Yarkend and Khotan, hearing of the capture of the town of Kashgar by Djengir, also rose in rebellion, slaughtered the Chinese garrisons, razed the fortifications and sent their detachments to the aid of Djengir, who now began to lay siege to the citadel of Kashgar.

The Khan of Kokan advances to his aid.

In the month of June of the same year (1826) the Khan of Kokan with an army of 15,000 men came to Djengir's assistance.

[1] A title of respect used in speaking of Beys, Hadjis and Poets.—*Trans.*

This reinforcement instead of proving useful was fruitful only of discord. The Khan of Kokan, after two unsuccessful assaults, turned back (he was at Kashgar 12 days altogether) and began to coin money with the inscription of 'Gazi,' or warrior for the faith.

Surrender by the Chinese of the citadel of Kashgar.

After a 70 days' siege the Kashgar citadel surrendered. The Mandarins committed suicide, and the garrison, consisting of from 8 to 10,000 men, was put to the sword, with the exception of 400 Doongans and Chinese who embraced Islam.

Failure of Djengir to gain the favour of the people.

After occupying Kashgar, Djengir introduced an order of things on the model of the Kokan Court. He abolished the Chinese style of dress, and put down Chinese customs of all kinds. Unfortunately he knew not how to take advantage of the people's love or of the ample means at his disposal. Instead of this he brought but harm to the people, for whose deliverance he had striven.

Operations of the Chinese against Djengir.

The Chinese, profiting by Djengir's inaction, concentrated, during February 1827, a considerable force in the town of Aksu, and with this they advanced against the town of Kashgar. Djengir went forth to meet them with a numerous but badly equipped army [1] composed of a heterogeneous mob devoid of any kind of discipline. The Chinese moved in military order, and met the enemy with artillery fire. After an ignominious fight Djengir's forces wavered. The first to fly were his Kokan volunteers and adventurers of every class. After these went the rest in headlong flight. The Khodja himself barely escaped capture, and got away to the mountains. His reign had lasted but nine months.

Defeat and flight of Djengir.

Pursuit of Djengir.

Having received orders from Pekin to take Djengir captive wherever he might be, even though they had to seek him either at Kokan or in Bokhara, the Chinese forces moved from the town of Kashgar to the Alai, where, report said, Djengir was concealed.

The strength of the Chinese forces told off for this campaign was put down at 20,000 men. For the march they were divided

[1] According to Valikhanoff, the Chinese army numbered 70,000 men, whereas Djengir Khodja's forces were computed at 200,000. These figures are evidently very exaggerated. At page 283 of Ritter's work, the Chinese forces are put down at 60,000.—*Author.*

into two columns. The one moved from Kashgar to Ooloogchat and through the Ton-Mooroon pass to the Alai. The other advanced from Kashgar to the town of Oopal, past lake Sarwi-Kool, and across the Kwizwil-Art pass to the same place. This movement took place during the autumn. The Chinese had no guns with them, for these they substituted *taifoors*. Traders accompanied the army, and flocks of cattle were driven after it. On arriving at an encampment, the Chinese on every occasion, for fear of a night-attack, excavated a shallow trench around their camp. These trenches in a circular shape exist up to the present time.[1] The Chinese forces remained for twenty days on the Alai, sending small detachments in every direction in order to discover Djengir Khodja's hiding place. The ruler of Kokan, Madali Khan, who was alarmed by the approach of the Chinese, gave orders to the Hakim of Andijan, Isa Datkha, to build two forts, Soofi-Koorgan and Kwizwil-Koorgan, on the caravan route between Kashgar and the town of Osh. His orders were carried out, and these forts, or, to speak more correctly, these posts were erected. Now their ruins alone remain.

Hiding place of Djengir.

Whilst the Chinese were searching for Djengir on the Alai, he had removed to the highlands of the river Tooyun, which crosses the road between the town of Kashgar and Forts Chakmak and Narwin. As soon as his hiding place became known to the Chinese, they withdrew from the Alai, and came by way of Ooloogchat to the town of Kashgar, where, after provisioning their forces for a fresh campaign, they moved towards the river Tooyun. Alarmed at the approach of the Chinese, the majority of Djengir's adherents fled, and he, whilst asleep, was bound by his friend Mamat, the Bek of Oopal, and delivered over to the Chinese. The Chinese rewarded Mamat Bek for his treachery by appointing him Bek of Khotan.

The Bek of Oopal makes Djengir over to the Chinese, and, for doing so, is appointed Bek of Khotan.

Djengir is sent to Pekin, where he is brutally tortured and put to death.

Djengir Khodja was sent to Pekin. The French missionary Mons. Huc [2] relates how Djengir, on being taken to Pekin, was confined in an iron cage and shewn to the people as a wild

[1] We have seen one of the ditches excavated round the bivouac of Chinese advanced posts at Ishna, situated 30 versts (20 miles) south of the Terek-Davan pass.—*Author*.

[2] Voyage dans la Tartarie par Huc.—*Author*.

beast. It chanced that the Chinese Emperor conceived the desire to see his conquered enemy. This desire caused great consternation amongst the higher officials of the Pekin Court; for they feared that Djengir would tell the truth as to the causes which led to his rebellion, and that he would relate all the severities which had attended its pacification. Such revelations, as implicating the laxity of the Chinese officials sent to Kashgaria, could not but have for such persons disastrous results. Meanwhile the Emperor's will could not but be attended to. The Mandarins found a way, however, of getting over their difficulty. They gave Djengir a poison which deprived him of the power of speaking rationally, and which, in fact, reduced him to a state of idiotcy.

When brought before the Emperor he foamed at the mouth and presented a repulsive appearance. He could not moreover reply to one of the questions that were put to him. By sentence of the judges his body was cut in pieces and given to the dogs.

Revenge taken by the Chinese for Djengir's insurrection.

Having done with Djengir, the Chinese proceeded to punish the other offenders. Those, however, who had sinned least suffered most. There now began executions, plunderings and confiscation of property.

Action taken by the Chinese against the Kokanese.

Thinking, and not without reason, that the Kokanese were the chief movers in the rebellion in Kashgaria, the Chinese, in order to revenge themselves, arrested all the Kokan merchants living at Kashgar, and adopted also a series of vexatious measures against all goods imported from Kokan. They furthermore entered into an agreement with the rulers of Bokhara and Koondooz for the transport of tea into their territories and to Afghanistan direct from China, thereby avoiding Kokan.

The Chinese fail to punish the Kara-Kirghiz.

It is interesting to observe that the Chinese, who were in need of cattle, took no steps to punish the Kara-Kirghiz, who had been the first to go over to Djengir and who had given him a refuge after his defeat.

Effect of the Chinese policy towards the Kokanese.

The blockade imposed by the Chinese on the Kokanese had such an effect on them that they laboured to bring about such results as would be quite unexpected by the sons of the Celestial Empire.

Madali Khan, the ruler of Kokan.

Madali Khan was at this time the ruler of Kokan. Although a man devoid of any great personal merit, he was surrounded by followers both capable and energetic. Such were the commanders of his army, Hak-Koolla and Koosh-Begi-Lashkar. The former was an Oozbek, the latter had been a Persian slave.[1] Thanks to these assistants the reign of Madali Khan became a brilliant epoch in the history of Kokan. By degrees almost all the Kara-Kirghiz and the Kirghiz of the Great Horde had acknowledged themselves feudatories of Kokan, whilst the mountain provinces of Karategin, Darwaz and Koolyab had been annexed to the Kokan dominions either by means of diplomacy or force of arms.

Madali Khan declares war against the Chinese.

Madali Khan soon became so sensible of the closing by the Chinese of all trade between Kokan and Kashgaria, that, in order to get rid of the vexation, he resolved to openly declare war against them.[2] Aware of the sympathy of the people towards the Khodjas, Madali Khan called from Bokhara Med-Yusoof, Djengir's eldest brother, and he gave out as the objects of his summons the deliverance of the Mahometans from the yoke of the infidels, and the restoration of Med-Yusoof to the throne of his ancestors.

Strength of Madali Khan's forces.

He collected for the proposed campaign very considerable forces. These consisted of 20,000 Kokanese, 15,000 Tashkentians, 2,000 mountain Tadjiks from Karategin and a few thousand Kashgarian emigrants. Altogether he had about 40,000 men and 10 small guns mounted, for the march across the mountains, on camels.

Plan of the campaign and success of the Kokanese.

This army, under the supreme command of Hak-Koolla, marched in September 1830 towards Kashgar. The Chinese, who could only place in opposition 3,000 men in the field, were utterly routed at Min-Yul, 44 versts (29⅓rd miles) from Kashgar.[3] In consequence of their defeat, the latter town was occupied

[1] He had been in the suite of the Lord-Lieutenant of Tashkent with the title of Bekler-Bek.—*Author.*

[2] Together with trade advantages a successful war brought Madali Khan the renown of the conqueror of the Chinese and of a combatant for the faith.—*Author.*

[3] Later on at this spot the *Badaulet* erected a small fort.—*Author.*

and Med-Yusoof established himself there. Hak-Koolla now commenced the siege of the citadel in which the Chinese garrison was shut up. Koosh-Begi-Lashkar set out to capture the other towns of Kashgaria. His operations were very successful, for in a very short time the towns of Yangi-Hissar, Yarkend, Khotan and Aksu acknowledged the sovereignty of Med-Yusoof. Soon, however, the entire instability of this sovereignty, founded more by the support of the Kokan forces than on the sympathy of the people, became evident. In the month of November 1830, in view of the unfavourable relations that existed with Bokhara, the Kokan forces were called back, and with them went Med-Yusoof, because he did not consider himself strong enough to cope with the Chinese single-handed. His reign over Kashgaria lasted 90 days. On this occasion the complete instability of the Chinese dominion was displayed even more clearly than during Djengir's insurrection. Another result of Djengir's campaign had been the emigration of several thousands of Kashgarians into Kokan territory.

The forces of the Kokanese are called back on account of unfavourable relations with Bokhara.

In the spring of 1831, Madali Khan opened a fresh campaign against the Kara-Kirghiz. His forces got as far as the highlands of the Narwin, and even penetrated to the province of Ili. In the year following, the Kokanese built Fort Koortka on the Narwin, and Fort Tash-Koorgan on the southern slopes of the Pamir. Kashgaria was thus encircled by the Kokan dominions, whence Chinese sovereignty was constantly threatened either by an inroad of Khodjas or by raids of Kara-Kirghiz.

Madali Khan marches against the Kara-Kirghiz.

Feeling themselves no longer in a position to fight with Kokan, the Chinese were obliged to change their policy towards her. In 1831, therefore, there appeared at the Court of the Khan of Kokan envoys with a request for peace. Madali Khan's return Embassy to Pekin, at the head of which was the merchant Alum Padsha, succeeded in completing an arrangement that was very advantageous to his own side.

Change of Chinese policy towards Kokan.

The following articles of the treaty, concluded by Alum Padsha, show how much the *Khodjas* were feared by the Chinese:—

Treaty concluded between China and Kokan.

I. "The duties on goods imported by foreigners into the six cities of Eastern Turkistan—*viz.*, Aksu, Ootch-Toorfan, Kashgar, Yangi-Hissar, Yarkend and Khotan, shall be for the benefit of the Kokanese.

II. "In order to collect these taxes, the Kokanese shall have in each of the abovementioned towns a trade inspector or *Aksakal*. This person shall be subordinate to a Kashgarian inspector. Each shall be the political representative of his own ruler.

III. "All foreigners visiting the six cities abovementioned shall be subject, in administrative and political matters, to the orders of the Kokan officials.

IV. "On their side the Kokanese must look after the Khodjas and not allow them to cross the frontier of their own territory; and in case of flight, they must refuse them a refuge."

Alum Padsha is appointed Kokan *Aksakal* to Kashgaria.

In the year 1832, Alum Padsha, who had gone as envoy to Pekin, was appointed the first *Aksakal* to Kashgaria. He received the post in the light of a contract. In course of time the privileges obtained by the Kokanese in Kashgaria were still more extended.

Results of the treaty for the Chinese.

Although the conditions of the treaty were not favourable to the Chinese, they nevertheless secured thereby a peaceful administration in Kashgaria for 15 years,—*i. e.*, up to the year 1847. Having obtained so vast an influence in Kashgaria, the Kokanese did not consider it expedient to support the pretensions of the Khodjas, over whom they really did exercise a strict supervision that slackened only in the year 1845, when the infant Khoodoyar Khan ascended the throne of Kokan. From this period disorder commenced in Kokan, and this state of affairs affected the Kokanese relations with Kashgaria. The Kara-Kirghiz, with the weakening of the Kokanese Government, began to make inroads into Kashgarian territory, and the Kokan *Aksakal*, Nomed Khan, whose duty it was to prevent them, took bribes and did nothing. The commotions in Kokan favoured the cause of the Khodjas.

Flight of the seven Khodjas from Kokan.

In the spring of 1847, seven Khodjas fled from Kokan to the mountains with several hundred adherents; they there collected a party, composed of a thousand well-mounted *Djigits*, and with these they resolved to promote an insurrection in Kashgaria. Katta-Turya (called also Khodja-Turya) was at the head of these Khodjas.

The other six were Katta-Turya's own brother Kitchkine-Khan, their cousins Vali-Khan-Turya and Tavakkal-Turya, Sabir-Khan-Turya, Ak-Tchagan-Khodja and Ishakhan-Turya.[1] More than half the party were Kirghiz, the rest were Kipchaks and a few Sarts.

The conspirators massacre the Chinese garrison of Min-Yul.

Their movements were in light marching order, as they had neither tents nor transport. On the eighth day from the town of Osh the conspirators reached the Min-Yul post, the first Chinese frontier station.[2] The hundred Chinese composing this garrison were killed, and the post thrown down. His band having received reinforcements *en route*, Katta-Turya appeared the same day before the walls of Kashgar. The Chinese, to the number of 3,000 men, according to custom, shut themselves up in the citadel, whence their weak and badly-executed sorties were beaten back. On this occasion the inhabitants of the town, taught by bitter experience, were not inclined to open the city gates to Katta-Turya until he had taken the citadel.

Katta-Turya appears before the walls of Kashgar.

Kokan merchants in Kashgar open the gates of the town to Katta-Turya.

The presence of Kokan merchants in the town aided the Khodjas. On the eighth day after Katta-Turya's arrival, Nomed Khan, the Kokanese *Aksakal*, and his party opened the city gates by night and let the Khodjas in. The first thing that they did was to slay all the Chinese merchants, to plunder their goods, and to appropriate their harems.

Katta-Turya is proclaimed ruler of Kashgaria.

Katta-Turya was proclaimed ruler of Kashgaria, and the remaining Khodjas were made governors of the neighbouring villages.

The Khodjas, who surrounded themselves with Kokanese and who gave themselves over to corruption, could not instil in others either devotion or fear towards themselves. Without personally troubling themselves about the administration of the country, they merely required that those about them should

[1] Ishakhan-Turya played a great part in the year 1865, during the reign of Poolat Khan: and later on, during the insurrection of 1876, he fled with Abdoolla Bek on learning the movements of the Russian forces on the Alai.—*Author.*

[2] At that time the Kokan boundary line reached as far as Koorgashin-Kani. Ooloogchat had not then been occupied by the Kokan troops, whose first post was at Soorfi-Koorgan.—*Author.*

procure for them as much money as possible without inquiring whence it came.

Neither were the hopes of the Khodjas as to a general rising in Kashgaria realized. Tavakkal-Turya, who was the most capable of all the Khodjas, advanced against the town of Aksu, whilst Katta-Turya marched against Yarkend. Meanwhile a Chinese army, collected from Kooldja, Ooroomtcha and Lian-Tchjei, and numbering over 200,000 men, had already reached Aksu and was marching towards the town of Kashgar. On reaching Fort Maral-Bashi, they halted there for the winter; but the cowardice of the Khodjas settled the business in favour of the Chinese sooner than they could have expected.

Katta-Turya, on hearing of the movements of the Chinese, marched his army back to Kashgar without going to Yarkend. The inhabitants of the former town, who had become incensed at the exactions made upon them and at the preference which Katta-Turya shewed for the *Andijans,* would not allow him to enter the place. Katta-Turya had a motley gathering of about 18,000 men, but the Chinese advanced-guard, numbering nearly 6,000 men, seemed sufficient to disperse this crowd. The Khodjas fled from the city, after having carried off the large stores of wealth that they had amassed during their sovereignty. After them went their army. The Chinese, who were satisfied with their easily-acquired victory, did not pursue the fugitives.

Flight of the Khodjas from Kashgar.

Revolt of the seven Khodjas and its effects on Kashgaria.

The events which we have related, known to the Chinese under the name of the "Revolt of the Seven Khodjas," would not have been important in its results except for the fact that it led to the emigration of 20,000 families,—*i. e.*, 100,000 souls from the towns of Kashgar, Yarkend and Aksu. The fugitives, fearing the wrath of the Chinese, fled to the mountains after the dispersed forces of the Khodjas. The greater portion of the exiles set out from Kashgar to Osh by the Terek-Davan pass, as the shortest way to the Khanate of Kokan. The flight took place in the month of January. Strong frosts set in, accompanied by heavy snow, and most of the miserable people perished. Eye-witnesses give the most harrowing details of their losses.

Sufferings of the fugitives from Kashgaria.

In front of all, mounted on good steeds, warmly clad, and furnished with every necessary, fled Katta-Turya with a party of about 2,000 adherents. He had with him some 16 camels laden with silver, which he had plundered. Having arrived at Soofi-Koorgan, 25 versts (16⅔rds miles) from the Terek-Davan pass and 105 versts (70 miles) from the town of Osh, Katta-Turya, no longer fearing pursuit, stopped to divide the booty with his companions. The division of the spoils was scarcely completed when a Sirkar of the Kipchaks arrived at Soofi-Koorgan from Kokan. The whole of the booty was once more collected and its value noted down. Katta-Turya's band was disarmed and its members dispersed to their several homes, whilst Katta-Turya himself was taken as a prisoner to Kokan.

Katta-Turya's band is disarmed by the Kipchaks, and he is taken as a prisoner to Kokan.

There came through Soofi-Koorgan, some 30 days after Katta-Turya's arrival at the same place, a crowd of almost naked fugitives, men, women and children, some on foot and some on horseback, and carrying their small possessions with them.

For the first ten days of their flight things went comparatively well with those of the poor people, who, by hastening to cross the Terek-Davan pass within that time, arrived for the most part safely at the town of Osh. After that, however, there suddenly set in strong frosts accompanied by heavy falls of snow. The fugitives, on getting into the snow, could scarcely direct their footsteps, but still they pressed forward. Those of them that stopped through exhaustion were at once frost-bitten, and then the steadily falling snow soon covered over their corpses. Many of those who attempted to move at night, lost themselves in the darkness and perished in the snow-drifts. These drifts were so large as to cover the whole caravan. As if to complete the sum of their misfortunes, hunger overtook the frozen fugitives.

The sufferings from this cause were so great that for a piece of bread or a cup of wheat-flour mixed with water a man would give up his overcoat. There soon appeared speculative hosts, who drove a brisk trade by pilfering the half-dead fugitives, thousands of whose bodies covered the Terek-Davan pass and the road on both sides of it. The bones of these unfortunates, notwithstanding that 30 years have passed since that time, lie about the spot even now.[1]

[1] We marched through the Terek-Davan pass in the months of October and March, when snow was on the ground. Nevertheless in one small cave, not far

The Kokan authorities took no especially warm interest in the fate of these sufferers, but they laboured principally to secure Katta-Turya's treasure. They also sent a guard of 30 *Sarbazais*, under an official of rank, to Soofi-Koorgan in order to guard the property of those who had perished and which lay buried in the snow.

Humane conduct of Ootambai-Koosh Begi, Bek of Margelan.

Aid was only given by Ootambai-Koosh Begi, Bek of Margelan. This man sent out at his own expense 300 horses from the town of Osh, and he thereby succeeded in saving 600 persons by placing two on each horse.

When spring came, crowds of workmen were taken out and made to dig, under the supervision of a guard. They unearthed many ornaments of various kinds and much money, especially copper.

The dead bodies were searched, and then thrown down, no one thinking it necessary to bury them. In the orders given from Kokan, it was only stated that the property of those who had perished was to be collected. Nothing was said about the corpses being buried, and therefore the workmen employed did not feel obliged to take upon themselves any extra labour. The one order given was very scrupulously attended to.

It was soon, however, found that the expectations as to finding much wealth would not be realized. Those who had perished had more copper-money than either silver or gold. The richer folk had either remained in Kashgar or had succeeded in reaching the town of Osh during the first ten days. The poor were the principal sufferers in the flight.

The Chinese re-establish their authority in Kashgaria.

The zeal of those who were carrying out the orders of the Kokan rulers was such that they even stripped the hides off the fallen cattle.[1] The Chinese again re-established their authority in Kashgaria, and with a patience in no way subdued, once more

from the summit of the pass and close to the *Darvaza*, we found fifteen skeletons of men, women and children whose bodies had rotted with the clothes they had on. In other places we saw many more skeletons—*Author*.

[1] The Kara-Kirghiz Mussulman Bi, chief of the Sartlar tribe, together with other eye-witnesses, gave me, when I was at Soofi-Koorgan, particulars of this calamity. They stated that the Kirghiz of the Sartlar tribe who wandered about the Terek pass for three years after this occurrence, would not drink water from the river Terek, as that river was filled with rotting corpses. Mussulman Bi had himself buried 300 bodies that were frozen close to his *Kibitka*. His brother had also buried 200 more in the neighbourhood of Koolyanka-Tookai.—*Author*.

began to introduce the order of things that had been on three successive occasions upset by the Khodjas. Again the people had to pay with their backs and with their property for the deeds of the cowardly and corrupt ambition seekers.

It had become more difficult for the Chinese to reconcile their interests with those of their neighbours, the Kokanese. Notwithstanding the dissensions that were taking place in Kokan, the Chinese considered it necessary to renew the conditions which had been settled by the treaty concluded in the year 1831. This concession, as displaying the weakness of the Chinese, made the Kokanese still more elated. They appointed as *Aksakal* to the town of Kashgar the same Nomed Khan who had let the Khodjas into the city. Moreover, they slackened the supervision over the Khodjas, and even stealthily assisted an agitation in their behalf. However, all those who joined Valikhan Turya and Kitchik-Khan in the year 1855-56 met with no success.

Valikhan Turya's successes against the Chinese.

Later on, the first mentioned repeated his attempts and with complete success. This was in April 1857. The garrisons of the Chinese advanced posts were massacred, with the exception of the native portion of them that went over to the side of the Khodjas.

Taken unawares the Chinese shut themselves up in the citadel of Kashgar. Valikhan Turya broke into the town at night, and his followers cried along the streets, "Hail Boozrook-Khan Turya."[1] The inhabitants rose and massacred the garrison of the town, consisting of Chinese and all the Chinese merchants. Valikhan Turya proclaimed himself Khan, and all the neighbouring hamlets sent deputations to acknowledge his title.

From all sides there began to pour in a heterogeneous mass to the standard of Valikhan Turya who managed somewhat skillfully to organize them into an army. This army was composed of infantry (*Sarbazais*) and cavalry (*Djigits*). The men were

[1] Boozrook-Khan Turya was the only son of Djengir. He enjoyed great popularity on account of his kind and peaceable disposition. Valikhan Turya determined to avail himself of this fact in obtaining easy possession of the town. Later on, the name of Boozrook-Khan appeared as a weapon in the hands of Yakoob Bek, who was bent on the same object.—*Author.*

variously clothed and were distributed under standards numbering 500 in each. Over each such body was a *pansat*.

The Government of Valikhan Turya worse for the people than that of the Chinese.

The people soon found, however, that the Government of this new Khodja was more oppressive than that of the Chinese.

Severity of Valikhan Turya.

Valikhan Turya having surrounded himself with Kokanese, treated the natives with disdain, and loaded them with taxes of unheard-of magnitude. Besides furnishing quotas of money and grain, the people were obliged to bear the labour of earthworks. Almost every day crowds of natives were sent out with spades and shovels to dam up the river Kizwil-Su in order to change its course so as to make it flow under the walls of Yangi-Hissar, where a Chinese garrison was shut up.

The inhabitants of the town and all the foreign merchants had to furnish copper vessels and horses for the army. All the workshops were taken up for the manufacture of arms. A certain Afghan superintended the cannon foundry, wherein were cast eight guns, in all probability, of inferior quality.

The disregard of their customs excited the people not less than did the imposition of taxes. Their women were forbidden to walk about the streets with unveiled faces, and with plaited hair. Any breach of this latter regulation led to the hair being cut off by policemen specially appointed for the purpose. All the males from six years and upwards were obliged to wear turbans, and to attend the mosque five times a day. On this subject, Valikhan displayed great cruelty. A day did not pass without the execution of several victims for breaches of this regulation. Having made on the banks of the river Kizwil-Su a pyramid of human skulls, both Chinese and Mussulman, Valikhan Turya steadily laboured to increase the size of this pyramid. One of his favourite pastimes was to cut off the heads of offenders with his own hand, and of opportunities there were none lacking. An unfortunate movement, a word, a yawn in the presence of the despot was sufficient to court death. The German *savant* Adolphus Schlagintweit was amongst the number of his victims, and his head went to increase the size of the pyramid. According to the information communicated to the Russian traveller, Mons.

Valikhanoff, who went to Kashgar two years afterwards, Schlagintweit was executed because he would not give the Khodja the papers addressed to the Khan of Kokan, with which he had been furnished in Bombay.

The remaining towns refused to recognize Valikhan Turya's sovereignty, and against them, *viz.*, against Aksu, Yangi-Hissar, Yarkend and Khotan, he sent forces. These succeeded in capturing the town of Yangi-Hissar only.

Aksu, Yangi-Hissar, Yarkend and Khotan refuse to recognize Valikhan Turya's sovereignty.

The reign of Valikhan Turya was happily not a long one. In the month of August 1857 (four months after his entry), a Chinese army entered Kashgar amid the joy of the inhabitants. Valikhan Turya's army fled, and after it went the ruler himself. On this occasion, 15,000 families fled after the Khodja to Kokan. The Chinese occupied Kashgar, but soon the joy of the inhabitants was turned into despair. The Chinese, for the first time during their possession of the country, endeavoured to outdo the ferocity displayed by Valikhan Turya. They seized the people's cattle, stores of grain and hay, burnt down their mosques, and overthrew the tombs of the Khodjas. The Kalmucks were especially foremost in the perpetration of every kind of atrocity. They stabled their horses in the mosques, killed the natives for no fault, and violated their women. The Chinese were at the same time active in torturing those who had taken part in the rebellion against themselves. The least suspicion that any one had participated in the insurrection or had served under Valikhan Turya was sufficient for him to be condemned to capital punishment. The innocent were subjected to severe tortures, and when in their agony they confessed to a crime that they had not committed, they were executed as *bonâ fide* offenders. The Chinese executions, whilst not less in number than those ordered by Valikhan Turya, differed therefrom only in this respect, the skulls of the victims were not added to the pyramid, but were placed in cages specially constructed for the purpose, and these cages were hung on poles so as to look like avenues to every street that led to the several gates of the town of Kashgar. The Russian traveller, who visited Kashgaria towards the end of the year 1859, *i.e.*,

End of Valikhan Turya's reign and restoration of the Chinese sovereignty.

Severity of the Chinese.

two years after the expulsion of the Khodjas by the Chinese, tells us that these avenues then remained.[1]

On this occasion, the Chinese, not seeing the advantage of obtaining a promise from the Kokan authorities that they would not allow the Khodjas to enter Kashgaria, were in no hurry to renew a treaty with Kokan that had been so disadvantageous to themselves.

Khoodoyar Khan of Kokan makes advances to the Chinese.

In the spring of 1858, Khoodoyar Khan himself despatched an Embassy to Kashgaria, by means of which he expressed his extreme regret on the occasion of recent events, and gave promises of various kinds for the future, asking at the same time for a renewal of the treaty of 1830.

The Chinese once more concluded an arrangement, and Nassreddin Sarkar, who carried out the negotiations with them, was appointed the Kokan *Aksakal* with the title of *Datkha.*

With regard to Valikhan Turya, he dwelt peacefully at Kokan, where, as a member of the local aristocracy, a Said, and a descendant of the Prophet, he was by Mussulman law exempted from bodily punishment or sentence of death.

End of the fourth attempt on the part of the Khodjas to set up their dynasty in Kashgaria.

Thus ended the fourth attempt of the Khodjas to restore their sovereignty over Kashgaria. On this occasion, the attempt only led to still greater loss to the country, and to the execution of several thousand persons, who were, for the most part, innocent. On this occasion, too, the principal offenders and participators saved themselves, and carried off their plunder, leaving the people, whom they had deceived, as victims in the hands of the Chinese.

[1] Complete details concerning the reign of Valikhan Turya are given in an article by Valikhanoff in No. 3 of the "Proceedings of the Imperial Russian Geographical Society for 1861." From this we have borrowed much of the information that we have herein furnished.—*Author.*

CHAPTER VI.

Some words on the Doongan insurrection in the Chinese Provinces of Shen-Si, Han-Su and Djoongaria — Rebellion in Kashgaria — Rasheddin Khodja — Habiboolla Khodja — Sadwik Bek — Boozrook-Khan — Arrival of Yakoob Bek in the town of Kashgar — His biography — Yakoob Bek defeats the Aksu and Yarkend troops sent against him — He captures the town of Yangi-Hissar and the citadel of Yangi-Shar — Suppression of the rebellion of the Kipchaks — Capture of Yarkend and Khotan — Yakoob Bek declares himself the ruler of Kashgaria — His march against the towns of Aksu, Koocha and Koorlia — Raid of the Doongans on the town of Koocha — Second movement against the town of Koonya-Toorfan — Third march of Yakoob Bek to Koonya-Toorfan for the purpose of engaging the Chinese forces — Failure before Hoomatai — Present condition of Yakoob Bek.

Mussulman insurrection in the western provinces of China and in Djoongaria and Kashgaria.

AFTER driving out Valikhan Turya in 1857, and again possessing themselves of the whole of Kashgaria, the Chinese did not long enjoy their victory. The Mussulman insurrection in the western provinces of China, Shen-Si and Han-Su quickly spread until it embraced the whole of Djoongaria, and afterwards, in 1862-63, Kashgaria. The Chinese were in a desperate condition. Many hundreds of thousands of them perished, and yet with unconquerable obstinacy they step by step, during the course of thirteen years, put down an insurrection that had spread as far as Tchoogootchak on the west, and Manas and Ooroomtcha on the south. In the year 1877, their armies besieged the town of Ooroomtcha, and opened a campaign against Yakoob Bek, their most talented and powerful opponent, who had ruled the events of the previous thirteen years.

Action of the Chinese thereon.

Mussulman population of China.

The Mussulman population of China is grouped in the provinces of Shen-Si and Han-Su, and numbers 5,000,000 souls.[1] The origin of these Mussulmans is variously accounted for. According to some, the date of their settling in the provinces of China goes back to the Eighth or Ninth Century, when the Chinese, after subduing the Uigur State, deported 1,000,000 souls to their deserted western provinces. In course of time, these Uigurs embraced the Mussulman faith, lost, through intermarriage with

Its origin.

[1] *See* Mons. Sosnovski's article in the "Military Magazine" for the year 1876, No. 10.—*Author.*

Chinese damsels, their primitive type, and now but little resemble their kinsmen who remained in Kashgaria. The same Mussulmans who peopled the western provinces of China afterwards formed the bulk of the people of Djoongaria and settled in the towns of Tchoogootchak, Kooldja, Manas, Ooroomtcha, Koonya-Toorfan, Barkooli and Hami. The people of Kashgaria, who are alien to these Chinese Mussulmans, begin on the west of Fort Karashar and the town of Koorlia. They take the name of the locality in which they dwell: thus we find Karasharians, Koochans, Aksutians, Kashgarians, Yarkendians and Khotanese.

The Chinese call their Mussulmans Hoi-Hoi-Tsian.[1]

Name given to the Mussulman insurrection in the Chinese provinces and the supposed derivation of that name.

In Kashgaria, the same Chinese Mussulmans are known under the name of Doongans, and the insurrection which they initiated is called the 'Doongan insurrection.' The derivation of the word 'Doongan' is not exactly known. According to oral tradition which I heard whilst in Kashgaria, the derivation of this name is sometimes traced to the epoch of Alexander of Macedon; at others to the days of Chingiz-Khan or of Tamerlane. It is thought, too, that, in the movement of bands of these popular heroes from the east to the west and from the west to the east, many of their soldiers remained both in Djoongaria and in the provinces of Shen-Si and Han-Su, and consequently received the name of *Toorgan*, which means "those left behind." [2]

Mons. Sosnovski believes that the origin of the word 'Doongan' relates to the commencement of the rising of the Chinese Mussulmans in the year 1861. According to him the insurrection first began in the neighbourhood of Fort Doongan, which is situated in the province of Shen-Si. The name of this fort, which was

---

[1] Mons. Heins, in his article in the "Turkestan Magazine" for the year 1867, No. 4, entitled the "Insurrection of the Doongans in Western China," supposes that the word 'Hoi-Hoi' is a corruption of the word 'Ooi-Goor.'—*Author.*

[2] The story as to the origin of the Doongans, which most merits attention and which I heard in the town of Koocha, is as follows:—When Chingiz-Khan advanced on Pekin he had in his army many Mussulmans from Eastern Turkestan. When he took possession of Pekin, he appointed his son Mangoo (or, as the Chinese call him, Mandjoo) governor of China. With Mangoo he left many Mussulmans in China, who from that time have received the name 'Toorgan.'—*Author.*

very often repeated in the first despatches sent to the Chinese, came perhaps to be applied to the participators in the rebellion.

But this idea is not based on probability, since the word 'Doongan' existed long before the insurrection of 1861.

Not being in possession of information that would enable us to arrive at a final opinion on the question as to the derivation of the word 'Doongan,' let us leave the matter to the considera-tion of specialists and turn to the facts in the insurrection itself.

Date of the beginning of the Doongan rebellion.

The rising began in the year 1861, during the last year of the rule of Sian-Fwin, in the province of Shen-Si, and from there it spread first to the province of Han-Su and thence to Djoongaria.

Cruelties which attended it.

The insurrection was signalized by the dreadful, and in places the total, destruction of the Chinese. The first attempts of the Chinese Government to put it down were not attended with success. On account of the extortions of the officials and the privations to which they were subjected, the Chinese detach-ments would sometimes go over to the side of the insurgents. The Chinese garrisons, for fear of being massacred one after the other, were obliged to shut themselves up in the citadels, and the insurgents, who were thus free to pour over the whole of the disaffected country, everywhere slaughtered the Chinese popula-tion. The hatred against the Chinese was so great that, accord-ing to Mons. Sosnovski, Mussulmans would themselves slay their own wives and children to prevent their falling into the hands of the Chinese. The same author tells us that the Chinese amply repaid the debt, for they mercilessly wiped out their enemies. On the occasion of the siege of the town of He-Djey, which lasted for seven months, 20,000 men were put to the sword by the Chinese on the fall of that place. Similarly at Si-Nin-Foo and at Tszin-Tszi-Noo, there were slain 9,000 and 50,000 men respectively, whilst a vast, a fruitful and a thickly populated tract was turned into a desert.

Rich towns became heaps of ruins.[1]

[1] I visited the town of Tchoogootchak in the year 1870. According to native statements, in that place alone and its environs 40,000 men perished at the hands of the Chinese. The town was one vast heap of ruins without a single inhabit-ant. Six years after this massacre the bones of the victims of the rebellion still lay in the streets of the town and in the fort ditch. A handsome Russian

Energetic action of the Chinese.

The action of the Chinese became energetic and swift only from the date of the appointment in 1868 of Tso-Tsoon-Tan as Governor-General of the provinces of Han-Su, Shen-Si and Djoongaria. Being aware, as Mons. Sosnovski tells us, that disorder principally proceeds from extortion, he selected trustworthy officials, made his soldiers contented and built a factory at Lan-Chey-Foo, where they now turn out breech-loading steel-guns and rifles on the newest system. The centres of the insurrection were one by one occupied by Chinese forces; and in January of the following year the road from Lan-Djey *viâ* Hami and Gootchen to Tchoogootchak presented an unbroken line of Chinese posts, whilst the rising in the provinces was crushed except that small bands of Doongans continued to wander about.

Effect of the first successes of the rebels.

The tidings of the success of the insurrection of the Chinese Mussulmans in Djoongaria, Shen-Si and Han-Su, quickly spread to Kashgaria and caused the population of that country to rise against the Chinese. The Chinese garrisons were weak, and, what was more important, were principally composed of Doongan soldiers, who, on the first intelligence of the rebellion of their kins-folk, took up arms against their employers, and with the aid of the local population massacred the greater part of those Chinese who did not contrive to shut themselves up in citadels. The rebellion was first discovered in the town of Koocha.

Rasheddin Khodja.

One of the inhabitants of this town, Rasheddin Khodja, who was the first to proclaim a *gazavat*, or holy war, in the year 1862, collected the people, and placing himself at their head conducted an attack on the Chinese garrisons. The Chinese were slain, whereupon Rasheddin sent his emissaries to all the towns of Kashgaria to get up a war against them. The Doongans joined the insurrection, and with their aid the Chinese garrisons in the towns of Karashar, Togsoon and Koonya-Toorfan

factory and the Russian church were thrown down. The Russian colony fled by night to Russian territory. It is related that the Russian priest's wife was taken in the pains of labour whilst flying, and that she died on the road.—*Author.*

were slaughtered. The people then recognized Rasheddin's sovereignty and proclaimed him Khan. Isa Khodja, Rasheddin's relative, was appointed Governor of the towns abovementioned. Rasheddin's two other relatives, Djalat-Eddin-Khodja and Boorkhaneddin-Khodja, set out for the towns of Aksu, Kashgar, Yarkend and Khotan, in order to exact from them Rasheddin's title of Khan. Before their arrival an insurrection had burst forth, and the Chinese garrisons had shut themselves up in the citadels. The people of Aksu were the first to recognize Rasheddin's title. One Sadwik Bek, of Kipchak[1] origin, was at that time an influential person in the town of Kashgar. After going out with his adherents to meet the Khodjas, he recognized Rasheddin as Khan, and his example was followed by all the inhabitants of the town of Kashgar. Having appointed Sadwik-Khan Hakim of the town, the Khodjas continued their journey to Yarkend.

Rasheddin is proclaimed Khan.

Sadwik Bek.

Now the Hakim of Yarkend, who had been appointed by the Chinese, was Niaz Bek. A great part fell to the lot of this man in the later revolutions that took place in Kashgaria.

Niaz Bek.

The commander of the Chinese forces composing the garrison of Yarkend, perceiving the murmuring both amongst the inhabitants of the town and the Doongan soldiers who formed part of the garrison, decided upon disarming the latter. News of this intention quickly reached the Doongans and caused them to rise in rebellion. They broke into the citadel at night, which contained the Chinese garrison consisting of 2,000 men. These they slew together with their families. A small body of Chinese escaped by beating off their assailants and regaining possession of the citadel. In the morning the Doongans rushed into the town and, aided by the inhabitants, plundered the houses and shops of the Chinese after killing the owners. It was evident, however, that the emissaries from Aksu obtained no great amount of success in this place, the inhabitants of which chose as their ruler Hazret-Abdurrahman,

Action of the Chinese military commander at Yarkend.

Its effect.

Failure of Rasheddin's mission to Yarkend and Khotan.

[1] According to other accounts Sadwik Bek was a Kirghiz, who appeared with his band in the town of Kashgar, and plundered both Chinese and Kashgarians with equal indifference.—*Author.*

an old moollah. They also appointed as his assistant the former Hakim of the town, Niaz Bek. The inhabitants of Khotan followed the example of the Yarkendians, slew the Chinese and chose as their ruler Habi-Boolla, who was also a moollah, and who had lately returned from Mecca. This man assumed the title of *padshah* (king) and began to coin money in his own name.

Places in Kashgaria left to the Chinese at the close of 1863.

At the close of the year 1863 the only places that the Chinese held in Kashgaria were the citadel of Kashgar, the town of Yangi-Hissar and the citadel of the town of Yarkend. Against the last-mentioned, detachments from Aksu and Yarkend were sent. To the aid of these detachments went also some Doongans. Nevertheless the citadel long withstood all the efforts of the besiegers, and when all the means of defence had failed, the Chinese commander and all his garrison heroically blew themselves up into the air.

Division of authority at Yarkend.

After this victory the Aksu Khodjas again demanded from the Yarkendians the recognition of Rasheddin's authority. The inhabitants would not consent to the demand. At length, after a long dispute, the Government was divided between Abdurrahman and the Khodja Boorkhaneddin. The former was supreme in the town, the latter in the fort, where were quartered the Doongans and some troops from Aksu. This state of things lasted until the time of Yakoob Bek.

Extent of Rasheddin's authority in the beginning of 1864.

In the beginning of the year 1864, Rasheddin's rule was recognized throughout the whole of Kashgaria with the exception of the town of Khotan.

Rasheddin Khodja was not the descendant of those Khodjas who had governed Kashgaria, and, we should add, who had brought upon her during the space of 40 years so much calamity (we speak of Djengir and of Valikhan Turya). Therefore, amongst the population of Kashgaria, it would have been easy to seek out those who were dissatisfied with Rasheddin, and who wished to place the government of the country in the hands of one of the numerous descendants of Appak

Boozrook-Khodja.

Khodja. Of these Boozrook-Khodja, Djengir's son, enjoyed the greatest amount of popularity. Amongst the people he was famous for his sanctity and for his kindness, but persons who knew him intimately were aware also of the weakness of his character, and of his complete incapacity. For this reason Sadwik Bek, the Hakim of Kashgar, of whom we have already spoken, could confidently reckon on making him a weapon in his own hands for the attainment of his own ends. He at once took advantage of Boozrook-Khan's popularity for this purpose. He then turned to Alim Kool, who was at that time Governor of Tashkent and Kokan, and begged him to send Boozrook, who was living at Tashkent, to Kashgaria, promising him easy possession of the entire country. Boozrook lost no time in going, attended by fifty men. With him went also Yakoob Bek in the capacity of *Lashkar-Bashi*, or commander of the forces that were to be formed.

Sadwik Bek takes advantage of Boozrook-Khan's weak character to work to his own ends.

Yakoob Bek.

Before continuing our exposition of subsequent events in Kashgaria, we will adduce some information which we have collected regarding Yakoob Bek, an historical personage without doubt and one who boldly stands out amidst all the rulers of the independent Asiatic States, who were contemporaries of his own.

Yakoob Bek's father was Ismet-Oolla, an inhabitant of Khodjent. He devoted himself to the repetition of various prayers over the sick. During a visit to the hamlet of Pskent, 50 versts (33⅓rd miles) from Tashkent, on the road to Khodjent, he married a native of that place and took up his abode in his wife's home. Yakoob Bek was the fruit of this marriage. I have not succeeded in determining with exactness the year of his birth. In the year 1876, Yakoob Bek had the appearance of a man of about 50 years of age. Those persons who were then about him said that his age was from 58 to 64, notwithstanding that grey hairs had only just begun to make their appearance. Soon after Yakoob Bek's birth, his father became divorced from his wife, who then married a butcher of Pskent, in whose house Yakoob Bek grew up. This is the reason that the people sometimes called him the butcher's son.

Genealogy of Yakoob Bek.

Having lost his father and his mother whilst yet a child, the young orphan, in order to gain a livelihood, became a *batcha*, or public dancer. The boy pleased a Kokan *sipahi* who was passing through Pskent, and this man took him off to the town of

Early life and livelihood of Yakoob Bek.

Kokan. Once there Yakoob Bek passed from hand to hand and acquired renown as a skilful and pretty *batcha*, until at last he was taken up by a certain Mahamed-Karim-Kashka, who was in the suite of Madali Khan of Kokan in the office of *chilim-chi* (or bearer of the *chilim* or pipe, a post corresponding to *valet de chambre*). I have chanced to speak with eye-witnesses who saw Yakoob Bek, at the time mentioned, in a great spectacle at Margelan, and they told me that he was then distinguished for his skill in dancing. According to the stories of these persons, Yakoob Bek was then a pretty well-formed and strongly-made boy, with a neck slightly short, fresh coloured face and beautiful eyes. He had many admirers.

To this period belongs the appointment of the *chilim-chi* Karim-Kashka to the office of Hakim of Khodjent and to that of *Parmanatchi*, corresponding to our rank of General. Asiatic potentates often appoint their servants, however menial, to the high office of Hakim preparatory to making them generals, and no one is surprised thereat.

Dissensions in the Khanate of Kokan.

An unsuccessful war with Bokhara cost Madali Khan his life. On his death there took place in the Khanate of Kokan a strife of parties, each of whom put forth its own pretender to the throne of the country. The Kipchak party triumphed and placed on the throne Shir Ali Bek,[1] a man of very small stature. He appointed as his minister one Mussulman-Kool, also a Kipchak, and a person who subsequently played an important role.

Mussulman-Kool.

Almost all the old Hakims were changed and slain. Amongst these also perished Yakoob Bek's patron Karim Kashka. After being for a short period without a place Yakoob Bek became the *batcha* of Nar Mahomed Koosh-Begi, Hakim of the town of Tashkent, and a Kipchak. At this period disorder still continued

[1] From the middle of the last century the Kokan meteors succeeded each other in the following order: Narboota-Khan (his brother's name was Khodja-Bek), Alim-Khan, son of Narboota-Khan, Omar-Khan, Narboota-Khan's second son, Madali-Khan, Omar Khan's son. On the death of Madali-Khan, Shir Ali Bek, a Kipchak, succeeded to the throne as we have said. He was afterwards called Shir Ali Khan. He was Khodja Bek's son and a brother of Narboota Khan.—*Author*.

in Kokan. Shir Ali Khan, after a reign of two years, was killed and Moorad, Alim Khan's son, succeeded to the throne. He reigned for nine days.

Mussulman-Kool was the rival of Moorad-Khan for the leadership of the Kipchak party. He slew Moorad, and having placed on the throne Khoodoyar Khan, Shir Ali Khan's infant son, began to personally administer the affairs of State. In order to obviate all pretensions on the part of Khoodoyar Khan's eldest brothers, he killed them. One of them only, Malya Khan, saved himself by flight. At this period Yakoob Bek had outgrown the age at which he could enchant the natives with his personal appearance or with his skill in dancing. His position would have become a difficult one, if fortune had not befriended him. Nar Mahomed, Hakim of Tashkent, became enamoured of his youngest sister (the butcher's daughter) and married her. Thanks to his influence, Yakoob Bek quickly attained the rank of *Makhram* (aide-de-camp), *Piyanj-bashi* (captain of fifty), *Yuz-bashi* (centurion) and *Pansat* (captain of five hundred) in succession.

Rapid rise of Yakoob Bek in consequence of his step-sister's marriage.

Soon after this, Yakoob Bek was appointed Bek of Ak-Mechet (Fort Perovski). In the year 1852, he had a skirmish with a Russian force and was defeated.[1] On his return to Tashkent he began to take an active part in all the subsequent agitations. His name, therefore, as that of an energetic and capable man began to be known to many.

He is appointed Bek of Ak-Mechet. As such, he takes part in a fight against the Russians.

Meanwhile Malya Khan had ousted his brother Khoodoyar Khan from the throne, which he occupied for three years until he himself was killed. The powerful Mussulman-Kool now

Execution of Mussulman-Kool.

[1] In the first account published by me in the "Military Magazine" entitled "Outlines of Kashgaria" on the subject of Yakoob Bek's biography, there has crept in a mistake. Misinformed by persons who were in attendance on Yakoob Bek, I wrote that he, on being appointed Hakim (Bek) of Ak-Mechet, heroically defended that place with a handful of men against a Russian force. This has been shewn to be an error. General Maksheyeff, Professor of Military Statistics, who took a part in the siege and storming of Ak-Mechet, has sent me a corrected statement borrowed from vast materials which he collected during his service in the province of Orenburgh. As this note is of interest, I have inserted it at length as a supplement to this chapter, and it will be found on page 182 and following.—*Author.*

asked for an army from Tashkent to aid in putting an end to the disturbances that were going on. This army was furnished and Yakoob Bek accompanied it. The army, on arriving at the town of Kokan, instead of obeying Mussulman-Kool, arrested him and made him over to Khoodoyar Khan, who, having grown up, had long fretted under the harsh guardianship of this time-server. Though he owed his throne to Mussulman-Kool, Khoodoyar Khan did not hesitate to execute him. His victim was fastened to a scaffold and blown from a gun loaded with a blank cartridge and placed at a short distance from his body. His clothes caught fire and the smoke suffocated him.[1]

Alim Kool.

Mussulman-Kool had no sooner disappeared from the scene, when his place was taken by another time-server, a man perhaps more energetic than his predecessor. This was Alim Kool, also a Kipchak.[2]

Appearance of the Russians.

Alim Kool having ejected Khoodoyar Khan seated on the throne Said Bek, Malya Khan's son. This took place in the year 1863 (?) at a time when new enemies, more terrible to Alim Kool than all the parties in Kokan that were hostile to him put together, made their appearance; these were the Russians who had already advanced to the town of Chemkent. Alim Kool, after leaving Kokan, set out for Tashkent in order to organize resistance to his new enemies. In Tashkent itself there was a very considerable party inimical to Alim Kool. In the ranks of this party Yakoob Bek occupied a prominent place. Having set out for Chemkent, Yakoob Bek bravely fought with the Russians and obtained considerable renown. This energetic and popular personage and a very formidable rival greatly alarmed Alim Kool, and he had already determined on getting rid of him by the means usually adopted by Asiatics,—*viz.*, murder, when a circumstance unexpectedly presented itself and not only saved Yakoob Bek, but gave his capacity and energy a wider sphere of action. Emissaries from the town of Kashgar from Sadwik Bek came to Tashkent with

Yakoob Bek appears as Alim Kool's rival.

---

[1] To say nothing of his body being blown to pieces by the force of the charge. —*Trans.*

[2] We were told that Mussulman-Kool was a *Sart Kipchak*, and Alim Kool a *Kirghiz Kipchak.*—*Author.*

the request that Boozrook-Khan Khodja might be sent thence to Kashgar. Alim Kool readily agreed to the request made to him and with Boozrook he also sent Yakoob Bek away from Tashkent. Boozrook Khan, accompanied by Yakoob Bek and Aldash Datkha,[1] Alim Kool's kinsman, and by fifty *djigits* and personal attendants, made his appearance in the year 1864 before the walls of the town of Kashgar,[2] and was gladly received by the inhabitants. Sadwik Bek gave over the government of the towns to Boozrook-Khan, hoping the while to play the most important part himself; but he soon saw that Yakoob Bek was opposed to his plans. Between the two rivals there now began a secret strife, which apparently could only end in the death of one or other of them. Yakoob Bek first of all succeeded in making a quarrel between Boozrook and Sadwik Bek, and then in causing the latter to fly. The victorious rival was now appointed *Batwir-Bashi* (commander-in-chief), and Mir Baba, an inhabitant of Andijan, *Esaul-bashi* (or second in command). The new commander-in-chief spent the first six months in collecting an army at the town of Kashgar. The nucleus of this force was represented by 400 Andjans. These, in time, brought large bodies of men. Yakoob Bek received all his recruits with kindness, liberally rewarded their leaders, and gave them commands over the soldiers raised from the neighbourhood of Kashgar. During the first year a force of several thousand men was furnished from the local population. The siege of citadels, which the Chinese were stubbornly holding, was carried on uninterruptedly, and served as a good military school for the new conscripts.

Alim Kool's method of getting rid of him.

Boozrook-Khan's reception by the inhabitants of Kashgar.

Yakoob Bek opposes Sadwik Bek's schemes.

Further advancement of Yakoob Bek.

The recognition by the inhabitants of Kashgar of Boozrook

[1] Up to the present time the Hakim of the town of Kashgar bears the title of Datkha.—*Author.*

[2] According to other information, there came with Yakoob Bek from Fergana from four to five hundred horsemen. After recruiting this band from the town of Kashgar to a strength of from three to four thousand men, he marched against the citadel of Yangi-Shar, situated at a distance of 7½ versts (5 miles) from the town of Kashgar, whence there went out to meet him Chinese and Doongans to the number of several thousand. A battle took place about a verst (⅔rds mile) from Yangi-Shar, on the banks of a canal leading from the Kizwil-Su. Placing his infantry in front, Yakoob Bek launched his cavalry on the flank of the main body of the Chinese who took to flight.—*Author.*

as Khan, coupled with his pretensions, as descendant of Appak Khodja, to the sovereignty of the whole of Kashgaria, called forth the opposition of Rasheddin Khodja, who was ruler of the country to the east of the town of Aksu, whilst Abdurrahman was ruler of Yarkend. The inhabitants of Aksu, Koocha, Yarkend and Khotan, whilst bearing in mind the inroads of the Khodjas of the Appak clan, Djengir, Katta-Turya and Vali-khan Turya, could scarcely be reckoned on to make a new attempt in favour of Boozrook. Forces both from Aksu and Yarkend advanced almost simultaneously on Kashgar with the object of driving out Boozrook, whose position had become critical. It was only owing to the energy of Yakoob Bek that he was able to hold his own. Leaving a small but well-equipped force to watch the citadel, Yakoob Bek went out to meet the army from Aksu, and, having defeated it at Khan-Arwik, energetically pursued its broken forces up to the hamlet of Yangabad. After this he returned and advanced against the Doongans and Yarkendians, who were still several marches from Kashgar. An engagement took place nine *tash* from the latter town, at Toozgoon. In speaking of the fight, eye-witnesses have exaggerated the enemy's forces by several thousands of men. According to their accounts, the Doongans approached to within a very short distance of Yakoob Bek's troops, and then directed against them a well-aimed fire which caused great loss. Yakoob Bek at once ordered several *sotnias* of his cavalry to attack the enemy's flanks. Having brought about, by this manœuvre, some degree of confusion, he now moved forward the rest of his troops and won the battle.

Rasheddin Khodja opposes Boozrook-Khan.

Boozrook-Khan's position is secured by the energy of Yakoob Bek.

Yakoob Bek defeats the Aksu and Yarkend troops sent against him.

It is stated that Yakoob Bek received three wounds in this engagement, and that he concealed the fact till the end of the fight, lest he should have depressed the spirit of his soldiers by appearing to be hurt. Following the routed enemy to the town of Yangi-Hissar, he took that place by storm after a siege that lasted 40 days. The greater part of the inhabitants and of the garrison perished in the siege and in the assault. About 200 soldiers and women and children turned Mussulmans, and thereby saved their lives. After the capture of Yangi-Hissar, Yakoob Bek sent envoys bearing gifts, and the news of his victory to

Captures Yangi-Hissar.

Alim Kool, who was at the time engaged in fighting the Russians. As part of his offerings, Yakoob Bek sent nine Chinese damsels. The envoys never even saw Alim Kool, for, before they came to Kokan, the tidings reached them that Alim Kool had been slain on the $\frac{9th}{21st}$ May 1865, in a battle with the Russians before Tashkent. The death of Alim Kool called forth new dissensions in Kokan, all of which indirectly served as a means whereby Yakoob Bek's position became still more secured.

Defeat and death of Alim Kool.

Fresh dissensions in Kokan aid in the aggrandizement of Yakoob Bek.

Said Khan of Kokan, who was advanced, as we have said above, to the throne by Alim Kool, on hearing of the approach of the Russians to Tashkent, moved with an army to the aid of that town. Before arriving there, he learnt that Alim Kool's forces had been defeated and he himself killed. Turning back, Said Khan was the first to fly to the town of Djizak, whilst a portion of his troops turned towards Kokan and proclaimed Khoodai Kool, a handsome boy, who sold girdles and turbans in the bazaar, Khan of that place. This boy was known to the people under the name of Bil Baktchi Khan. The new Khan did not reign long. Taking advantage of Said Khan's march towards Tashkent, Khoodoyar Khan, who, after his expulsion by Alim Kool, had dwelt in Bokharian territory, moved with some troops of that State, and with a body of Turkmans to Kokan. Bil Baktchi Khan, without waiting for Khoodoyar Khan's approach, fled in September 1865, with 7,000 horsemen, 30 large guns and 400 infantry soldiers armed with falconets first to the town of Osh and then across the mountains to Gultcha, and so on *viâ* Kizwil Koorgan to Soofi-Koorgan. At this point the roads divide: one leads through the Terek-Davan pass to the town of Kashgar; the other through the Shart pass to the Alai. The route adopted over the mountains was a strange one, because the army had to take heavy guns by a bridle path in the following direction. Both the army and the guns marched in one day from the town of Osh to Langar, 30 versts (20 miles). Here a slight attack of Khoodoyar Khan's cavalry vedettes was repulsed. From Langar the cavalry moved on the following day by the direct road leading to Gultcha,[1] traversing 33 versts (22 miles).

Khoodai Kool or Bil Baktchi Khan.

His flight.

Roads leading from Gultcha to Soofi-Koorgan.

[1] The Russians have erected Fort Gultcha on the same spot.—*Author.*

The guns and convoys moved by a more circuitous route through the Tchigirtchik pass, where they halted for the night, reaching Gultcha, a distance of 43 versts (28⅔rds miles), in two days. At Gultcha, the whole force remained for ten days, and then moved on Soofi-Koorgan. The distance between Gultcha and Soofi-Koorgan, 22 versts (14⅔rds miles), was accomplished by the cavalry in one day, and by the artillery in three. To each gun eight horses were harnessed, and 30 infantry soldiers (*sarbazais*) looked after it. Wherever the road was narrow, the guns were dismounted and dragged along the ground. In the neighbourhood of Belyaooli, where a bridge broke down, two guns were lost, so that only 28 were left to bring into Soofi-Koorgan.

Khoodoyar Khan pursues Bil Baktchi.

Khoodoyar Khan, with an heterogeneous army, supplemented by 300 Turkmans, set out from the town of Osh to pursue Bil Baktchi, twenty days after the latter had left the same place. On the first day, Khoodoyar Khan's forces reached the Tamgik pass, 40 versts (26⅔rds miles); on the second day, they arrived at Gultcha, and on the third, at Soofi-Koorgan. Khoodoyar Khan left in the Tamgik pass all his transport and four small guns. From Gultcha his forces moved in light marching order, each man being provided with four small loaves only in the way of food.

Bil Baktchi's forces consisted of three distinct elements, Kirghiz, Kipchaks and Sarts. The latter were the *sarbazais* with the falconets and the gunners. The only thing in common amongst them was that all were devoid of the necessary courage to fight with the same equally heterogeneous body as themselves that was advancing against them under Khoodoyar Khan. As soon as Khoodoyar Khan's Turkman advanced cavalry appeared

Bil Baktchi's forces scatter.

in the neighbourhood of Soofi-Koorgan, Bil Baktchi's camp was broken up, the Kipchaks flying to the Terek-Davan pass, and the Kirghiz, taking Bil Baktchi with them, making for the Alai through the Shart gorge. The Sarts, on seeing their comrades take to flight, stood firm and directed their falconets at them as they ran. The whole then joined Khoodoyar Khan's party.

Return of Khoodoyar Khan to Kokon.

The fugitives were not pursued for a long distance, and after taking 80 prisoners, Khoodoyar Khan returned homewards.

Together with the Kipchaks there had come to Kashgar Boozrook-Khan's cousin, Katta-Turya, who was Governor of Kashgar during the revolt of the Khodjas, Bik Mahomet, who commanded the Tashkent army, after Alim Kool's death, and Mirza Ahmet Koosh-Begi,[1] formerly Hakim of Tashkent.

All the Kipchaks entered Boozrook's service, and thus Yakoob Bek's army was considerably increased. His siege operations too against the citadel of Yangi-Shar became more successful. In the autumn of 1865, Yakoob Bek entered into negotiations with Ho-Dalai, commandant of the Chinese forces, relative to the surrender of the fortress, and he promised that if all the Chinese would embrace Mahometanism, their lives should be spared. Ho-Dalai agreed and apprized the Amban, Governor of Kashgar, who was likewise shut up in the fortress, of his intention, advising him to do the same. But the Amban would not seek his safety by sacrificing either his duty or his religion, so together with some of his followers he blew himself up into the air, and thus by heroically courting death expiated the cowardice and faint-heartedness which he had displayed throughout the rebellion. Hearing the sound of an explosion, Yakoob Bek at once sent his forces to storm the place. A portion of the garrison perished, but about 3,000 Chinese soldiers and women and children were forcibly converted to Mahomedanism. The houses of Yangi-Shar were given over to pillage for a space of seven days.

Yakoob Bek enters into negotiations for the surrender by the Chinese garrison of Yangi-Shar. The Chinese Commandant Dalai turns traitor.

The Chinese Amban of Kashgar refuses to follow his example and commits suicide.

Capture of Yangi-Shar.

After this victory, Yakoob Bek began to make less use of Boozrook's name, for during a series of splendid feasts given by him to the population of Kashgar, he received the honours given only to the ruler of a country.[2] The weak and characterless Boozrook, who had given himself up to debauchery notwithstanding the halo of sanctity which surrounded him, and with which all his admirers would still surround him, was little able to oppose Yakoob Bek, and therefore from the very first he had given into his hands the general administration of affairs.

Yakoob Bek begins to set Boozrook-Khan aside.

[1] He lives still in Kashgar, but has no great amount of influence.—*Author.*

[2] During these festivities he married Ho-Dalai's daughter and placed her father over those Chinese who had embraced Mahomedanism, giving him the power of life and death over those subject to him.—*Author.*

The Kipchak party in Kashgar opposes Yakoob Bek.

But there were certain influential Kipchaks who envied Yakoob Bek and who were not pleased at his aggrandizement. They, therefore, only waited for a favourable opportunity to snatch the power out of his hands. An opportunity soon came.

Yakoob Bek marches against the town of Yarkend.

Yakoob Bek, after the capture of Yangi-Hissar, marched against the town of Yarkend. A little before this, a detachment of his troops had taken possession of Fort Maral-Bashi, which is situated between Kashgar and Aksu. He had also succeeded in gaining the neighbouring hamlets, and was ready to direct against

Insurrection of Kipchaks in Yakoob Bek's camp.

the defenders of Yarkend a final blow, when an insurrection amongst the Kipchaks burst forth in his own camp. Not considering themselves in a position to openly withstand Yakoob

The Kipchaks fly, taking with them Boozrook-Khan.

Bek, they seized Boozrook-Khan and fled with him to the town of Kashgar, where they gave out that Yakoob Bek's power had been overthrown. Yakoob Bek's position was now desperate and one which called for all his lively energy if he would issue triumphantly from these circumstances. Without losing a minute,

Yakoob Bek returns to Kashgar.

he left Yarkend and returned to Kashgar. The Kipchaks, on hearing of his approach, shut themselves up together with Boozrook-Khan in Yangi-Shar.

He enters into negotiations with the rebel Kipchaks.

After an unsuccessful attempt to take their refuge by an exhibition of strength, Yakoob Bek entered into negotiations with the rebels. Bek Mahomet, who had instigated the revolt, required that Yakoob Bek should swear on the Koran that he would grant full liberty to all the Kipchaks to go whither they would. Yakoob Bek swore to do so. According to the conditions subsequently arranged, the malcontents went out at one gate of the citadel, whilst Yakoob Bek's forces entered in at the other. With the Kipchaks fled, or, as others say, was carried off, Boozrook-Khan.

Yakoob Bek offers the Khanship to Katta-Turya.

Not feeling himself sufficiently strong, having regard to a prospective struggle with the remaining cities of Kashgaria, to set forth without the standard of the Appaks, Yakoob Bek

Perfidious conduct of Yakoob Bek.

He chastises the Kipchaks.

offered Katta-Turya, who had taken no part in the revolt of the Kipchaks, the Khanship in place of Boozrook. He then, in spite of his oath, followed the fugitive Kipchaks to Kokan. Many of his enemies were overtaken and slain. Yakoob Bek, however, soon perceived that his new Khan was but little disposed to be the same willing weapon in his hands that Boozrook was. Being one of those persons who never hesitate to employ any kind of means for the attainment of their own objects, Yakoob Bek found a way out of his difficulty. Katta-Turya was poisoned after a reign of four months. At the sumptuous ceremonials which he inaugurated at the funeral of the deceased, Yakoob Bek walked in front of the bier, shedding tears and wearing a girdle as a symbol of his grief. Katta-Turya was interred side by side with Appak.[1] The repentant Boozrook now returned and was again proclaimed Khan.[2]

And poisons Katta-Turya.

Having subdued the Kipchak revolt, Yakoob Bek advanced again against Yarkend. Khodja Boorkhaneddin, who commanded the Yarkend Army, was gained over by Niaz Bek, and the latter was at this time assistant to the ruler Hazret Abdurrahman. He therefore refused to fight against Yakoob Bek, saying that he had been sent to free Yarkend from the Chinese, and that nothing could be said against the recognition of Boozrook-Khan. Thus it was that with Niaz Bek's aid Yakoob Bek gained possession of Yarkend after a very short fusillade. The Moolla Yunoos-Djiana-Shahaul-Datkha was then appointed Hakim of the town. A native of Tashkent, this man served as a writer to the merchants of his native town, and by his skill in caligraphy and in composition, acquired some renown. Appraisers of Yunoos's talents have told us that if he wished, however dry might be the subject on which he wrote, he could move the reader to tears. The Moolla Yunoos had been advanced to the rank of Datkha by Alim Kool, and he was ruler of Yarkend up to within a recent date.

Yakoob Bek again advances against Yarkend.

Yakoob Bek gains possession of Yarkend with the aid of Niaz Bek.

From Yarkend Yakoob Bek moved on Khotan. On arriving at this place he announced that he did not want to fight, and that he would allow its ruler, Habi-Boolla Khodja, to remain.

Yakoob Bek advances against Khotan.

[1] Katta-Turya's son, Hakim Khan Turya, was afterwards Hàkim of the town of Koonya-Toorfan.—*Author.*

[2] I have chanced to learn the sort of role that was played by the population of Kashgar during all these revolutions. I have been told, for example, that the people joyfully welcomed Katta-Turya's elevation to the Khanship. But I do not believe this statement, because no causes for their joy could exist. The revolt of the seven Khodjas was still in the memories of many, and it is therefore difficult to place credence in Katta-Turya's popularity.—*Author.*

The latter, placing confidence in Yakoob Bek's word, went out to meet him with a sumptuous *dastar-khan* and was kindly received by Yakoob Bek at his camp. He was further assured that the personage to whom he was paying a visit, had come to Khotan not for war but in order to pray at the tomb of the Imam Djafari-Sadwik, a descendant of the Sainted Ali. The credulous Habi-Boolla remained in Yakoob Bek's camp to pass the night, during which he was slain by his host's orders. The inhabitants of Khotan, on hearing of the death of their beloved ruler, became enraged at Yakoob Bek's perfidy, and, rising, went out beyond the city, walls to attack the murderers. Even the women armed themselves with whatever thing came in their way, and fought by the side of the men. Yakoob Bek fell on the undisciplined mob of Khotanese, and putting it to flight, pursued it back to the city, into which he forced an entrance, and of which he gained possession after a terrible fight.

Yakoob Bek treacherously slays Habi-Boolla, the ruler of Khotan.

Yakoob Bek gains possession of the town of Khotan.

Niaz Bek is appointed Hakim of the town.

Niaz Bek, who had aided Yakoob Bek in obtaining possession of Yarkend, was appointed Hakim of the town. He also ruled in the same place until recent times.

Yakoob Bek's conquests during 1866-67.

Thus during the year 1866-67, Yakoob Bek had united under one sovereignty the Circles of Kashgar, Yangi-Hissar, Yarkend and Khotan.

Boozrook-Khan is exiled by Yakoob Bek.

Boozrook-Khan, in whose name all these conquests were made, was by degrees completely set aside, until, at last, Yakoob Bek proposed that he should undertake a pilgrimage to Mecca. He had of course only to obey. Accordingly he set out for Kashmir, whence he made his way to Fergana, where he still lives in the hamlet of Kinagez, in the Kokan district, near the hamlets of Karaul-Tube and Kash-Tigerman.

Yakoob Bek is proclaimed Khan and receives the title of 'Badaulet.'

Without mixing in politics Boozrook-Khan lives like a hermit, supported by the offering of his co-religionists, passing his days in fasting and prayer. After Boozrook's departure, Yakoob Bek was proclaimed Khan, with the title of *Badaulet*, or "the fortunate one."

Yakoob Bek's sole rival at this time.

His sole rival now throughout Kashgaria was Rasheddin, whose sovereignty was still recognized by the inhabitants of Aksu, Koocha and Karashar. Yakoob Bek had scarcely returned from Khotan when he marched his forces, in the summer of 1867, against Rasheddin, who resided at the town of Koocha.

Yakoob Bek's route from Kashgar to Koocha lay by Fort Maral-Bashi, which he had occupied a little time beforehand, and by the town of Aksu. Regarding Yakoob Bek's capture of the latter place we have various information. Some say that he moved from Maral-Bashi to it, and took it after a stubborn resistance. Others maintain that he left it in his rear and moved straight on Koocha, and that it was, after he had taken the latter place, that the inhabitants of the former submitted to him without opposition.

Uncertainty attending Yakoob Bek's capture of Aksu.

After Yakoob Bek had captured Yarkend, Rasheddin Khodja sent from Koocha for his kinsman Boorkhaneddin who had refused to fight against his rival, and, having got possession of him, placed him in confinement. But as soon as he heard of Yakoob Bek's movement against himself, he released his victim, whom he caressed and appointed chief of all the quotas furnished by Koocha, Bai, Koorlia, Karashar and Shaar which he had collected to resist Yakoob Bek. The strength of all these bands amounted to several thousand men.[1] Boorkhaneddin went out to meet Yakoob Bek, but only to go over with all his following to his side. Yakoob then came to the town of Koocha, and, in order to get possession of it, resorted to the same cunning as he had practised at Khotan.

Rasheddin imprisons Boorkhaneddin who had refused to fight against Yakoob Bek, and then releases him in order that he may lead his troops against his rival.

Boorkhaneddin goes over to Yakoob Bek.

On the approach of Yakoob Bek's forces, Rasheddin sent emissaries to inform him that their master had freed his father-land from the Chinese; but that against Mussulmans he had no wish to fight. Yakoob Bek replied that he had come to the town with the sole object of prostrating himself at the tomb of Khan Hazret Maulan, Rasheddin's ancestor. Upon this Rasheddin went out with a *dastar-khan* beyond the city walls to meet his rival.

Midway between the camp and the town both dismounted from their horses and embraced. Rasheddin was invited to visit Yakoob Bek's camp, and that very evening he was murdered. On hearing of the death of their Khan, the inhabitants of Koocha surrendered without a fight, and Yakoob Bek appointed Isa Khodja, his last victim's brother, Hakim of the town.

Rasheddin is treacherously murdered by Yakoob Bek, who takes possession of Koocha.

[1] According to information not unworthy of credence the strength of these bands was 80,000 men.—*Author.*

From Koocha Yakoob Bek marched to Koorlia, which also fell to him without a struggle. Thus all the towns of the country with a Kashgarian[1] population became united. Yakoob Bek now entered into negotiations with the Doongan chiefs relative to a boundary line between their respective countries.

A boundary line is agreed upon between Yakoob Bek and the Doongan chiefs.

A boundary line was agreed upon which passed through Ooshag-Tal, which lies 50 versts (33⅓rd miles) to the east of Fort Karashar.

Forming the town of Koorlia, Fort Karashar, the hamlets of Boogoor and Yangi-Hissar into a Circle, with the town first named as a capital, Yakoob Bek appointed Mir-Baba Datkha, a native of Andijan, Hakim thereof.

Yakook Bek returns to Kashgar.

Yakoob Bek then considered the work of the subjugation of Kashgaria at an end, and so he returned, *viâ* Koocha, to the town of Aksu, where he appointed Hakim Khan Turya[2] as Hakim. He then set out for Kashgar with the intention of engaging himself in the consolidation of the sovereignty which he had set up.[3]

The Doogans do not adhere to their agreement.

But on this occasion he was not destined to remain for long at home. The Doongans of Koonya-Toorfan, Ooroomtcha and Manas were not disposed to respect the boundary line which they had agreed to. Collecting in considerable numbers, they advanced first against Karashar and the town of Koorlia and then against Koocha. The inhabitants of Koorlia were plundered of everything they possessed.

The Doongans defeat Hakim Khan Turya.

Hakim Khan Turya, Hakim of Aksu, on learning the movements of the Doongans, sent to Kashgar to inform Yakoob Bek thereof, and advanced himself to the town of Koocha, collecting reinforcements *en route*. Having received these from Aksu, Koocha, Bai and Shaar, he moved out against the Doongans. An engagement took place at a distance of 14 versts (9⅓rd miles) from Koocha in the neighbourhood of Ootch-Kar. In conse-

[1] In the towns of Koonya-Toorfan, Togsoon, Ooroomtcha and Manas, the Doongans predominate; in the Karashar Circle the Kalmucks.—*Author*.

[2] The son of Katta-Turya whom he had murdered.—*Author*.

[3] It may be supposed that it was at this time that Yakoob Bek received Col. Reintal at Kashgar, for that officer was sent there in the year 1868 by General-Lieutenant Kolpakovski, Governor of the Province of Semriaitchensk.—*Author*.

quence of treachery on the part of the Sharians, the Doongans came off as complete victors. Hakim Khan Turya's loss in killed was reckoned at several thousands. Even now on this spot whole lines of the graves of his soldiers are to be seen.

The Doongans pillage the town of Koocha.

After pursuing the defeated enemy, the Doongans gained an entrance into Koocha, which they pillaged and partially burnt. One Akmoolla-Sirkar, who in the time of the Chinese was a Bek, led the Doongans, and in the plunder of Koocha did much good by restraining those over whom he had placed himself.

Yakoob Bek sends a force against the Doongans.

The Doongans after a short stay in Koocha separated, some to return to their own country, others to take up their final abode in the place. The latter then chose Hakims for the different towns in Kashgaria from among the local inhabitants who had assisted them. The newly-chosen officials were told to go and wrest their respecti ve Circles from the grasp of Yakoob Bek. Meanwhile the defeated Hakim Khan Turya had retired to the town of Aksu, to which Yakook Bek had already come. The two together made preparations and collected troops with which to undertake further fight against the Doongans. Yakoob Bek appointed Mirza-Ahmet Parmanatchi and his eldest son Bek Kooli Bek leaders of an army which he sent against the town of Koocha.

The Doongans are defeated and Koocha is once more occupied by Yakoob Bek's army.

The first skirmish which this force had with the Doongans took place in the neighbourhood of Bai, whilst the first engagement was fought at a distance of one march from the town of Koocha on the Aksu road and near the hamlet of Kooshtam. The Doongans were defeated and Koocha was once more occupied by Yakoob Bek's army. On Yakoob Bek's arrival, Alayar Bek was appointed Hakim of the town.

Complete rout of the Doongans.

The Doongans in their retreat pillaged the town of Koorlia for the second time, carrying off therefrom some young women and driving off cattle. They then remained in the neighbourhood of Karashar and began to collect fresh forces to resist Yakoob Bek's advancing army. A second engagement, more important than the first, took place near Danzil, between the towns of Koorlia and Karashar, about a march from the former and some 15 versts (10 miles) from the latter place. The Doongans were completely defeated, but not till Yakoob Bek had lost 500 men.

Yakoob Bek prepares to alter the former boundary line.

On returning to the town of Koorlia, the 'Badaulet' did not desire to rest content with the boundary line which the Doongans had agreed to on the former occasion, for he dreaded, and not without reason, fresh attacks by his enemies. He therefore determined to possess himself of the towns of Koonya-Toorfan and Ooroomtcha, and for this purpose he began to prepare another army.

The nomad population of the Koorlia Circle consisted of several thousand Kalmucks, of the Torgout and Koshoot tribes. Since the beginning of the Doongan insurrection these Kalmucks had joined the rebels, and in return for their services had received possession of the fruitful valley of the Haidwin Kooya, and of the lands adjoining lake Bagratch Kool, close to Fort Karashar. (On the maps this lake is incorrectly called Boston Nor.) The Kalmucks, after pillaging the settled population of Karashar, took up their abode in the places which they had appropriated. Hearing of Yakoob Bek's advance to the town of Koorlia, the Kalmucks once more pillaged that town and then concealed themselves in the mountains. When the town of Koorlia fell to Yakoob Bek for the second time the Kalmucks decided on submitting to him. Accordingly, their ruler, a woman of the Torgout tribe, made her appearance in the *Badaulet's* camp with tokens of submission. The offerings that she made to Yakoob Bek consisted of 1,000 camels, 1,000 horses, 500 sheep and 45 *yambas* of silver (each worth 108 roubles or about £36). With the queen came her army composed of several thousand men, some armed with bows and some with rifles.

The Kalmucks submit to Yakoob Bek.

Yakoob Bek received the queen kindly and readily accepted the Kalmucks as subjects. He then promised that their religion (Buddhism) should not be interfered with.

He moreover directed Khodja Mirza, a native of Pskent, whom he had appointed Hakim of Koorlia, to be especially circumspect in dealing with his new subjects.

Before we leave the Kalmucks we should add that, soon after Yakoob Bek's arrival at Kashgar, the queen behaved somewhat rudely to the Hakim, and then with all her tribe of Torgouts decamped across the mountains to the Kooldja frontier, after plundering the town of Koorlia. She there accepted Russian protection. At the present day only a small number of Kalmucks of the Koshoot tribe roams over the neighbourhood of Karashar.

Information regarding Yakoob Bek's compaign against the towns of Koonya-Toorfan and Ooroomtcha.

The information which I have contrived to procure regarding Yakoob Bek's campaign against the towns of Koonya-Toorfan and Ooroomtcha is very contradictory. Notwithstanding the freshness of these events, I was unable, whilst collecting details concerning them during my stay at Koorlia, to arrive at the truth either from Kashgarians who had taken part in the campaign or from the natives of the towns visited. I must, therefore, put forward two very complete but dissimilar accounts. According to the first, Yakoob Bek, after moving from the town of Koorlia, took Koonya-Toorfan without a fight, and then started for Ooroomtcha. At 16 versts (10⅔rds miles) from that town his advanced guard met one evening the advanced posts of the Ooroomtcha forces.

Yakoob Bek called back his vedettes and encamped for the night, keeping close to his main body.

Situation of the town of Ooroomtcha.

The town of Ooroomtcha lies on some high ground, and is watered by three branches of the same stream. The 'Badaulet' followed the bed of this stream.

His forces were divided into five columns (*lashkars*). Each column was led by a *lashkar-bashi*. In the first column there were eleven standards, a battalion of red *sarbazais*, and eight guns. This column was commanded by Jamadar-Parmanatchi.

The second column consisted of eleven to twelve standards, and was led by Niaz-Hakim-Bek-Datkha.

The third column consisted of ten standards, and was led by Abdoolla.

The fourth column, consisting of nine standards, was commanded by Omar-Kool Datkha, who later on marched for the second time to Ooroomtcha with Yakoob Bek's son, Bek Kooli Bek.

Yakoob Bek commanded the fifth column in person. This consisted of twelve standards. Each standard represented from 200 to 250 men, and was commanded by *pansats*. Each group under a standard was also divided into bodies of a hundred men under a *Yuz-Bashi*.

The strength of from 53 to 54 standards would represent

from 11,000 to 15,000 men. Besides these, with the army there would be several thousand retainers.

The troops of the several columns were composed of *Kara-Koondaks* and *Djigits*.

The former are infantry, mounted on horses and armed with flint muskets. The latter are cavalry partially furnished with fire-arms.

In Jamadar-Parmanatchi's column only was there regular infantry, numbering from 5 to 700 men. He had also 150 mounted Afghans.

Yakoob Bek's opponents placed in the field 20,000 Doongans. As soon as morning broke both sides sent out their vedettes to open fire. The Doongans were the first to advance. Yakoob Bek met them with three columns drawn up, so as to cover his right flank, centre, and left flank, keeping between each column a branch of the Ooroomtcha stream. Yakoob Bek's columns were in *échelon*, and each had its line of skirmishers. Two columns were in reserve.

On nearing the enemy, the Kara-Koondaks ran forward and delivered their fire. The standards in each of the advancing columns moved forward gradually. As the fight raged, both sides got mixed up in one confused mass that surged now this way and now that. Yakoob Bek remained with the reserves, whence, through a telescope, he watched the progress of the fight. Perceiving that the enemy made especial attacks on his right flank, and that he had already succeeded in pressing it back, Yakoob Bek ordered his column to mount. He then led them in person to reinforce his fighting line. At the same time his *Makhrams* (aides-de-camp) were sent off to all the columns with the news that reinforcements were coming up under the personal command of Yakoob Bek, and that a general advance was to be made. By this timely succour of his right flank, Yakoob Bek retrieved the day ; the Doongans fled, the column that remained in reserve to the last was the only one employed to pursue the enemy.

The loss was considerable on both sides. Out of the 150 Afghans not more than half remained alive.

The day following the battle Yakoob Bek sent his emissaries to the town of Ooroomtcha to tell the Doongans that their master did not wish to lay siege to the town, that he did not desire more bloodshed, that he came to fight for the faith, and therefore that with them, as with all Mussulmans, he desired to remain at peace. He demanded only a very slight form of acknowledgment of his power. Some days afterwards a return mission bearing rich offerings made its appearance in Yakoob Bek's camp, and conveyed the assent of the inhabitants to the surrender of the town. The *Badaulet* at once entered Ooroomtcha, and was very affable to his recent antagonists. He appointed Sooleiman Bek, brother of the former Khan of the place, Hakim of the town, and after a stay of twenty days in camp outside the town, he returned to Koonya-Toorfan, where he celebrated his new victory. His occupation of the town of Ooroomtcha took place in the year 1869-70.

According to other information, Yakoob Bek got possession of the towns of Koonya-Toorfan and Ooroomtcha in quite a different manner.

During the insurrection of the Doongans, Shoosha Hoon, Amban of the Liyai San Circle, fled to the *Badaulet*, and was very kindly received by him. After the attack made by the Doongans on Koocha, the *Badaulet* advanced against them, taking with him Shoosha Hoon, who collected about 8,000 Chinese who had escaped destruction, and induced them to accompany Yakoob Bek in his march against Koonya-Toorfan. When this place fell, Yakoob Bek sent Shoosha Hoon against the town of Ooroomtcha, giving him a large number of his own troops. He himself then followed, making Ooroomtcha in one march.

Shoosha Hoon, aided by some of Yakoob Bek's troops, took Ooroomtcha, Hoomatai (Homoodi), Moori (Moorooi), Tchatai (Kitai), Manas, Sanji and Liansai (?) All these places were taken after a fight, and were first of all made over to Shoosha Hoon to govern.

Yakoob Bek changes his policy towards his Chinese auxiliary.

After gaining possession of these towns with the aid of the Chinese, Yakoob Bek changed his policy towards those who had helped him. He began to bully the Chinese, and to court the graces of the Doongans who inhabited the conquered towns. The Chinese troops were dismissed, and the garrisons of these towns were formed partly from Yakoob Bek's own troops and partly of Doongans. At length the government of all the places abovenamed was entrusted to two Doongan chiefs, Shikho and Dakho, to whom Shoosha Hoon had to declare himself subordinate.

Results of this change.

The affronted man fled with 500 Chinese to Pekin, where he besought the *Bogdwi Khan* for 8,000 soldiers, with whose aid he pledged himself to get back all the Doongan towns.

Yakoob Bek makes Aksu his capital, and devotes his time to domestic affairs.

After settling his affairs in the eastern towns of his sovereignty, Yakoob Bek returned to the town of Aksu, which he made his capital. The next five years he passed here were devoted to the domestic affairs of the State that he had founded. One of his chief labours was to secure his frontiers on the side of the province of Semiraitchensk and of the Khanate of Kokan. The construction by the Russians of Fort Narwin greatly annoyed him, and he protested against the occupation by us of part of the Narwin river, which he considered was the natural boundary between his possessions and Semiraitchia. The construction of the very strong fort of Chakmak between Fort Narwin and Kashgar, on the road leading through the Tooroogart and Terek passes, belongs to this period.

Boundary between Kashgaria and Kokan.

On the side of the Khanatc of Kokan, the boundary question had been raised by Yakoob Bek somewhat before this date. Taking advantage of Khoodoyar Khan's weakness, Yakoob Bek had begun to advance further and further towards the mountains, establishing one post after the other. In the time of Madali Khan, the Kokan frontier line passed through Koorgashin-Kani, 88 versts (58⅔rds miles) from Kashgar. Yakoob Bek advanced, first to Ooksalwir, then to Ooloogchat, where he built a fort and established a centre for all the Kara-Kirghiz population. Not satisfied with Ooloogchat, he subsequently shifted his advanced troops to Forts Nagrachaldwi, Yegin and Irkeshtam in succession. The annexation of the Khanate of Kokan by the Russians was the only thing that stopped continued progress on the part of Yakoob Bek towards the north. It is very possible that if Khoodoyar Khan's reign had lasted for several years more, Yakoob Bek would have crossed the Terek Davan, and taken his advanced posts to the town of Osh.

In the year 1866, the small mountain State of Sari-Kol declared itself a feudatory of Yakoob Bek, but subsequently its ruler Alaf Shah refused to recognize Yakoob Bek's government, in consequence of the general disturbances that took place in Shignan and on the Pamir. Accordingly, in the year 1869, an expeditionary force was sent from Yarkend against the town of Sari-Kol. Alaf's forces were defeated, and he himself was slain, whilst a considerable portion of his subjects received orders to move their homes to Yarkend and Kashgar, where the fittest of them were enrolled in the military service as *sarbazais*.

Yakoob Bek sends a force against the State of Sari-Kol.

In the year 1872, a fresh insurrection of Doongans interrupted Yakook Bek in his labours for the settlement of Kashgaria. This time he entrusted the subjugation of the rebels and their punishment to his eldest son, Bek Kooli Bek, who advanced rapidly against the town of Ooroomtcha, laid siege to it, and after terrible bloodshed gained possession of it.

Fresh insurrection of the Doongans.

From Ooroomtcha, Bek Kooli Bek went to the town of Manas, of which he also got possession. After leaving small garrisons in the conquered towns, and after executing several hundreds of rebels, Bek Kooli Bek returned to Aksu, where his father received him as a conqueror with great honour.

Bek Kooli Bek returns after suppressing the revolt.

From 1872 to 1876, Kashgaria experienced a degree of quiet to which it had long been unaccustomed. During this period, Yakoob Bek was greatly taken up with the armament and training of his forces. It was during the same period, too, that he received a Russian Embassy under Colonel Kaulbars and two English Embassies, and that he sent his own Envoy to India and to Constantinople for the purpose of obtaining a recognition of his title of Amir both from the English and from the Turks. But it was during the same period also that the Chinese, with methodical measurement and step by step, were moving to put down the Doongan insurrection. They reached the town of Manas, which they besieged and took. News of this victory of the Chinese compelled Yakoob Bek, after leaving his eldest son, Bek Kooli Bek, in Kashgar, to move out to meet his enemies, and prevent, if possible, their obtaining possession of the towns of Ooroomtcha and of Koonya-Toorfan.

Period of rest for Kashgaria.

The Chinese once more advance against Kashgaria.

Both at Manas and the two last-named points, Yakoob Bek had only weak garrisons which could not offer any resistance to the Chinese, whilst in the Doongans he could not repose any special confidence.

Yakoob Bek moves against them.

Collecting all the forces he could from Kashgar, Aksu and Koocha, Yakoob Bek advanced *viâ* Koorlia, Karashar and Togsoon. His forces amounted to from 12,000 to 15,000 men. During the movements of Yakoob Bek, the Chinese had marched from Manas to the town of Hoomatai. As a reinforcement to the small garrison of this town, the *Badaulet* sent 600 well-mounted and well-equipped horsemen with four *pansats* under the command of Azim Kool. Yakoob Bek himself followed, but at several marches' distance. The Chinese forestalled Yakoob Bek, for, before his reinforcements arrived, Hoomatai was taken and destroyed, and a large number of its inhabitants killed. The Chinese, who were now in considerable force, fell upon Azim Kool's weak detachment. The Kashgarians fought desperately, but the greater number of them, including Azim Kool, were laid low, only about 100 escaping to bear the unfortunate news to the 'Badaulet.'

The Chinese take Hoomatai and defeat a detachment of Yakoob Bek's troops.

Azim Kool.

Regarding the personalty of Azim Kool, and this particular defeat, I have been told some interesting and characteristic details.

Known as a brave and energetic man, Azim Kool was nevertheless for a long time in disgrace on account of a quarrel which he had with Khodja Mirza of Pskent, who was then Hakim of the Koorlia Circle.

The two quarrelled whilst in the presence of Yakoob Bek. Azim Kool reproached his antagonist with being too conceited and with having a short memory that failed to enable him to recollect his recent trade as a bootmaker in the village of Pskent. Upon this, the Mirza retorted, "Why art thou so proud, seeing that not so long since thou spunest coarse yarn at Alti-Arwik?" (close to the town of Kokan). Both were right, since, before they came to be enrolled amongst the nobles of Kashgar, one of them was a bootmaker, the other a weaver, in his native place.

Still Azim Kool so far forgot himself on receiving this retort that he drew his sword and ran at the Khodja Mirza in the presence of Yakoob Bek. On being disarmed, he was sent to the town of Koorlia, where he lived in banishment for nine months until Yakoob Bek came there. Having sent for Azim Kool, Yakoob Bek forgave and embraced him, hoping no doubt to benefit by his bravery in the campaign on which he had himself started.

In order to give Azim Kool an opportunity of distinguishing himself, Yakoob Bek appointed him to command the reinforcement, of which we have already spoken.

When masses of Chinese and of Kalmucks surrounded the Kashgarians, one of the four *pansats*, Mahomed Said, advised Azim Kool to retire, but he answered, "It is better to die once than to again lick the dust from the feet of the 'Badaulet.'"

A close combat now ensued. Azim Kool fought like a mad man and would answer no proposals of surrender. Wounded and lying on the ground he discharged his rifle, and then raising himself on his knees continued to make cuts with his sword. At last one of the Kalmucks shot him with an arrow. Said, the *pansat*, now succeeded in getting through the ranks of the enemy with about a hundred of his men.

The Chinese advance against Ooroomtcha.

After the capture of Hoomatai, the Chinese moved towards the town of Ooroomtcha.

As the Chinese forces advanced, thousands of Doongan families abandoned their abodes and fled to seek the protection of Yakoob Bek, who sent the greater number of them to the frontier towns and raised from amongst them a body mustering 10,000 men, whom he made over to the garrison of the town of Koorlia.

The winter of 1876-77 put an end to military operations before the main body of Yakoob Bek's forces could measure its strength with the Chinese. Both sides felt the great want of provisions, and each was obliged to withdraw its more advanced line of posts.

Relative positions of the Chinese forces and of Yakoob Bek's army.

The Davantchi ridge divided the combatants. The advanced post of the Chinese was the town of Ooroomtcha, which was held by 6,000 men. Yakoob Bek's advanced post was Fort Davantchi with a garrison of 800 men armed with quick-shooting rifles and two rifled guns.

Effect of the winter halt on Yakoob Bek's soldiers and personal adherents.

The winter did not bring with it any accessions of strength to Yakoob Bek's army, nay,—as regards the *morale* of that army, it lost in power. Desertion had increased, and had begun to enrol in its ranks persons in whose devotion Yakoob Bek had been always able to trust. The first of such who fled were Sadwik Bek, a former Hakim of Kalpin under the Chinese administration, and who had been a *Yuz-Bashi* in the town of Aksu under Yakoob Bek; Bakwish Mirab Bek, who had also served under the Chinese as *Mirab-Bek* in the village of Yar-Bashi-Djam and others. These two persons, on flying from Koonya-Toorfan to the Chinese, were very kindly received by the Chinese Commander-in-Chief Shoosha Hoon, who appointed[1] the former Hakim of Kashgar, and the latter Hakim of Yarkend. Following the example of these persons, there deserted to the Chinese during the winter of 1876-77 Yakoob Bek's treasurer, Ashir Akhoon. This man took away all the treasure of which he had charge and forty-one picked *djigits*. Then followed in the same direction the brothers of the Hakims of Koocha and of Kashgar, the brother of Yakoob Khan, Yakoob Bek's Envoy to Constantinople, Hamil Khan who now lives at Tashkent, and many others. There deserted too from the close of 1876 to February 1877 (old style) 400 soldiers.

Further misfortunes of Yakoob Bek.

Besides the loss of his treasure, and of people of whose services he stood in need, the same winter brought fresh misfortune to the 'Badaulet.' A store-house containing provisions and powder, which he had built at Siapoor, on the road between Togsoon and Fort Davanchi, was burnt to the ground. In this store-house, there were 80,000 *chariks* (about 1,440,000 lbs) of flour, and 17,000 *chariks* (about 3,06,000 lbs) of groats. The cause of the fire was not ascertained, though it was supposed to be the work of an incendiary.

Some additions to the biography of Yakoob Bek.[2]

Correction of certain statements made in the biography of Yakoob Bek.

In an article inserted in the "Military Magazine" entitled 'Outlines of Kasgharia," Mons. A. N. Kooropatkin very vividly and circumstantially gives us the biography of the famous Yakoob Bek of Kashgar, as based on information, collected by him on the spot, from persons in close communication with that remarkable man. Nevertheless there are mistakes in the narrative and these have been repeated more than once in other Russian publications, statements to the effect that Yakoob Bek on being

[1] Prospectively it may be presumed.—*Trans.*

[2] *Vide* allusion on p. 161.—*Trans.*

appointed Hakim of Ak-Mechet heroically defended that fortress in the year 1853 with a handful of men against a Russian army. Now the fact is that Yakoob Bek was not Hakim, but only Bek, of the place named, which was subordinate to the orders of the Hakim of Tashkent; that he was not at Ak-Mechet in the year 1853, when the fort was besieged and taken by storm by a Russian force under General Aide-de-Camp Perovski; that he was not even there on the $\frac{\text{20th July}}{\text{1st August}}$ 1852, when Colonel Blaramberg attacked it. The only occasion on which Yakoob Bek had a skirmish with the Russians was on the $\frac{\text{4th}}{\text{16th}}$ March 1852 at Ak-Gerik, not far from Fort Aral. On this occasion he had a force ten times stronger than that of the Russians. He was then defeated with great loss, consequently he did not display any special bravery. Soon after that he was recalled from Ak-Mechet.

The only occasion on which Yakoob Bek ever encountered the Russians in the field.

I will here introduce some particulars, which I have already published in various articles during the last fifteen years, both regarding the engagement at Ak-Gerik and concerning the activity displayed by Yakoob Bek during the time he was at Ak-Mechet.

Ak-Mechet and Yakoob Bek's predatory excursions.

About the year 1850 there began to be some talk at Orenburgh about the Kokan Fort of Ak-Mechet and about its Bek Yakoob, who directed his myrmidons to carry on plunderings and pillage amongst the Kirghiz subject to Russia. The Sultan ruler of the eastern portion of the Kirghiz horde in the Ahmed-Djanturin section of the Orenburgh Government, one of the most enlightened Kirghiz of the age, expressed himself in a letter in the following manner about Yakoob Bek:—"He does not know to-day whether he will plunder his neighbours to-morrow or not. All his actions depend upon sudden orders which he may receive from the Koosh-Begi of Tashkent, to whom he is subordinate, and who may be in need of money. In any such case the Bek of Ak-Mechet immediately sends out a band, which is always ready, to plunder the Kirghiz and to take away their last piece of property. It is only those members of the horde who satisfy without a murmur all the heavy exactions of the depredators that are not subjected to violence."

At the close of the year 1849, an Ak-Mechet band, consisting of 100 Kirghiz of the Kipchak tribe under the leader Bookharbai, rode in and plundered the Oolootaw post. They drove off a number of horses belonging to the Baganalin tribe of Kirghiz and carried off as prisoners several Siberian Cossacks. Of these Milushin and Batarwishkin, when they returned from a Kokan prison in the year 1852, related, amongst other things, that "when they were taken to Ak-Mechet on the $\frac{19th}{31st}$ December 1849, Yakoob Bek expressed himself satisfied with the plunder, but scolded the Kirghiz because they had not taken alive all the Cossacks whom they had surprised. Of the horses that were driven in, he took half for himself and divided the remainder amongst the robbers."

On the night of the $\frac{16th}{28th}$ February 1850, an Ak-Mechet band carried on depredations in the neighourhood of Fort Aral, plundering twenty Kirghiz *auls*, in which they killed six persons and from which they drove off 1,000 horses and 25,000 sheep.

On the night of the $\frac{25th\ August}{6th\ September}$ of the same year, another band from Ak-Mechet, numbering 400 men under the leadership of Bookharbai, plundered some Kirghiz nomads in the neighbourhood of Kazal, killed eleven of them and drove off 934 horses, 555 camels, 139 cows and 20,800 sheep. Major Damis, Commandant of Fort Aral, took revenge for this raid by capturing and destroying on the $\frac{9th}{21st}$ September Kosh-Koorgan, a place under the charge of Yakoob Bek, to whose assistance some more Kokanese soon came.

Major Damis, the Russian Commandant of Fort Aral, makes a reprisal for the raid of Yakoob Bek's band.

In February 1851, the Ak-Mechet band of robbers drove off from Russian Kirghiz, who were encamped at Kara-Koomakh, 2,500 horses, 1,900 camels and 70,600 sheep. In revenge for this the Russian Kirghiz, to the number of 90 men, raided on the Kirghiz encamped in the neighbourhood of Kokan-Koorgan or Fort Djoolek.

On the evening of the $\frac{3rd}{15th}$ March 1852, a fresh band of robbers pillaged 100 *auls* of Kirghiz nomads at Ak-Gerik. This band, which was under the leadership of Yakoob Bek himself, consisted of the Kokan garrisons subordinate to him,—*viz.*, Djoolek,

Ak-Mechet, Koomwish-Tchin, and Kosh-Koorgan and of Khivan Khodjanias: also of Kirghiz nomads from the same neighbourhood. The Kokanese numbered about 1,000, and the Khivans about 130. The latter had joined the band for the purpose of carrying off Sultan Ir Mahammed Kaswimoff (Ilikei) who had returned to us from Khiva. The band collected at Koomwish Koorgan, and after crossing the Sir-Darya at Kosh-Koorgan followed its right bank.

Major Engman, Russian Commandant of Fort Aral, proceeds with a force to punish the raiders on Ak-Gerik.

Major Engman, Commandant of Fort Aral, on receiving news of the raid on Ak-Gerik, started from the fort the same evening with a party of 22 infantry soldiers mounted on horses, 74 Cossacks and a howitzer with its crew. The next day he was joined by 17 Kirghiz, and at four in the afternoon he came up with the raiders at Akcha-Boolak. Major Engman opened fire from his howitzer. The enemy extended and, surrounding his detachment on all sides with a double chain of skirmishers, came well within rifle-fire; but Major Engman's artillery and rifle-fire combined caused the raiders to keep further back. Notwithstanding this, many of the enemy rode up to the small Russian force and engaged the Cossacks at the lance's point. The firing lasted till nightfall.

Yakoob Bek's band retreats to Kosh-Koorgan.

Next day at dawn it was found that the raiders had left the battle field. They had made a hurried move to Kosh-Koorgan, taking with them only a small part of the plundered cattle. The Kokanese carried off 100 camels and 2,000 sheep, and the Khivans, 6 camels and 300 sheep. The rest of the livestock, to the number of 53,000 sheep, a few horses, camels and cows, were restored by the Russians to the plundered Kirghiz. In the affair of the $\frac{4th}{16th}$ March we had four men wounded, whilst the enemy's loss amounted to 100 Kokanese and 3 Khivans killed, very many wounded and amongst the number the leader Bookharbai.

Yakoob Bek's anxiety for his unprotected posts.

Yakoob Bek's hasty flight was due not so much to the heavy loss suffered by his band, as to the surprise at the sudden and unexpected appearance of a Russian detachment, to the stoicism evinced by that detachment in the fight and to the fear lest the Russians should move up the Swir in order to destroy the posts subordinate to him and which he had left unprotected.

24

Yakoob Bek is recalled from Ak-Mechet to Tashkent.

After the engagement at Ak-Gerik, Yakoob Bek was recalled from Ak-Mechet. He arrived with his suite at Tashkent on the $\frac{11\text{th}}{23\text{rd}}$ April, and on the $\frac{20\text{th April}}{2\text{nd May}}$ he presented to Nar Mahammed Tart, Hakim of Tashkent, gifts that were valued at 1,000 ducats (about £140), as stated in the journal of the merchant Klutchareff, who was living at the time in Tashkent.

Oppression of the Kirghiz agriculturing class.

Soon after Yakoob Bek's departure, Bontch Osmolovski, who had taken part in the expedition to Ak-Mechet under Colonel Blaramberg, collected on the spot some very interesting particulars regarding the relation of the Ak-Mechet Kokanese with the neighbouring Kirghiz agriculturists and husbandmen, particulars which clearly show to what a degree the burden of the yoke of ignorant Asiatic despots can reach.

Osmolovski says: "The Kokanese divide the taxes taken from the Kirghiz into two classes—the *ziaket*, which is the tax on cattle; and the *heradj*, which is the tax on grain of all kinds.

"In opposition to all Mahometan laws which limit the levy on cattle to a fortieth part, the Kokanese take daily, by means of force, six sheep from a *kibitka*, and from the richer Kirghiz twice as many. Amongst the number so taken the so-called gifts do not enter. These are *presented* by the Kirghiz to the chief tax-gatherer and to his assistants.

"From grain the Kokanese take every third crop. From certain Kirghiz, who wander about the forts, in exchange for the *heradj* on green corn they take baked bread and millet gruel. The *heradj* taxes comprise the levies on wood, charcoal and hay. They exact yearly from each *kibitka* 24 sacks of charcoal, four loads of *saksaul* and 1,000 sheaves of reeds and grass. From those Kirghiz whose homes lie distant from the Kokanese fortified posts, in exchange for these exactions, the Kokanese take either cattle or grain according to a valuation which they themselves fix.

"Besides the *ziaket* and *heradj* taxes, the Kirghiz are subjected to the following burdens:—

"Free labour for the Kokanese, *i.e.*, the cultivation of fields and orchards, repairs to fort-walls and the like. Each *kibitka* has to send monthly for this purpose one man, who has to give his labour for nothing. The distant Kirghiz, in consideration of their release from this kind of forced labour, have to furnish more cattle.

"The cleaning of stables and stalls, &c., in the fortified posts, takes place six times in the year. Kirghiz are driven out to perform this duty. As a rule, those are taken who chance to be at the time in the neighbourhood of the posts, no regard being paid to a roster.

"In case of a war or a raid, every able-bodied Kirghiz must, on being told off by the Kokanese, serve at his own expense and supply his own horse, however protracted the particular service may be.

"The heaviness of the imposts and of the dues is increased still more by reason of the raids on the part of the Kokanese who, leading as they do an idle and depraved existence, often ride up to the *auls* of the Kirghiz and defile their women, or, in defiance of the ordinances of the Shariat, marry such women.

"All this has combined to bring about poverty and slavery amongst the Kokan Kirghiz."

Such relations between rulers and ruled are very common in the East, and they are cultivated in various degrees amongst the majority of Asiatic despots. Yakoob Bek was no exception to this rule. Like others he manipulated the administration of the Ak-Mechet tract exclusively with one aim—*viz.*, the squeezing and pilfering of the unhappy husbandmen to the last degree. Still, even he spared some of the flying Kirghiz from fear that they would change their places of abode, and that he would not then have at hand bands wherewith to carry on his plundering expeditions amongst those distant Kirghiz who were under Russian rule. Except this idea, it is difficult to find another motive in his Ak-Mechet mode of action which did, indeed, result in political service, not to the Kokanese, but to us Russians. Yakoob Bek was the first to call our attention, directed as it was up to that time exclusively on Khiva, to the side of Kokan, and he was the cause of our moving up the Sir-Darya, and of our occupying Ak-Mechet, Turkestan, Tashkent and Kokan in turn. He was then the first to call us to the not-to-be-deferred fulfilment of that Central Asian problem which has been imposed on us by the force of historical expediency.

A. MAKSHEYEFF.

CHAPTER VII.

The Kashgarian army — Its organization, complement, commissariat, armament, training and nature of employment — Its numerical strength and distribution on the $\frac{1st}{13th}$ February 1877 — Conclusions to be drawn therefrom.

First standing army in Kashgaria.

THE first attempt at forming a standing army in Kashgaria relates to the sixtieth year of the present century, when the Khodja Valikhan Turya ruled over the country. Aided by a few hundred exiles from the Khanate of Kokan and by some Kara-Kirghiz, Valikhan Turya occupied the town of Kashgar in April 1857, slaughtered those Chinese whom he found there, proclaimed himself Khan of Kashgaria, and was recognized as such both by the inhabitants of Kashgar and by the surrounding population. His swift successes drew to him crowds of new adherents, part of whom came from Yarkend, Khotan and Aksu, and part were Kara-Kirghiz and Kokanese. The Chinese, according to their custom, shut themselves up in the citadels and awaited reinforcements, which never came. Valikhan Turya at once set himself energetically to work at the organization of his forces. All those who had volunteered their services, and who were capable of bearing arms, he arranged under standards, placing 500 under each with a *pansat* to command them. His troops were divided into infantry (*sarbazais*) and cavalry (*djigits*). They were fairly well dressed in some sort of uniform and were taught to move with a certain degree of order, and to act together on certain words of command. Their armament was very varied. The best armed, both of the infantry and cavalry, had matchlocks with a flint and steel apparatus for igniting the powder, but the majority of the infantry carried lances or short javelins, swords, &c., &c.

Valikhan Turya organizes his forces.

The number of volunteers falls off.

Soon, however, the number of volunteers for Valikhan Turya's army fell short of the demand, and then the population of the town of Kashgar and of the neighbouring villages was obliged to furnish as recruits all the young men who were fit for the service. This measure, whilst it increased to a considerable extent the numerical strength of the army, excited great discontent amongst the people. It nevertheless reduced the already small cost of Valikhan's military forces. Besides having to furnish recruits, the people were likewise called upon to supply *gratis* horses, cattle, provisions, forage and fuel for the use of the troops. All the skilled workmen were taken to manufacture cannon, or to prepare the dress and equipment of the soldiers. A foundry was opened in the town of Kashgar, where, under the direction of a certain Afghan, eight guns were soon cast. A want of copper in his foundry caused Valikhan Turya to seize all the copper-vessels which could be found amongst the local inhabitants, or amongst the foreign merchants. The manufactured guns were now attached to a battery which was very badly worked.

Forced enlistment substituted.

Discontent caused thereby.

Exactions from the people for army purposes.

A cannon foundry established at Kashgar.

During four months of uninterrupted exertion, Valikhan Turya got together a fairly strong army, and with this he proposed to enter into a struggle with the Chinese, who had already begun to advance from Aksu, Koocha and Kooldja towards the town of Kashgar. The first collision shewed the entire worthlessness of Valikhan's troops. Almost before they met with opposition, they all gave signs of wavering, whilst many of them ran away. Valikhan Turya followed his fugitive soldiers and contrived to reach Kokan, in company with a few adherents who had stood by him. The inhabitants of Kashgar then opened the city gates to the Chinese forces.

Valikhan Turya meditates a fight with the Chinese.

His army is dispersed in the first engagement, and he himself flies to Kokan. Kashgar surrenders to the Chinese troops.

In the subsequent commotions in Kashgaria, commencing with the year 1870, and known under the name of the "Doongan Insurrection," both the inhabitants of the country and the Doongan troops took part in the struggle against the Chinese sovereignty. Now a considerable portion of the troops, with whose aid the Chinese had maintained their dominion over Kashgaria, was recruited from the same source.

The Doongan insurrection.

Principal element in the Chinese forces.

The rebels were, however, without any organization except in rare instances. Whenever they sent aid from one town to another, this aid would be furnished in the shape of loosely put together and badly armed bands, undisciplined and devoid of all feeling of heroism.

The rebels without organization.

Spread of the "Doongan Insurrection."

By the year 1863, the insurrection against the Chinese had taken possession of the whole country. The people, who joined the Doongans, compelled the Chinese to shut themselves up in the citadels. Sadwik Bek, a Kipchak, seized the power in the town of Kashgar, but not considering himself strong enough to carry on a struggle against the Chinese, he besought the aid of Alim Kool, who was then ruling over both Tashkent and Kokan. This aid was furnished to him in the year 1864 in the person of Boozrook-Khodja, with whom came also Yakoob Bek, in the capacity of *lashkar-bashi* (commander-in-chief). Attached to Boozrook were from 50 or 60 *djigits* and seekers of fortune. By degrees Yakoob Bek pushed aside the weak and incapable Boozrook-Khan and took into his own hands the power at Kashgar, until in the same gradual way, during the ten years which followed, he had subordinate to his own rule the whole of Kashgaria from the town of Keria to Koonya-Toorfan, including Khotan, Yarkend, Kashgar, Aksu, Koocha and Koorlia.

Sadwik Bek. Alim Kool, ruler of Tashkent and Kokan. Boozrook-Khodja; Yakoob Bek. Yakoob Bek sets aside Boozrook-Khan and by degrees subordinates to himself the whole of Kashgaria.

First military operations of Yakoob Bek.

The first military operations entered into by Yakoob Bek comprised the siege of the citadel of Kashgar (Yangi-Shar), two campaigns against Yarkend, and a campaign against Khotan. In these operations, his troops were composed of every kind of nationality, Kashgarians, Kara-Kirghiz, Kokanese, &c., &c. All were very badly armed and but poorly clothed. The fact, however, of Yakoob Bek's having been strong enough to seize the power raised up for him many foes not only amongst the population but in the army.

Heterogeneous composition of his army. Foes of Yakoob Bek amongst the population and in his own army.

The Kipchaks revolt.

Thus, the want of success attending his first campaign against the town of Yarkend resulted in an insurrection of those Kipchaks who were in Yakoob Bek's army.

The Kara-Kirghiz element of Yakoob Bek's army is eradicated.

After them, the most disobedient and most restless element in Yakoob Bek's forces was the Kara-Kirghiz. These he eradicated.

Yakoob Bek is unable to reckon upon the sympathy of the people. He therefore places his dependence on the army.

Having seized the power over all the cities of Kashgaria, here by force, there by fraud, Yakoob Bek could not count on the sympathy of the people, and therefore from the commencement of his reign he resolved to lean on the army and to make it the privileged and dominant class in the State.

The original organization that Yakoob Bek gave to his army, and which is preserved in its principal features up to the present day, differs in no sense from the organization long ago built up in all the independent Central Asian sovereignties.

Original organization of Yakoob Bek's forces.

The army was divided into infantry (*sarbazais*), cavalry (*djigits*) and artillery (*topchis*). The fighting unit was the *sotnia*, under the command of a *yuz-bashi*. The *sotnia*, comprising from 40 to 60 men, was divided into *half sotnias*, over which were placed *piyand-bashis* (one over each). The *half sotnias* were again divided into sections of ten, and over each of these was put a *da-bashi*.

The army is divided into infantry, cavalry and artillery.

Subdivisions of the several branches.

The resources of the country furnished Yakoob Bek with provisions and materials for the clothing of his troops, except cloth (which was imported partly from Russia and partly from India), powder, lead and unmanufactured iron. Yakoob Bek stood in special need of firearms and cannon. Such of the former as he had were principally flint muskets, got partly from the independent States around, and partly manufactured in the local workshops. Beside flint muskets, Yakoob Bek contrived in the year 1868 to procure a small supply of sporting guns, with one and two barrels. Yakoob Bek's artillery was in a very bad condition.

The resources of the country how far capable of meeting the wants of the army.

Yakoob Bek's need of firearms and of cannon.

As soon as he had established relations with the English and with the Turks, Yakoob Bek found out a source whence he could equip a portion of his troops with good rifles, both percussion and repeating. Shaw's mission and the two under Forsyth had made him acquainted with perfected systems of firearms. These persons had brought him as gifts several hundred breech-loading rifles on the Snider system, Enfield muzzle-loaders, revolvers and several specimens of magazine equipment. Mr. Forsyth also invited Yakoob Bek to send an Embassy to India to the Viceroy, which would find a way through India to Constantinople. He at the same time opened a road along which even now goes on a fairly active trade in arms with Kashgaria.

Yakoob Bek establishes relations with the English and with the Turks and procures rifles from them.

The English missions under Messrs. Shaw and Forsyth in connection with the equipment of Yakoob Bek's army.

Trade in arms between India and Kashgaria.

The desire of the English to include Kashgaria in a neutral zone, which should separate their possessions in India from the Russians in Turkestan, induced them to resort to the same measures in the case of Kashgaria as they have long practised

The English desire to include Kashgaria in a neutral zone separating their possessions in India from those of the Russians in Central Asia.

in other countries. Such measures have for their object the making of the neutral zone in question as impenetrable as possible for Russians, should the latter be forced to advance their frontiers in Asia still further towards the south. They consist, too, in furnishing the independent rulers of Afghanistan and of Kashgaria with arms and instructors and in concluding defensive alliances with such rulers. In order to gain a political supremacy, England very skilfully seeks the right of maintaining at independent courts her own agents under the title of residents or commissioners. For the attainment too of a trade monopoly she makes use of the powerful means at her disposal through her numerous factories.

Measures adopted by the English in furtherance of their desire.

Yakoob Bek takes advantage of English policy in this respect.

Yakoob Bek contrived to take full advantage of the interference of the English in his affairs, and for many years improved the organization of his army and also its equipment and training.

Colonel Baron Kaulbars, the first Russian Envoy to Kashgaria, and his report to the Governor-General of Turkestan on the Kashgarian army.

In the year 1872, Colonel Baron Kaulbars, the first Russian Envoy to Kashgaria, was present at parades of Yakoob Bek's army, and in his letters to the Governor-General of Turkestan he thus wrote on the subject:—

"They began by shewing me the Chinese and Doongan infantry, numbering 3,000 men. The character of its manœuvres is of the defensive order. The chief strength of this infantry lies in being able to deliver a ceaseless and deafening fire from the *taifoors*.

"They then shewed me the *sarbazais*, who fire very accurately at a mark. They had a bronze gun with which they made several successful shots at a distance of not less than 1,000 paces.

"In conclusion, I was shewn a field-battery of six guns, which manœuvred with some degree of skill by English signals and words of command. Amongst other movements they several times performed that of going through a retreat, accompanied by firing without stopping to take aim and without arranging the sights of the gun.

"From 50 to 60 horsemen and as many infantry soldiers formed the escort of the battery. The latter are armed with English rifles and bayonets. The commandant of this battery is an Afghan, and attached to it are some Hindoo officers and three Afghan trumpeters. Its instructor is a Russian or Tatar deserter."

After the above parades Baron Kaulbars was allowed to see the barracks of the Kashgarian troops. According to our Envoy's opinion, the artillery barracks were modelled on the European style. Along the line of guns a sentry paced with a drawn sword in his hand. The rank and file when addressing their superiors in rank did not stand but sat down. The private dwelling-house of the commandant of artillery was not like an ordinary hut. In a word, Baron Kaulbars finishes the narration of all that he saw by remarking that in everything is traceable English influence.

The Russian Colonel Reintal sent in the year 1875 to Kashgaria.

In the year 1875, Colonel Reintal was sent to Yakoob Bek to convey to him some presents from the Tsar. During his stay of three days in the town of Kashgar, Colonel Reintal succeeded in witnessing a parade of the Kashgarian troops, and in collecting some information regarding the strength of Yakoob Bek's forces. On his return to the town of Tashkent, he presented his report to the Governor-General of Turkestan. The substance of this report is as follows:—

Colonel Reintal's report on the Kashgarian army.

"1. The English have given Yakoob Bek a large number of percussion rifles; these I have seen. One of these weapons which I handled is so badly preserved that it is now almost impossible to distinguish whether it is a rifle or a smoothbore.

"2. Yakoob Bek has built a foundry in which muzzle-loading rifles are converted into breech-loaders. Without doubt this foundry was built by aid received from the English. 4,000 rifles have been so converted. I suppose that on the parade at which I was present on the $\frac{15th}{27th}$ May 1875, about 6,000 infantry soldiers were armed with breech-loading rifles. I saw one of these. Its breech block did not draw out, but opened from left to right. In the breech block there is a needle, which on the fall of the trigger is struck by the hammer.

"The foundry turns out sixteen rifles a week.

"3. In Kashgar, there are several powder manufactories in which very good burnished powder is prepared.

"4. In Kashgar, there is a common foundry. I saw four newly-cast rifled-guns being proved. In Kashgar, there is also a special factory where they prepare elongated cartridges for these guns.

"Yakoob Bek liberally rewarded the English for a successful trial of explosive charges, especially of grenades.

"5. I saw only one battery at Kashgar. It consisted of six guns; of these four were new mountain guns, which with their carriages were packed on three horses. Besides these attached to the infantry were sixteen guns. Some other guns and 18,000 troops had been sent to the towns of Manas and Ooroomtcha.

"6. The infantry marches well; its principal formation is the square. The extended formation is now being taught. This has recently been introduced by Yakoob Bek, and is the weak side of his infantry.

"7. The cavalry manœuvres well together. Its armament is varied. On the parade which I saw there were about 1,500 cavalry soldiers.

"8. There are many English workmen in Kashgar.

"9. Turks are the instructors of Yakoob Bek's army. I saw two of them.

"10. There is to be soon introduced a new uniform for the infantry which is to resemble the Russian style."

Colonel Reintal's report not quite accurate. Improvement in the armament of Yakoob Bek's forces undoubtedly due to English aid.

Colonel Reintal's information appears to be somewhat exaggerated, nevertheless it does not admit of doubt but that the considerable improvement in the armament of Yakoob Bek's forces which has been attained up to the year 1875 has been arrived at with English aid.

Russian Embassy of 1876-77 in a better position as compared with all which had preceded it to collect information regarding the military strength and resources of Kashgaria.

Our Embassy of 1876-77 as compared with all which had preceded it, was placed in the most favourable circumstances for collecting information regarding the military strength and resources of the *Badaulet*. Setting out, as that mission did in October 1876, from the town of Osh, it passed through Kashgar, Aksu, Bai and Koocha to the town of Koorlia and Fort Karashar, traversing 1,250 *versts* (811⅓rd miles) in the dominions of Yakoob Bek in one *journey*. At Kashgar, the members of the mission witnessed several parades of the Kashgarian troops, inspected their barracks, and saw parades also at Bai and at Koocha, besides a camp of exercise held by the *Badaulet* in the neighbourhood of the town of Koorlia. Finally, during its sojourn on the borders of Kashgaria for nearly six months, the Embassy had several opportunities of verifying by various questions the information already collected regarding Yakoob Bek's army. Nevertheless, the collection of accurate information in indepeudent Asiatic States, in consequence of the extreme suspicion of the local authorities and of their wish to hide the truth, is attended with such difficulty that I cannot be assured of the complete accuracy of the information given below; so beforehand I wish to apologize for mistakes, which I hope will not be important, that may, perhaps, have crept into the narrative.

Difficulty of obtaining *accurate* information on any subject in independent Asiatic States.

Possible inaccuracies in the information obtained by the Russian mission to Kashgaria of 1876-77.

The particulars collected by the Embassy regarding the forces of the *Badaulet* present some interesting details concerning their organization, complement, equipment, armament, periods of service, commissariat, training and manœuvres.

In conclusion, I have endeavoured to approximately determine the numerical strength of the 'Badaulet's' forces, and their distribution over the country, and to draw up a general summary of their value as a military machine.

Division of the military classes of Kashgaria into infantry, cavalry and artillery, including *taifoorchis*.

All persons in Kashgaria who belong to the military class are called *sipahis* by Yakoob Bek, and are divided, according to the branch of the service with which they serve, into infantry (*sarbazais*), cavalry (*djigits*) and artillery (*topchis*). Besides the *sarbazais* and *djigits*, there are also the *taifoorchis*, who on account of their armament, which consists of long heavy flint matchlocks (like those employed formerly in Russian forts), one to every four men, and of their designation, are a kind of body that more closely resembles artillery than infantry.

The standing army and the Doongan levies.

The *sarbazais, djigits* and *taifoorchis* compose the standing army. Besides these, Yakoob Bek has formed in his eastern towns,[1] for service against the Chinese, levies of Doongans.

Regular and irregular troops.

The various branches of the Kashgarian army are not classed as regular and irregular, still, having regard to their training,

[1] Ooroomtcha, Manas, Koonya-Toorfan. The two first named were occupied by the Chinese in the year 1876.—*Author.*

armament and equipment, the *sarbazais* and a portion of the *djigits* and *topchis* alone can be considered regular.

The active army of Kashgaria.

All Yakoob Bek's soldiers belong to the active army.

New subdivision of the infantry into *tabors* and *booluks*.

(*a.*) The *infantry* (*sarbazais*). Since Turkish instructors came to Yakoob Bek a few years ago, the Kashgarian infantry, instead of its former subdivision into *sotnias* and standards, has been divided into *tabors*. Each *tabor* again is divided into eight *booluks* of thirty file each. The real strength, however, of a *booluk*, in consequence of the army not being up to its full strength, varies from fifteen to thirty file.

Subdivision of the cavalry into *tabors* and *takims*.

(*b.*) The *cavalry* (*djigits*). The greater portion of Yakoob Bek's cavalry during the last years of his life has likewise received the organization introduced by Turkish instructors. As have been the *sarbazais*, so too have been the *djigits* divided into *tabors*. Each *tabor*, which as regards numbers is equal to two Russian squadrons, is divided into eight *takims* of from fifteen to sixteen file a piece.

Relative strength of *sotnias* and of *standards*.

Besides this subdivision, the old divisions by *sotnias* and standards have been maintained in the greater part of the *djigits*. *Yuz-bashis* commanded the former unit and *pansats* the latter. The strength of a *sotnia* varies from forty to hundred men. A standard consists of from three to six *sotnias*.

In the infantry and the cavalry the double rank formation has been adopted.

Amount of artillery in the Kashgarian army.

(*c.*) *Artillery.* In the Kashgarian army there are two batteries, each of six guns forming separate military units. In the first of these which Colonel Kaulbars saw, there are smoothbore guns of local manufacture, carrying shot of about 12 lbs weight. The second is a 3-pounder mountain battery containing rifled breech-loading guns.[1]

Strength of the ordinary escort for the guns.

The guns of the second battery were imported from India a few years ago. They are at the outposts notwithstanding that five of them are ineffective, the breech mechanism being out of order. Each battery has an escort of about fifty horsemen and about as many foot soldiers. Other guns also of local manufac-

Guns attached to bodies of infantry.

[1] According to other information, there are eight guns in this battery, of which four are breech-loaders and four muzzle-loading guns.—*Author.*

ture have been served out to the infantry. Attached to two *tabors* of red *sarbazais*[1] of the guard there are sixteen guns, or eight guns to each. Other *tabors* have but two guns a piece.

The *taifoorchis* whence recruited.

(*d.*) *Taifoorchis.* This kind of soldier is recruited exclusively from the Chinese and the Doongans. A group of four soldiers forms the crew of a *taifoor*, the length of which is about a *sajen* (7 feet) and its bore something less than one inch. Five *taifoors* comprise a section. Every section has its own standard and an escort of five men armed with ordinary flint muskets.

Length and bore of a *taifoor*. Subdivision and escort of *taifoorchis*.

The several grades and their titles in the infantry, cavalry and artillery.

In the infantry, cavalry and artillery the following are the grades and their respective titles. The lower ranks are of two degrees, the *da-bashis, piyand-bashis;* the grade of officer is confined to the *yuz-bashis* or centurions and the *pansats*. The first mentioned is a sort of under officer, the second a staff officer. The highest military title is that of *lashkar-bashi*. He commands from five to ten *pansats* and corresponds to the European commander of a division.

Kashgarian army recruited at first by voluntary system of enlistment. Compulsory system substituted for it.

At first Yakoob Bek was satisfied with those who offered their services both from amongst his own people and from foreigners for the filling up of his army. Soon, however, the number of those who volunteered their services did not meet the demand for recruits, and so Yakoob Bek was obliged to adopt a compulsory system of military service, keeping the voluntary system as but an aid in filling up the ranks of his forces.

Obligation of service. Number of yearly recruits variable. Recruits how distributed.

Obligatory service fell on all males who had reached fifteen years of age. The number of recruits furnished yearly varied according to the requirements of the service. The recruits who were drawn were assigned to the several Circles, towns and villages. The burden of the compulsory system was especially heavy on a family consisting of two or three brothers, of whom one was taken. A son could be taken in place of his father. The age fixed for recruits was from 15 to 30 or even 35.

Yakoob Bek's army of greater strength than the population could supply without being overburdened.

In consequence of the continual wars, now with his neighbours, now for the subjugation of his own people, Yakoob Bek was obliged to keep up an army of greater strength than the population could furnish without overburdening itself. More-

[1] One of these *tabors*, at the time of our stay in Kashgaria, was at the advanced posts, the other was at the town of Kashgar.—*Author*.

over a corrupt administration made this burden still more heavy. For some years a forced enrolment was carried on throughout whole towns and villages. They seized and made over as soldiers even foreigners who came to the country merely as traders,[1] or as leaders of caravans. This forced enlistment led to desertion to such an extent, that the vacancies in the ranks of Yakoob Bek's forces often remained unfilled.

Abuses of the compulsory system of enlistment and their results.

Foreign element in the Kashgarian army, of what classes composed.

Of those foreigners who entered the Kashgarian army of their own free will, the first place belongs to exiles from the former Khanate of Kokan, people known in Kashgaria under the general name of *Andijans*, to exiles also from Bokhara and from Russo-Asiatic territory. Yakoob Bek's preference for exiles from Western Turkestan is easily understood. The Andijans were his first allies after his appearance in Kashgaria. He was moreover, himself, a native of Pskent, a village near Tashkent. Besides which these same Andijans undoubtedly comprised the most intelligent and the bravest part of Yakoob Bek's army. It can therefore be understood why they enjoyed such privileges as they did in Kashgaria. The best places in the government of the country and in the army were occupied by Andijans, who formed a very powerful party in Kashgaria, on which Yakoob Bek could thoroughly depend. In fact, so long as fortune attended Yakoob Bek, the ranks of this party steadily increased; but on the first failures occurring in the year 1876, when the struggle with the Chinese began, the weakness of this prop was sufficiently manifest. Of those who had come to Kashgaria to seek their fortunes and a livelihood, many, after Yakoob Bek's first failures, had ceased to believe in his star, and only waited for a favorable opportunity for making off in time to their own country with the wealth which they had plundered. Amongst the individuals who abandoned Yakoob Bek at the very outset of his failures, may be counted some of those who were nearest to his person.

Yakoob Bek's preference for foreigners from Western Turkestan.

Privileges accorded to them.

Whilst prosperity lasted, they were numerous and faithful, but when adversity came, they fell away.

Heterogeneous composition of Yakoob Bek's army.

Besides the exiles from Western Turkestan, there served also in the ranks of Yakoob Bek's army, Afghans, natives of India,

[1] At the time of our stay in Kashgaria, several of our own Tashkent subjects came to me with complaints of some of their members having been forcibly taken for soldiers. See page 63.—*Author.*

a few Turks, Chinese, Doongans and Kirghiz. Yakoob Bek highly prized the Afghans as good soldiers. They took service principally in the artillery and in the red *sarbazais*. There were also one or two *sotnias* composed of Afghans. The workmen in the rifle and cannon factories were also Afghans.

The value put upon Afghans as soldiers.

The number of natives of India in Yakoob Bek's army was very limited. They preferred to employ those of the race that they had in the artillery.

Natives of India.

Yakoob Bek's Turks came from Stamboul in the capacity of instructors. They introduced the Turkish system, but they were not able to do much. For this reason many of them, whose hopes had been disenchanted, were not slow to return to their own country. One of their number built in the town of Kashgar a factory, where he prepared very good caps for percussion firearms.

Turkish instructors.

A cap factory in Kashgar.

The Chinese, serving in Yakoob Bek's army, were the remnants of the Chinese forces that were destroyed during the insurrection in Kashgaria in 1863-64. By embracing Mahometanism they saved their own lives, but both they and their children had to serve for twelve years in the military service. The Chinese were the *taifoorchis* of the army, and as such represented the weakest part of Yakoob Bek's forces. Besides their services as *taifoorchis*, the Chinese were made to perform all the menial offices in the army.

Chinese mercenaries in the Kashgarian army. Origin of their appearance.

The Chinese perverts to Mahommedanism made to perform menial offices.

The Doongans in Yakoob Bek's army were the remnants of those who had served under the Chinese in garrisoning the towns of Kashgaria. They, too, were enrolled as *taifoorchis*, but some of them also entered the cavalry. Their position was somewhat better than that of the Chinese, though they, in like manner, were regarded with suspicion. The Chinese and Doongans had leaders appointed from amongst their own number. The Kirghiz and Kara-Kirghiz readily volunteered for service in Yakoob Bek's cavalry. They were employed principally in the garrisons of the distant posts, and as runners or couriers in the postal service.

Whence the Doongans in Yakoob Bek's army came.

Their position a little better than that of the Chinese.

The Kirghiz and Kara-Kirghiz.

How employed.

Lastly, in Yakoob Bek's army there were a considerable number of slaves who had been taken in wars with the various independent and minor potentates whose territories bordered on the west and south of Kashgaria.

Slaves in the Kashgarian army.

Service in the army or its substitute.

Service in the Kashgarian army was for life. Those who were not fit to serve in the active army, were either made to work in the fields or to pasture the State cattle.

Nature and extent of rewards for good service.

Rewards for service consisted of money, robes, rifles, promotion, and finally release from further service. The amount of the money rewards was completely discretionary. For the rank and file they never exceeded 50 *tengas*, *i.e.*, 5 *roubles* or about 12*s.* 6*d.*

Usual form of rewards.

Rewards by the bestowal of robes or rifles was the form usually practised by Yakoob Bek, when any one was personally presented to him on the completion of any particular service. The robe would be a *khalat* of value that would vary according to the rank of the recipient. Simple soldiers would be given chintz or *adrias*[1] *khalats*: *yuz-bashis* would receive either cloth or silken robes: on *pansats* would be bestowed robes made either of cloth of the best quality, or brocaded stuffs, or it might be of velvet.

When the rewards took the form of firearms, double-barrelled sporting guns or revolvers were usually given. The latter were generally preferred.

The rewarding of officials depended on the ruler's will, and was not guided either by length of service or by seniority.

Promotion how regulated.

Promotion to *da-bashi* and to *piyand-bashi* was in the hands of the *pansats*. Promotion to *yuz-bashi* and to *pansat* rested with Yakoob Bek, who, at his inspections, could promote a man from the ranks direct to the grade of *pansat*, and in like manner degrade a *pansat* to the ranks. The further promotion or rewards of *pansats* consisted in either farming to them, or bestowing on them, tracts of land, sometimes whole villages; in appointing them to offices at court, or to places in the administration. The highest offices, such as *toksobas*, *Bek-toksobas* and *Beks* were thus open to them. Persons appointed to fill posts in the general administration of the country could, at the same time, retain their military positions and commands over such portions of the army as might be distributed over the district entrusted to them.

[1] Semi-silken flowered material.—*Trans.*

Highest military rank in the Kashgarian army.

The highest military rank which could be reached in the Kashgarian army was that of *lashkar-bashi*, which corresponds to our commander of a division. He had under his command from five to ten *pansats.* In consequence of political combinations, Yakoob Bek endeavoured, as far as possible, to send those portions of his army that were recruited from his eastern provinces to the western borders of his dominions, and *vice versâ.* In return for good service, every private soldier had the right to claim in time of peace one month's leave.

Distribution of the army, subject to political conditions.

Leave privileges of the private soldier in time of peace.

Regulations affecting leave of absence.

A man on obtaining leave would be furnished by his commandant with a pass; this he had to show, on arriving at the place to which the leave was granted, to the local *Aksakal.* It was also considered a reward to transfer a soldier for service in his native town.

Uniform furnished by the State.

All those serving in the Kashgarian army received a State uniform which is described below:—

Uniform of the sarbazais.

The *sarbazais* had a long double-breasted *kaftan* of a reddish cloth, with metal buttons. On the shoulders, stars were embroidered in various colours. Those *sarbazais* whom we saw had parti-coloured *kaftans*, but some of them wore ordinary *khalats.* A few were attired in the uniform of Turkish soldiers consisting of a frock coat of thick black cloth braided with red, of loose trowsers of the same material, with a red stripe. The rest of the infantry had leathern *chambars* [1] of a yellow colour and ornamented with braid.

The head coverings were tall cone-shaped hats, made either of cloth of various colours, or of felt edged with fur, or the skin of the Russian otter. The *kaftans* were fastened with wide girdles made of leather, with white embroidery, and secured with silver buckles. At the waist hung several wallets of one pattern. On the right side was a small pouch for odds and ends, such as thread, needles, an awl, a pocket knife, &c. On the left side there hung a leather-covered powder horn, bags for bullets and for caps, three cartridge cases, each holding five cartridges, and a horn containing tallow for lubricating the particular firearm.

---

[1] This word is probably the same as *sambar. Sambar* skin garments are well known in India.—*Trans.*

Uniformity as to head-dress.

The *sarbazais*, *djigits* and artillerymen all wore the same description of head-dresses and girdles.

The artillery uniform.

The artillerymen had kaftans of a blackish cloth or felt material. Red stars were embroidered on the shoulders.

The cavalry uniform.

The cavalry wore *khalats* of various colours and materials, such as chintz, semi-silken or silken webs, *mata*, &c. The ends of the upper garment were tucked inside the leathern *chambars* or pantaloons.

Dress of the *taifoorchis*.

The *taifoorchis*, whether Chinese or Doongan, were dressed in *khalats* made of *mata* of various colours, but principally grey.

A towel made of *mata* appeared to be the headdress of the greater number of this class of soldier. One end of this towel was allowed to hang down the back. The foot covering of the *taifoorchis* consisted of blue stockings and thick shoes. Those of the infantry, cavalry and artillery soldiers were wide tipped boots made of soft leather with thick soles.

Periods for which the several articles of uniform and equipment were supposed to last.

Horses and saddlery furnished by the State and never replaced.

The period for which a *kaftan* had to last was from one to two years, *chambar* half a year, boots four months. Every year a change of under-clothing was served out and every two years a *poshteen*. To the cavalry two *khalats* were issued every year. The horse and the saddle were furnished by the State and were supposed to last for ever. As a fact all the articles, the issue of which was fixed by regulation, were issued very irregularly, so that the soldiers very often went about in tatters and in worn out boots.

Armament of Yakoob Bek's troops.

Yakoob Bek's forces were armed, the *sarbazais* with firearms, the *djigits* with carbines and swords, the Doongan horsemen with lances. Those artillerymen who served the guns had swords; those who formed the escort of the guns had firearms. The *taifoorchis* composed of Chinese and Doongans had *taifoors* and their escort was furnished with firearms. All the persons in command, from the *yuz-bashi* downwards, had firearms, swords, pistols and, in some cases, revolvers.

The greater portion of the firearms in use in Yakoob Bek's army consisted of flint muskets of various lengths and bores. These, together with the small number of percussion arms in the possession of the same army, were, as a rule, of small bore. They were heavy too on account of the Chinese sights that were fastened to the piece for the purpose of insuring aim and because they were weighted with iron ramrods.

System of rifling.

In many of them the rifling consisted of a few straight incisions in the barrel of the piece. In loading it was necessary to force the bullet down with some sharp blows of the ramrod. The accuracy of these pieces was very fair up to 200 paces. Their range sometimes exceeded 1,000 paces. The unfitness of this kind of weapon is patent and is comprised in the delay which occurs in loading, in the necessity of dismounting for the purpose of firing, in the insufficiency of range and accuracy of the piece in question.

Range and accuracy of the firearms in use.

General unfitness thereof.

Number of weapons of foreign manufacture in use in the Kashgarian army.

In point of numbers the percussion arms, both smoothbores and rifles, occupied the next place in Yakoob Bek's army. Amongst the number of the latter that we chanced to see and to hear of, there were about 8,000 Enfield rifles with bayonets, with a bore of about $\frac{5}{8}$ths of an inch, stamped "Tover,[1] 1864," and in some cases 1867. A considerable portion of the cavalry and several *tabors* of infantry were armed with this description of weapon. Yakoob Bek procured these rifles from India a few years ago.

The remaining percussion firearms belonged to two categories: 1. Sporting weapons, with single and double barrels, of foreign workmanship; these were mostly marked "Joseph Brown and Son, London," some too were from the Russian factory at Toola: 2. Percussion rifles or smoothbores of local manufacture.

Of both the one and the other description the number was not considerable, but it is difficult to determine what that number was. The sights of the double-barrel smoothbores of local manufacture were arranged for shooting up to 600 paces (!!)

Percussion firearms of local manufacture.

The percussion arms that were prepared in the local factories were of two patterns: smoothbores in shape like an Enfield, with several straight cuts in the barrel and short pieces with a length of barrel corresponding to the Berdans of the Russian cavalry.

Rough manufacture but fair results.

Both patterns were very roughly turned out, still it must be acknowledged that they lasted well and were fairly accurate at

[1] *Sic* in original. Tower (meaning Tower of London) is probably the word which the author wishes to use.—*Trans.*

short ranges. They had a bore of about ⅗ths of an inch. The weight of the longer specimens was 10 lbs, that of the shorter from 6 to 7 lbs. They had no bayonets attached to them, but were fitted with iron ramrods and with sights for shooting up to 600 paces. The stocks of these weapons were not ornamental at all. On the right side of the butt, a small piece of wood lifted up and displayed a small cavity for holding grease and rags for lubricating the piece. Over the breech-end of the barrel the name of the maker was cut in Turkish letters.

Issue of breech-loaders to Yakoob Bek's troops.

According to information which I gathered, Yakoob Bek in January 1877 arranged that 4,000 breech-loaders should be served out to his troops. Part of these rifles had already been issued and part were in store at Yarkend.

The first consignment of these weapons, to the number of 2,200, had been brought from India some two years before, together with 8-rifled 3-pounder mountain guns, 4 breech-loaders and 4 muzzle-loaders. The breech-loaders which we saw at Kashgar were in the possession of the soldiers forming the escort of Datkha-Aldash, Hakim of Kashgar. Those at Koorlia were Enfields converted on the Snider system. They had three grooves and were fitted with three-sided bayonets. We noticed, however, a few weapons, apparently on the same system, with French bayonets or sabres like those attached to rifles of the Chassepot patent.[1]

Cartridges for the same.

The cartridges, for the rifles on the Snider system that we saw in Kashgar, were central fire on the Boxer-Henry principle. Specimens of these cartridges have been taken to Tashkent.

Apparatus supplied, for attaching to Enfields converted on the Snider system.

Except in the case of the Sniders, extractors had not been provided. Yakoob Bek received a consignment of the necessary mechanism, and this was fitted in the local workshops to the rifles of local manufacture. I saw one such weapon, it was a smoothbore, of coarse workmanship, but the extractor had been fitted to it with a fair amount of skill. Several persons, on being questioned by us, exclaimed with one voice that the con-

[1] Both the French and the English first adopted (in the year 1867) as a temporary measure the Snider system with some modifications; with them the head of the hammer is not flat but concave.—*Author.*

verted Enfields and the breech-loaders came from Stamboul, and they added that these weapons had been sent by Abdool Aziz as a present to Yakoob Bek and as a token that he had accorded to his country the protection of Turkey. Another revelation, more detailed and perhaps more worthy of credence, tells us that Yakoob Bek commissioned his Envoy in Constantinople, Said Yakoob Ishan Khodja, to buy and to send to Kashgaria 12,000 rifles and some guns. Relative to the place where such rifles were to be bought, Ishan had no definite directions, but he had powers to act in the matter within his own discretion. Further revelations tell us that Ishan Khodja received whilst at Constantinople (whence is not known) 6,000 rifles and six guns. These he took with him through India to Kashgaria. The remaining 6,000 rifles were not delivered to him because he had not money enough to pay for them. On arriving at Tibet in the year 1875, Ishan Khodja was not allowed to go on until he had paid the duties on the guns, &c. This duty amounted to 30 *yambas* (or about 3,200 roubles or £400). Having sent on Ismail Effendi to procure the required amount, Ishan Khodja remained in Tibet. Yakoob Bek, on hearing of the detention of Ishan and of the guns, immediately sent off the 30 *yambas* which had been demanded. These he collected from merchants. He at the same time proceeded to make fresh requisitions for money to send by the hands of Ismail Effendi to Ishan, to pay for the remaining rifles left in Constantinople. The rifles already purchased by Ishan Khodja were partly breech-loaders and partly muzzle-loaders.

Source of supply of breech-loaders and converted Enfields.

Above we have reckoned that the whole number of breech-loaders in Yakoob Bek's possession was 4,000. It is probable, though, that one or more of the consignments sent by Ishan Khodja entered into this total. Notwithstanding the information in my possession, I still will not take upon myself to decide the question as to what extent the English had a part in furnishing Yakoob Bek with perfected firearms. The Turks, who have lately adopted the Henry-Martini system for their army, would seek to get rid of their rifles on the Snider system, and therefore they would be in a position to sell a portion of such rifles to Yakoob Bek. In like manner the

Number of breech-loaders in the possession of Yakoob Bek, and how far England took a part in furnishing him with perfected fire-arms.

The Turks would not be likely to have supplied such, though in a position to do so.

English, in India, whose sepoy troops are all now armed with rifles on the Suider system, continue to manufacture such rifles up to the present moment. It is, indeed, difficult to believe that the Turks, a considerable portion of whose forces are still armed with percussion and even with flint muskets[1] would find it advantageous to sell breech-loaders to Yakoob Bek. Nevertheless we, up to this time, possess no direct information as to the part taken by the English in furnishing Yakoob Bek with rifles. We only know that English trade agents, such as Shaw, and English Envoys, such as Forsyth, took with them as presents for Yakoob Bek several hundred rifles and revolvers and some specimens of magazine equipment. We know too that Ishan Khodja, the Kashgarian Envoy, remained for some time in London, with what object we have not discovered, and yet, before finally deciding the question as to who furnished Yakoob Bek with arms, whether English or Turks, or both, we must await more circumstantial information.

Trade in arms with Kashgaria continued to a very recent date.

To what has been said above, I will add the undoubted fact that a trade in arms with Kashgaria has continued up to a very recent date.

On the $\frac{\text{23rd December 1876}}{\text{4th January 1877}}$, we met on the road between the towns of Koocha and Bai, at one march distant from the latter place, five carts, each drawn by from four to five horses, laden with boxes of rifles. These carts were going to Fort Togsoon, where the rifles were to be issued to the troops.

On the $\frac{\text{7th March}}{\text{19th March}}$, we met at the village of Yangabad, between the towns of Koorlia and Karashar, a caravan of twenty camels; of these ten were laden with long wooden boxes, two on each camel, containing arms. On two camels four guns in cases were being carried. It may be supposed that these were the 3-pounder breech-loading mountain guns. As we have remarked above, Yakoob Bek possessed one battery of six such guns. Two camels were laden with the wheels of the guns, and also

---

[1] During March 1875, when I was paying a visit to the Turkish sea port towns of *Volo* and *Salonica*, I saw in the former 1,000 soldiers armed with percussion muskets, and in the latter sentries with worn out *flint muskets*.—*Author*.

on each animal was a box of ammunition. Two other camels were carrying four gun carriages. On the remaining four camels were sixteen small but well-packed boxes of ammunition. The men attached to the caravan told us that behind was following a large caravan with rifles and ammunition. These caravans, as also the carts which we had first met, had been despatched from Yarkend, where both guns and ammunition are kept in store. Islam Bek, the Hakim of Togsoon, told us that, at the close of the year 1875, he brought from Tibet and deposited in store at Yarkend 780 boxes of gun ammunition and rifle cartridges. He had with him a party of thirty-six *djigits* and 40 mule-drivers. Two men died in consequence of the labour undergone in the difficulties met with on the road and 76 mules were lost through the same cause. According to Islam Bek's statement, this ammunition was sent by the Turks from Constantinople to India, whence the English undertook to forward it on to Yakoob Bek.

In Tibet (was it not at Ladak ?) the English agent put pressure on Islam Bek until he paid him as a bribe 3 *yambas* (325 roubles, £40).

The road from Ladak to the town of Yarkend was traversed in 36 days.

Steel weapons and their quality.

With regard to the steel weapons which we saw, the swords were very mediocre as to quality, but of good shape. Most of the sword blades were of local manufacture, but we found a few which had been imported from India.

The officers of the Kashgarian army how armed.

It has been remarked above, that the officers of the Kashgarian army, besides having muskets and swords, were furnished with pistols and in some cases with revolvers. With regard to the pistols, nothing need be said since they were sufficiently bad; but concerning the revolvers it may be observed that though the number of these weapons in Kashgaria was limited, it was steadily increasing, thanks to Yakoob Bek's exertions and to the intense desire to obtain them manifested by every *yuz-bashi*. Colt's and Lefauchaux's systems were those most frequently met with. Those of the latter pattern that we saw quickly became useless, either on account of an insufficient supply of their cartridges or, still oftener, from their mechanism getting out of order.

Payment and victualling of the army of Kashgaria.

The payment and victualling of the army in Kashgaria were not regular or subject to any fixed rules. The amount of pay issued to the troops depended on whether they were on the march, or were stationed in barracks in the several towns, or were at the advanced posts, but chiefly on the condition of Yakoob Bek's cash deposits.

The scale of pay how considered.

The scale of pay was also subject to the questions—Were the particular troops kept up at the cost of the State or were they furnished by private individuals? In the latter case the scale would stand at a minimum.

Scale of pay of the several ranks.

Under favourable circumstances the following rates of pay were issued: To a private soldier from 3 to 15 *tengas* (from 30 *kopaikas*, or about 9*d*. to 1 rouble and 15 *kopaikas*, about 3*s*. 9*d*.) a month; to a *da-bashi* 20 *tengas* (about 5 shillings), and to a *piyand-bashi* 25 *tengas* (about 6*s*. 3*d*.) per mensem. *Yuz-bashis* and *pansats* received revenues derived from land or payment in kind or in money at the discretion of Yakoob Bek. A *yuz-bashi's* expenses would amount to 30 *roubles* (£3 15*s*.) a month. Artillery soldiers were paid at a higher rate. The pay of many of the *djigits*, who entered the service of their own free will, was discretionary with Yakoob Bek.

Issue of rations.

With regard to the rationing of the army, several methods were practised in Kashgaria. The issue of rations was twofold:

1. Two cakes (in weight about 1½ lbs.) were issued daily to each soldier, and a dish of *pilau* was divided amongst several men, who messed together according to commands. Once a month each soldier received one pound of tea.

2. Each soldier received for the month 2 *chariks* (about 32 lbs.) of flour, 1 *charik* (16 lbs.) of groats, and 1 or 2 *chariks* of meat.

Alternative issue, in lieu of issue in kind, to married soldiers.

Instead of the issue in kind to soldiers, especially those who had families, small plots of land were allotted to them, and they could thus raise a crop at an expenditure of 15 *chariks* of corn for seed. The occupant of such a piece of land, even if he was not able to cultivate it himself, would still receive half the crop, and this would amount to about 80 *chariks* for the year. The families of the rank and file received allowances from the State only in cases of extreme poverty.

The extent of such allowances would not exceed for one family 100 *chariks* of green corn. This would give each member of the family about two *chariks* of flour and one *charik* of groats per mensem. In cases of poverty, the families and parents of soldiers would be freed from all or from certain imposts and duties.

Allowance of food to horses.

Troop horses, whilst halting, would receive per diem two sheaves of clover and a bundle of straw amongst three. Corn at the rate of 50 *chariks* for the year would be issued to each horse. On the march a horse would receive from three to four sheaves of clover or of hay, if such were procurable, and four *djins* (about 10 lbs.) of green corn. During the movement of large forces through desert countries, the horses would receive the green corn only, and this would be reduced to an allowance of 7½ lbs. instead of 10. Instead of clover, sheaves of young reeds, sedge grass, a grass called *tchi*, or straw would be issued. Maize was largely used for horse's fodder, and also *djoogara* and barley.

Issue of clothing to the Kashgarian soldier.

The issue of clothing to the Kashgarian soldier was, under favourable circumstances, as follows:—*Every year:* One inner chintz *khalat*, one upper ornamented *khalat*, one *kaftan* made of either *mata* or cloth, two pairs of leathern *chambars;* one, two or three pairs of boots, one or two changes of linen.

Every two years: One *poshteen*. Amongst the articles issued to the soldier for an indefinite period, were his firearm, his belt with all its appurtenances and his saddle. His horse too was not replaced until it was quite inefficient. All allowances were received from the *pansats* and were passed on to the detached posts by the *yuz-bashis*.

Channel of supply.

Each *pansat* received from the *sirkars* the quantity of corn required for a given number of horses. The issue was checked by receipts, which had to be given to the *sirkars* for a given quantity of corn. These receipts were filed. The *pansats* received the firearms and the yearly kit from the *daulat-khanas* or stores, which had been established in all the large towns of Kashgaria.

Allowances in fixed quarters.

On arriving at fixed quarters, instead of receiving issues of corn, the *pansats* would have allotted to them tracts of State land. These tracts were cultivated partly by the soldiers and partly by hired labour. The cultivation of such lands was a burden that fell heavily, especially on the Chinese soldiers, because they were made to work *gratis*. Besides the State lands the *pansats* had made over to them droves of horses and of cattle which were pastured in the mountains. Those who took service with the *pansats*, either for working in the fields or for pasturing cattle, received 3 *roubles* (7*s*. 6*d*.) per mensem.

Method of transport in the Kashgarian army.

Every *pansat* had at his disposal the following means of transport :—Several camels, from 10 to 15 horses and five carts.

The most simple method of maintaining bodies of troops in Kashgaria.

The most simple method of maintaining bodies of troops, and one that was most often practised in Kashgaria, consisted in farming out to each *pansat*, *togsoba* and *bek* one or more villages, the income from which went to keep up a given number of soldiers. Under such an arrangement, the arms, and sometimes the uniform, were issued by the State, all other allowances, whether pecuniary or material, being at the expense of the occupant of the leased land.

Examples of this system.

Such an arrangement was made, for example, with the *togsoba* of Fort Ooloogchat, who administered the mountain region extending from the frontier of the Russian province of Fergana to the exit from the mountains at Kashgar, and who had under him more than ten small posts.

In return for the maintenance of from 700 to 850 *djigits*, who composed the garrisons of these posts, the *togsoba* collected a fixed tax from the sparse population of nomad Kirghiz, that wandered over the district under his rule. In like manner the Beks of Kashgar, Aksu, Khotan, Yarkend and other places, who held their provinces under the same system of tenure, were obliged to maintain a fixed number of *sarbazais* and of *djigits*.

The system one of oppression.

The latter method of raising soldiers was very hard upon those who served, since they received no fixed remuneration but just what their masters were pleased to give them. Indeed they very often were hungry because they received no pay, and were burdened with field and various domestic works.

The troops how located.

In the towns and at the detached posts the troops occupied barracks. These took the form of detached blocks (*koorganchis*).

Each block comprised several huts, surrounded by a common wall. Around these blocks were built rows of smaller huts, which were also occupied; ten men lived in each hut. Certain blocks were made over to the families of the soldiers, the soldiers themselves occupying other quarters. The divisions of the blocks were kept clean, but the detached huts were dirty, hot and too confined for the number of people occupying them. The married quarters were respected, and no one was allowed to enter them without invitation. Before the barrack system was introduced, the soldiers used to live in small and very light tents made of *mata;* ten occupied one tent. In the town of Koorlia we saw a camp of from 2,500 to 3,000 picked soldiers of Yakoob Bek. In the months of December, January and February, they were still in tents with 10 and 11 degrees of frost on the ground. They had scarcely any fuel and an insufficiency of warm clothing. Their beds consisted of a small quantity of straw covered over with felt. Another felt served as a general covering for all the occupants of one tent. When in barracks the soldiers were occupied daily, Fridays excepted, with their drill. Their parades lasted from 5 to 11 o'clock in the day. After the parade, they were kept from 1 to 2 hours under arms waiting for their dinners. Sometimes after dinner parades were instituted, but as a rule the soldier's time after dinner was taken up with working in the State fields, orchards, or workshops and with various domestic duties. They had but little leisure time at their disposal. Leave from barracks lay with the superior officers. On Fridays all the troops assembled at the principal mosque to attend the *Djooma-Namaz* or Friday's prayer.

The soldiers how occupied.

Leave from barracks how granted.

Religious service on Fridays attended by the troops.

Disciplinary punishments, as imposed on the Kashgarian soldier, took the form of arrest and of flogging with rods or leathern thongs.

Disciplinary punishments.

The powers conferred on the several officers to inflict punishments were not clearly defined. In this particular, complete license reigned. For criminal offences those who served in the army were subject to trial according to the ordinances of the *Shariat* as interpreted by the *Kazis*. For a first offence, say for stealing, detention in prison was awarded; for a second, severing of the arm at the wrist; for a third, death.

Powers conferred on the several officers to inflict punishments not defined.

Criminal offences subject to the ordinances of the *Shariat*.

Capital punishment rarely resorted to in Kashgaria. Death by hanging the most usual form of capital punishment.

Capital punishment, in spite of the prevailing opinion to the contrary, was rarely resorted to in Kashgaria. Death by hanging was the method most generally followed. Gallows, for a number of persons varying in size according to the extent of the town or village, were erected everywhere in the most conspicuous places. These generally were the first object that met the eye on entering a town or large village.

Before concluding the account of the condition of the Kashgarian soldiers I will here introduce some statements of different persons which I have recorded.

Statements regarding the condition of the Kashgarian soldier.

During our stay at Fort Ooloogchat, one of the soldiers attached to our escort told us that he was a native of the town of Khotan; that seven years before he had been pressed into the service; and that during the whole of that time he had been detained at Fort Ooloogchat. His family was at Khotan. Throughout his previous service he had not once received any pay. According to the statement of this man, the rations of the garrison of Ooloogchat consisted of two cakes, of which they ate one in the morning and kept the other for dinner. Two sheep were killed evey day for the men's dinner. One of these the *togsobas* and *yuz-bashis* kept for themselves; of the other they made a broth mixed with peas for the whole garrison consisting of from 70 to 80 men with their families and about 100 unmarried soldiers; the married men set aside their portions of this broth in separate cups.

Rations of the garrison of Ooloogchat.

Uniforms and arms furnished by the State very irregularly served out.

The uniform and arms furnished from the State workshops and stores in the town of Kashgar were very irregularly served out.

Portion of the soldiers' pay only issued.

The *togsobas* only issued a part of the pay due to the soldiers.

Garrison discontented.

The greater portion of the garrison was discontented and of opinion that the people were better off under the Chinese. Under them the soldiers at any rate did not suffer. Only the *Andijans* and the inhabitants of Pskent (Yakoob Bek's birthplace) lived well, it was said, under the present *régime*.

Deserters to Russian territory made over to the Kashgarian authorities by the

In the year 1875, two persons who had fled to Russian territory were made over to the Kashgar authorities by Musulman Biĭ, chief of the Sartlar tribe of Kara-Kirghiz, subjects of

Russia, who wander over both sides of the Terek-Davan pass. The offenders were executed and Musulman Biĭ received a reward from the Kashgarian authorities.

Sartlar tribe of Kara-Kirghiz.

A little before this two persons were cut to pieces by order of the *togsoba* for attempting to escape. Although the *togsoba* had no right to inflict capital punishment, he was allowed to so act by the personal will of Yakoob Bek.

Other persons punished for attempting to escape.

Certain soldiers, forming the garrison of the town of Kashgar, related that Aldash-Datkha, Hakim of that town, kept his soldiers (to the number of 800) almost in the same condition as those of the *togsoba* of Ooloogchat, *viz.*, without pay.

Garrison of the town of Kashgar in the same condition as that of Ooloogchat.

Shkokoff, a Russian agent, who had lived for a long time in the town of Kashgar, said that neither Kashgarian soldiers nor officers ever appeared as purchasers in the bazaar, and that after their uniform had been issued, they would sell it and also their *poshteens* and boots for a mere song and remain themselves in a tattered condition.

Testimony of Shkokoff, a Russian agent residing at Kashgar.

On our return journey from Koorlia to Koocha, we travelled for several marches in company with a *djigit*, a native of Yarkend. This man, amongst many interesting particulars relating to recent collisions between the Kashgarians and the Chinese, told us that he had served for five years in succession at the advanced posts. During this period, he received two cloth *kaftans* and 25 *tengas* (2 *roubles* and 50 *kopaikas*, 6*s.* 3*d.*) Rations had never been issued, and the soldiers at Koonya-Toorfan had sometimes been obliged to beg alms. On account of sickness he had been permitted to go to Yarkend, but only on condition that he joined the garrison of that town. They gave him money to buy a mule to take the place of the horse which he had lost, and on this animal he rode with us. They took from him the powder and the bullets of his flint musket, which he carried, leaving him but two charges for the road. To admit of the unhindered progress of this man to Yarkend, he had been furnished with a pass and a paper showing that he had the right to procure provender for his mule at the stations on his route.

Story of a *djigit*, a native of Yarkend.

Beyond the town of Koocha we met another man on leave who was returning to Yarkend on foot, with his flint musket on his shoulder. He corroborated what his comrade had said.

The story corroborated by another man returning to Yarkend.

Information gained through the soldiers of the several guards which were furnished to the Russian Embassy.

During all our halts in the several towns of Kashgaria, they furnished us with a guard of Kashgarian soldiers to wait on us as a mark of respect. At first they would speak boastfully of their condition and talk of the liberality of Yakoob Bek, exaggerating the pay and allowances which they received; but on closer acquaintance with us, they would become more open, and, as a rule, bitterly complained of their fate and of the evil deeds of their officers.

Attendance of the members of the Russian Embassy at parades of the Kashgarian troops.

Our attendance at the training of the Kashgarian army relates to the towns of Kashgar, Aksu, Koocha and Bai. At Koorlia, notwithstanding the considerable force which was there stationed during the period of our stay, we never once witnessed a parade.

Number and duration of such parades.

At Kashgar, where there were upwards of 5,000 men, the training went on on the most systematic manner. Every day at 5 o'clock in the morning all the soldiers were drawn up in front of their barracks. Twice a week the several branches of the service paraded together on a large field facing the town of Yangi-Shar. Four times a week all the troops in turn took part in target practice, and thus each branch of the service had the chance of attending this practice once or twice a week.

System on which the Kashgarian troops were trained—a mixed one.

Up to a recent date the training of the Kashgarian troops was on a system which was a mixture of Afghan, English (as taught by Hindoos) and Russian, with changes that had been introduced by Yakoob Bek himself. Of late years Turkish instructors had appeared, who took the training into their own hands, with the exception of that of two *tabors* of red *sarbazais*, who adhered to the old system of training. The new instructors introduced new forms only, leaving the essence of the matter what it was before.

Teaching of the new system.

With regard to the infantry, the new training inculcated the manual exercise, especial skill in preserving an unbroken front, and in marching. The cavalry were taught changes of front, to ride past at the walk and at the trot, column of threes and sixes and dismounted exercise. Extended order for the infantry, the attack and outpost duty for the cavalry, did not enter into the course of training. Neither was any attention paid to manœuvres over mixed ground or to the complex evolutions of the several branches of the service. For the teaching of such it would have been necessary to await the arrival of other instructors more skilled and possessed of knowledge than those sent by the Turks.

Account of the manœuvres witnessed by Kuropatkin at Kashgar, Bai and Koocha.

In order to make the reader better acquainted both with the character of the training and with the Kashgarian troops, whose occupations we had opportunities of witnessing, I give below an account of some of the manœuvres which I saw in the towns of Kashgar, Bai and Koocha.

Parade of the Kashgarian army near Fort Yangi-Shar.

Amongst other occasions, I happened to attend a parade of the Kashgarian army near Fort Yangi-Shar on the $\frac{\text{6th November}}{\text{18th November}}$ 1876. This parade took place on a piece of ground, two *versts* (1⅓rd miles) long and about a *verst* (⅔rds mile) wide. This extent was bounded on the south by a portion of the walls of Yangi-Shar and on the east by the Igiz canal.

The troops, to the number of about 3,000, were drawn up in a large square, the northern face of which was formed by cavalry (two *tabors* or 16 *takims*), the western and southern by infantry (three *tabors* or 24 *booluks*, with eight guns). On the eastern face were red *sarbazais* with eight guns and four *takims* or half a *tabor* of cavalry. About 400 Chinese were drawn up in front of the cavalry on the northern face and the same number of Doongans in front of the infantry on the western face. Both were armed with *taifoors*. All the troops were faced towards the interior of the square. In the centre stood Yakoob Bek's son, Bek Kooli Bek, with his staff, consisting of an instructor, a few *yuz-bashis* and *makhrams*. The latter, young boys of from 15 to 17 years of age, performed the duties of aide-de-camp. At the most conspicuous part were the red *sarbazais* formed in column of eight *booluks* with eight guns. An Afghan, by name Jamadar Parmanatchi, commanded this column.

Dress of the red *sarbazais*.

The red *sarbazais* were dressed in long red and green cloth *kaftans* reaching to within a short distance of the ground and greatly interfering with their movements. To the wide leathern belts which they wore hung several cartridge boxes. *Chambars* of a yellow colour had gone out of wear. On their heads they had conical hats with fur trimming made of the skin of the

Russian otter. The greater portion of the arms which they carried were Enfield rifles fitted with bayonets, but we also saw a small number of firearms of local manufacture.

Formation of the *sarbazais*.

These *sarbazais* were in *booluks* numerically very weak, *i.e.*, they were composed of 15 instead of 30 files. The eight guns attached to this body reminded us of Russian 18-pounder howitzers. Some of them were only 12-pounder guns. The carriages of these guns had the appearance of being strongly made although of rough workmanship. Some were painted green. The guns rested on their carriages by means of trunnions after the English fashion and each was drawn by two horses. The crew of each gun was composed of five footmen, who carried no arms at all, and of two horsemen.

Carriages of the guns strongly made but of rough workmanship. The guns how placed on the carriages.

Number of men to work each gun.

Arrangement of the guns.

The guns were placed at intervals between the *booluks*, so that the whole eight were on the left flank. Taking their orders from Jamadar Parmanatchi, all the manœuvres of this *tabor*, both infantry and artillery, went on simultaneously.

Square formation of the red *sarbazais*.

The first formation of the red *sarbazais* that we saw was the square. The front face was made up of four *booluks* and five guns, the rear face of two *booluks* and one gun, and the flank faces of one *booluk* and one gun each. The flank and rear faces were formed of the *booluks* deployed into line with the guns in the middle. This original formation was, however, considerably varied according to the several words of command given by Jamadar Parmanatchi. Sometimes the front rank would double to the right and left of the front face, forming a sort of screen for it. At other times the size of the square would be increased by sending the rear rank of the front face to prolong the flank faces. Sometimes again the size of the square would be decreased by taking the two *booluks* at the ends of the front face and by placing them on the flank and rear, thus making those faces four deep instead of two. During the manœuvres the guns were moved by the hand, the carriages being left inside the square. When the square was moved forward or backward or to the flanks, the guns were again placed on their carriages, and this operation was performed in a rapid manner.

When firing was going on from all sides of the square, the men worked fairly well together. After firing, however, they did not load with regularity. They were taught to do so as if all had quickshooting rifles when such was not the case. After the firing from square had taken place, small bodies of men were sent out. These, after moving slowly forward, covered the front, preserving intervals between themselves. The firing of these skirmishers was carried out by command of Jamadar Parmanatchi.

Working of the men when firing.

Skirmishers sent out to cover the front of the square.

The square appeared to be Jamadar Parmanatchi's principal form of instruction of the red *sarbazais*, to whom he gave the words of command in the Afghan language. The same manœuvres were repeated several times.

The square, the principal form of instruction of the red *sarbazais*.

Besides the square the *sarbazais* carried out deployments, moved to the front and rear and formed column of companies. The description of column most used was that which preserved the wheeling distance. In these movements the guns were on the right flanks of the *booluks*. The pace in marching was very short, and the men started with the left foot. All the movements were very slow, but regular as to pace and step, and the intervals beween the *booluks* were preserved.

Other formations.

Whilst Jamadar Parmanatchi was drilling his *tabor* he was attended by a bugler on foot, who sounded very skilfully the various calls. These reminded us of our own bugle sounds.

The various calls sounded by a bugler.

The manœuvres of the red *sarbazais* had no connection with those of the other portions of the force assembled. In like manner, these several portions all drilled independently.

The manœuvres of the several bodies independent one of the other.

The rest of the infantry made up into 24 *booluks* or three *tabors*, was drilled under the guidance of Bek Koolwi Bek. His orders were conveyed to the men by the Turkish instructor, who flew about from one end of the field to the other on his sorry steed like one asphyxiated with the fumes of charcoal.

Bek Koolwi Bek directs the movements of the infantry.

These three *tabors* were composed of recruits, of whom there were 30 file in each *booluk*, *i.e.*, they formed a body just double the number of red *sarbazais*. Two of these *tabors* were being drilled together and the other by itself.

The three infantry *tabors* composed of recruits.

The uniform of the soldiers consisted of ordinary *khalats* of embroidered *mata* with the ends let into yellow *chambars*, belts

Uniform of the soldiers.

Variety of firearms. Inferiority of the guns in possession of the artillery.

with wallets, like those worn by the red *sarbazais*. Amongst the firearms was noticeable a very great assortment. Apparently, flint muskets predominated. The eight guns in the possession of the artillery were inferior in respect of manufacture and equipment to those attached to the red *sarbazais*.

Movements how carried out.

The movements were carried out in columns by *booluks* with intervals somewhat greater than the front of such *booluks*. In these movements the men were not always in step, but they moved with regularity. The *booluks* closed and opened out on the march, halted and deployed fairly well and in good order. The *sarbazais* held their rifles on the right shoulder, the small of the butt resting on the nape of the neck with the arm nearly outstretched.

The standard of the training of the recruits not a high one.

The training of the recruits was confined to working together in closed ranks. It was apparent that the standard at which they had arrived was not a high one.

Infantry words of command.

The infantry words of command, with the exception of those given to the red *sarbazais*, were in the Turkish language. As we have observed above, those addressed to the red *sarbazais* were in the Afghan tongue.

Force of cavalry.

The cavalry that we saw consisted of nine separate bodies, corresponding to our squadrons, and *sotnias*. Eight of these manœuvred together and two separately.

Division of the cavalry.

Each *sotnia* was divided into two troops containing from 15 to 16 files apiece. These troops bore the designation of *takims*, eight of which went to form a *tabor*. Altogether two and-a-half *tabors* attended the parade.

Dress and armament of the cavalry.

The cavalry were dressed in *khalats* of various colours with the skirts let into *chambars*. Their armament consisted of firearms, principally percussion, with fixed bayonets and of swords. Amongst the firearms were some breech-loaders. The men slung their firearms round their necks. The drawn swords which we saw in possession of the officers were of very good quality.

Condition of the horses.

The cavalry horses were good and well-fed. Most of them were *karabairs, i.e.*, a cross between the Kokan *argamak*—a breed of stallion—and the Kirghiz mare.

Manœuvres of the cavalry.

The cavalry manœuvres were confined to the formation of columns of threes and of *takims*, and to the movements of such columns at a walk and at the trot. The distance between the several bodies was sometimes more sometimes less. Circling was performed in fair order. The flank, which formed the pivot in the circle, moved on its own ground, whilst the outer flank increased its pace. The men sat firmly in their saddles; nevertheless, in every movement one or two of them fell. These having remounted each time overtook their comrades. Neither the attack, nor dismounted drill, nor skirmishing, was practised although the men had been taught the second form of exercise. At the end of the parade the cavalry moved past us by *takims*; these were commanded by Moolla Kabool, *yesaul-yuz-bashi*, a native of the town of Andijan. After him followed several officers at the head of the *takims*, who saluted with their swords.

Besides the infantry and cavalry, the Chinese and Doongan *taifoorchis* were being drilled on the same parade ground. Of the training of this kind of soldiery we will speak below.

Chinese and Doongan *taifoorchis*.

The parade of all the troops terminated with a discharge of blank cartridges. The aides-de-camp of the *Bek-Batcha*[1] now galloped in every direction and soon all the troops were formed up in line. The cavalry were at some paces in rear of the infantry. The guns were placed in between the *booluks* of infantry.

The whole parade finishes with a discharge of blank cartridge.

At a signal from the Bek-Batcha all the troops opened fire. During this the front rank of the red *sarbazais* knelt down, and the cavalry fired over the heads of the infantry.

The troops fire by signal.

The guns were discharged as often as possible without aiming before each round.

Method of firing off the guns.

The infantry, except the red *sarbazais*, fired slowly. Their pieces were then lowered to the ground and the charges pressed home with the ramrod. In the case of the flint muskets the powder dropped about and was strewn over the regiment.

Slowness of the infantry fire.

A deafening and disorderly fire continued for about ten minutes. It then ceased almost in one moment at a signal given by the Bek-Batcha.

Firing ceases by signal.

During the parade silence was preserved, which was broken only by the violent shouting of the officers. It was only after the firing that talking in the ranks was heard.

Silence is preserved.

---

[1] As Bek Koolwi Bek was called.—*Author.*

Number of soldiers present on the parade.

The number of soldiers present at the parade was approximately as follows:—

		Men.
1.	3 *tabors* or 24 *booluks* of infantry, with from 28 to 30 files apiece	1,600
	1 *tabor* or 8 *booluks* of red *sarbazais*, with 15 files in each	300
	Total number of men in the four *tabors* of infantry ...	1,900
2.	$2\frac{1}{2}$ *tabors* or 20 *booluks* of cavalry, with 14 files in each	700
3.	16 guns with 32 files and about 80 drivers ...	100
4.	Chinese and Doongan *taifoorchis*, about 400 of each	800
	Total number of men ...	3,500

The parade unintelligible from a military point of view.

As a whole, the parade presented a very pretty and picturesque scene, but from a military point of view it was completely unintelligible.

Display of the kind of treatment experienced by the people who came to look on at the parade.

I will finish by an observation which characterizes Kashgarian manners. During the parade many of the inhabitants had collected to look on. These persons were let alone for a long time, when suddenly, by somebody's order, several of the mounted boys (*makhrams*) rode at them and began to drive the people off the ground. One man was even struck with the buttend of a firearm, and two or three others were kicked by the horses and fell to the ground.

The members of the Russian Embassy inspect the barracks of the Kashgarian troops.

On the $\frac{11\text{th}}{23\text{rd}}$ November 1876, we rode out to inspect the barracks and to attend the private parade of the red *sarbazais*. These barracks are situated a short distance from Fort Yangi-Shar, and about a *verst* ($\frac{2}{3}$rds mile) from the house occupied by the Embassy. The commandant of the red *sarbazais*, Jamadar Parmanatchi, met us at the gates, and after the usual compliments, conducted us to his official residence. The barracks, which were occupied by the *tabor* of red *sarbazais*, and by the men attached to the eight guns that we saw on the previous parade, were divided into four

Arrangement of the barracks

sections or blocks built in lines one behind the other. In front of the first block the guns were arranged under a canopy, the crew of each gun being drawn up in front of it. Under a canopy were also placed three mortars of local manufacture. One of these threw a shell of about 70 lbs., and the other a shell of something under 18 lbs. At the flanks and rear of this block and of the others there were small huts which were occupied by the soldiers and their families. These huts were kept very clean. At all four blocks were seated rows of soldiers with their firearms on their shoulders and with their eyes fixed on the ground. The greater portion of their firearms were muzzle-loading rifles bearing the Tower-mark.

And of the guns.

Huts of the married soldiers.

Attitude of the soldiers during the inspection of their barracks.

Long cloth *kaftans*, in many cases much worn, left the neck and part of the breast open and bare.

Clothing.

Boots of goatskin, which were much trodden down.

Foot coverings.

The appearance of the soldiers, amongst whom we leisurely passed, was not attractive. These men were in their prime, and yet they looked haggard and ill rather than healthy. It may be affirmed without mistake that the average age of the soldiers whom we saw was from 30 to 35. There were several younger men, but there were also old men of 50. About a hundred Afghans and Hindoos and several Doongans could be distinguished from the others, who were natives of the country. The commandant of the *sarbazais*, Jamadar Parmanatchi, was, according to his own statement, 73. He was yet a vigorous old man, of middle height, slim and with a slight stoop, with an energetic and very agreeable expression of countenance. During his military career he had served for 50 years in the Sikh army, and had fought with them against the English. He had then set out to seek his fortunes in Central Asia. Having entered the Kokan army he fought against the Russians at Chemkent, and finally, when the Russians occupied Tashkent, he came to Kashgaria, where by his military capacity he won the favour of Yakoob Bek. He was considered the commandant of the Kashgarian artillery, although he had only eight guns under his command.

Unattractive appearance of the soldiers.

Jamadar Parmanatchi.

When he was *lashkar-bashi*, he commanded from eight to ten standards (about 4,000 men) of infantry and cavalry.

Jamadar Parmanatchi had, he said, eleven wounds. He nevertheless enjoyed good health.

His uniform.

His uniform consisted of a *kaftan* of fine English red cloth fastened with silver clasps on his breast, a wide girdle, ornamented with round silver-plates, from this hung a sword of the best quality. At the back of his belt was placed a revolver, on the piston system, probably Colt's. On his head he had a conical-shaped hat of violet coloured velvet trimmed with marten's fur.

His official residence.

The official residence of Jamadar Parmanatchi was a four-storied house, in which his staff also lived. On the halls were hung firearms of different kinds, double-barrelled flint muskets and one breech-loader.

Private parade of Jamadar Parmanatchi's red *sarbazais*.

After the usual *dastar-khan* had been offered to us in Jamadar Parmanatchi's house, we requested him to show us a private parade of his soldiers. Accordingly there soon appeared at the first block of barracks about 70 *sarbazais* with "ordered arms." On the word 'silence' the whole came to attention, drew their heads back, threw out their chests and slightly shuffled their feet. On the word "arms at ease" all threw up their pieces together to the left shoulder, seized the butt with stretched out arm and "presented" and "ordered arms" in a manner very similar to that practised by Russian soldiers.[1] After the manual exercise was over they shewed us some wheeling and marching past. Wheeling on one foot, the *sarbazais* raised the other somewhat high whilst marking time on the ground. On the word "slow march" the first steps were made on the ground by marking time. The movement forward was made with the left foot. In marking time the legs were raised very high with the bend of the knee almost directly at right angles. The pace was very short. The body was held erect with the head slightly raised. The movements, with some exceptions, were made in time and with the head erect. The ranks were composed of sections with from five to ten men in each. The right was the directing flank of the

The "manual exercise."

Wheeling and marching past.

[1] In this motion the bayonets of the rifles stood out more from the shoulder than with us.—*Author.*

sections. In breaking into sections it was evident that they took especial care to confuse each part of the movement. Wishing to show off, the Jamadar rapidly changed the formation, during which his men circled round him, made leaps, struck their feet together and went through a number of antics. This part of the parade reminded us of a dance. It became so mixed up that at last the *sarbazais*, without crowding, beat each other on the neck and exchanged abuse. A certain *yuz-bashi* got particularly angry, and several times struck those men who had lost their places hard blows with the butt-end of a musket. An Afghan, who played the clarionet, and who, though in attendance on the Jamadar, was in a tattered *khalat*, considered himself an authority whose duty it was to control matters. This person, perceiving the confusion that was going on in the formation, ran hither and thither freely bestowing his blows.

Extraordinary character of some of the manœuvres.

A *yuz-bashi* makes himself conspicuous.

An Afghan attendant on the Jamadar does the same.

Having seen a parade of the infantry we begged them to show us an artillery parade. After repeated refusals, the Jamadar at length agreed and directed the two end guns to be moved out from under the canopy and the gunners to form up in their places. The guns were bronze smoothbores of local manufacture. One was an 18-pounder, and the other a 12-pounder, but both were much shorter than Russian guns. The carriages were of the naval pattern; one of them was painted green. The raising mechanism consisted of a screw fastened strongly to the sides of the carriage. The thread of this screw was let into the breach part of the gun. The wheels of the carriage were roughly made, but strong; they had thick tires.[1]

An artillery parade.

Description of the guns and of the carriages.

The gunners were variously dressed, some were in black woollen *kaftans*, others were dressed like the *sarbazais*. The uniform of all was dirty.

Clothing of the gunners.

At each gun stood seven men, of whom two or three had swords of different patterns in steel scabbards. From five to six men, forming the escort, were armed with muzzle-loaders.

Crew and escort of the guns.

[1] These tires were fastened on with nails on the Chinese pattern. The heads of these nails were coarse and angular, projected out a good deal, and impeded the progress of the carriage. The same kind of tires are used for the wheels of *arabas*, or tilted carts.—*Author.*

Distribution of duty.

Of the seven men who formed the gun's crew, one carried the sponge, one the match, one the charge, one was the man who placed the charge in the gun, one stood with the needle to prick the charge (the same fired the charge or inserted the fuse). Finally two men, apparently orderlies, took no part in the proceedings at all.

Nature of the parade.

The parade consisted in going through the motion of loading and firing. All the numbers went through their work fairly well by word of command. The loading was carried out with much shouting. The numbers ran out and ran back with jumps and great gesticulation.

Manner of loading.

The man with the sponge especially distinguished himself in this respect. Generally speaking, the loading was performed in the same way as we used to carry it out not long ago when we had smooth-bore guns. It was difficult to keep from smiling at the comic zeal which accompanied each movement.

Distress of the gun's crew after firing ten rounds.

After ten rounds the gun's crew appeared to be completely out of breath.

Change of numbers.

By command of the Jamadar the numbers were now changed, and the loading continued, although less skill and some confusion were apparent. A change was made five times until each man had performed the duties of each number.

Awkwardness of a gunner and rage of the Jamadar thereat.

It chanced that one old gunner, to whose lot it fell to carry the sponge, put all the rest out. This awkwardness, completely unexpected, so enraged the Jamadar, that he pulled out his sword and with curses rushed on the offender. The poor fellow, pale with fright, expected to be struck. Happily the matter terminated with threats only.

Amenities of the parade.

Another time one of the men struck a gaping comrade on the neck with the linstock. The latter took the linstock when it came to his turn, and darted to his place with an air of offended dignity. When the time came to load, thinking it a good opportunity, he turned towards the man who had touched him, and who was now carrying the charge and struck him full in the face.

End of the parade.

Having carried out the process of loading an indefinite number of times, Jamadar Parmanatchi at length informed us that the parade was at an end.

Parade of the Chinese troops.

Some days after this, *viz.*, on the $\frac{14th}{26th}$ November, we chanced to see in Kashgar a parade of the Chinese troops. They took us past the gates of Fort Yangi-Shar to the quarter occupied by the Chinese soldiers. From afar a quantity of standards shewed us the spot where the *taifoorchis* were drawn up. We rode out to a vast and well-cleared square, the rear face of which was occupied by a line of troops. In front of them was a canopy under which Dalai, the commandant of the Chinese troops, awaited us. In the middle of the square were the bandsmen. On our approach, Dalai came out to meet us and invited us to take our seats on the carpets which had been spread under the canopy. Dalai was a decrepit old man of 66 years of age. He had no hair on his face except a straggling grey beard. His countenance was of the characteristic Chinese wrinkled type. He had on a rich *khalat* of green silk trimmed with fur, warm yellow trousers with fur lining, and a conical hat made of some thick material. On his knees as he sat on the carpet lay a double-barrelled gun of inferior quality. A Kashgarian youth acted as interpreter. Two or three Chinese of from 16 to 18, with small parti-coloured flags in their hands, acted as aides-de-camp, and carried his orders to the troops.

Dalai, the commandant of the Chinese troops of Kashgaria.

Dalai's previous history.

About 13 years before, Dalai commanded the Chinese garrison in the town of Kashgar, where, on the outbreak of the rebellion against his Government, he shut himself up in the citadel (Yangi-Shar). Yakoob Bek laid siege to the citadel, but, perceiving the want of success that attended his endeavours to take the place, he entered into negotiations with Dalai, who, at the price of treachery and the change of his religion, purchased his own life, for, during the subsequent storming of the citadel, he, with his accomplices, went over to the side of Yakoob Bek, whilst the *Amban* of Kasghar, with those Chinese who remained faithful, heroically blew himself up into the air.

His position as a pervert not a good one at first.

At first Dalai's position was not a particularly good one, but afterwards, having become Yakoob Bek's brother-in-law, he began to be treated with some respect, which was, however, only superficial.

Inspection of the *taifoorchis.*

Having partaken, according to custom, of the inevitable *dastar-khan,* which on this occasion consisted of numerous Chinese dishes, we set out for the right flank of the troops, along whose front we then passed. The *taifoors* to the number of about 200 were placed within an even line of props. The men who served them sat two on each side. Standard-bearers, with large three-cornered flags of coloured materials, were distributed among each set of five *taifoors,* and they also sat in a straight line. Neither the men serving the *taifoors* nor the standard-bearers had any sort of weapon. Behind the *taifoors* there was a line of sharp-shooters, one for each *taifoor,* armed with ordinary flint muskets. These men had about 20 square-shaped flags, which were intended to frighten the enemy's horses.

Five *taifoors* composed a section, on the right flank of which sat an under-officer armed with a flint musket. Some of the sections, however, had on their right flanks *yuz-bashis,* who were armed with double-barrelled rifles and swords.

As we passed along the front we were struck with the plain, and often ugly faces of the soldiers who were seated before us.

Pure Chinese predominated, but *Kachirs*[1] or mixed breeds entered largely into the number of the men whom we were inspecting. (They call the offspring of a marriage between a Kashgarian and a Chinese woman a *Kachir.*) The leaders of tens and the *yuz-bashis* were principally such. Amongst the soldiers were some very young men, almost boys, and likewise some old men. As a rule, moreover, the men were younger than the infantry, and especially than the red *sarbazais.*

Uniform of the Chinese soldiers.

The uniform of these Chinese soldiers produced an impression not less dull than did their faces. Only a small portion of them had on new wadded *khalats,* embroidered with *chekmen.*[2] The greater number had old worn and torn *khalats* of *mata.* Their foot coverings—Chinese shoes (cloth with leathern soles)—were much trodden down. The headdresses were conspicuous for

[1] Properly speaking the word signifies a mule.—*Author.*

[2] A cotton web of local manufacture, very durable.—*Author.*

their variety. Those who wore *chekmèn khalats* had conical hats trimmed with fur.

The majority, however, had only a piece of *mata* which was fastened round the head, so that the folds protruded over the ears. Some had for a headdress a conical-shaped cap of some striped material which reminded us of ancient head-pieces.

Offices of the men forming the crew of each *taifoor*.

Of the four men who formed the crew of each *taifoor*, one had a belt filled with about ten wooden cartridges. The second was the sponger out; the sponge was an iron rod with a bundle of hair tied to the end. Numbers three and four had to carry the *taifoor* and to form themselves into a sort of carriage when it was fired off. Not long ago, the Chinese troops presented a much more original appearance. They were dressed in Chinese cloaks, with wide sleeves, and wore armour and tiger skins in order to frighten the enemy's horses.

Former dress of the Chinese troops.

Escort of the *taifoors*.

The escort of the *taifoors* were spearmen and pikemen. With the troops were many flags of various sizes and shapes. The band consisted of a large number and of different sorts of instruments.

Yakoob Bek's treatment of the Chinese soldiers captured in war.

Yakoob Bek turned all the Chinese soldiers whom he captured in war into Mussulmans, gave them a native dress and formed bodies of *taifoorchis* of all who had been spearmen and pikemen. Of the Chinese musical instruments he retained the drum and the tambourine only.

Commencement of the parade.

The parade commenced with the signal "to rise." At a sign from Dalai the drummer gave one roll on his drum. All the men then got up, placed their *taifoors* on their shoulders and prepared to move off.

Movements carried out by waving flags.

Dalai now took from one of his aides-de-camp two small flags, of which there appeared to be six shapes. He held one flag up in the air and placed the other behind him. On this signal, half of the *taifoorchis* went to the right and half to the left, and keeping their right and left shoulders forward, began to deploy from both flanks into two lines. At the head of each line a standard was carried. Behind this marched five *taifoorchis* in single file. Then there was another standard followed by another set of five *taifoorchis*, and so on. The commanders of tens and of hundreds marched on the flanks of their respective commands. The escort and its flags remained stationary.

Method of carrying the *taifoors*.

On the march a *taifoor* was placed on the shoulders of every two men, the foremost of whom held it with a cloth fastened round the barrel. This cloth was not removed when the *taifoor* was discharged, so that the aim must have been interfered with. During the march the pace was marked at intervals by the dull beating of a drum. On arriving at the spot where the band stood, the lines of *taifoorchis* wheeled to the right and left, so as to clear the obstacle, again closed in and continued the movement. This manœuvre, on account of its measured pace and the monotonous beating of the drum, put one in mind of a funeral procession rather than of a military movement. When the manœuvre was to terminate, Dalai lowered the arm which held the flag up in the air.

Character of some of the manœuvres.

Method adopted for insuring proper step being kept in marching.

Whenever those in rear got out of step, the drummer would, by Dalai's order, sound the pace, whereupon all quickened the step to the proper time. The taps on the drum gradually became more rapid, until at last a roll was beaten. This was the signal for those who were not in their places to double up.

Nature of other movements.

The second manœuvre consisted of a movement forward, backward and in an advance of the sharpshooters. The attack was made sometimes with and sometimes without firing. In either case, each set of five *taifoorchis* marched in single file preserving the dressing. The sharpshooters, who had formed up in rear, as soon as the *taifoorchis* were halted, ran forward and covered the front. In front of the skirmishers again ran a number of Chinese whose business it was to wave flags in a frantic manner. On the signal 'fire' (which referred only to the sharpshooters) the sharpshooters delivered their fire, and then on the signal 'retire' they shouted and brandished their firearms. The Chinese who were in front of the line of sharpshooters lay down, but continued to wave their flags in a still more frantic manner. The idea was that an attack of cavalry had been beaten back.

Position of the men carrying the *taifoors* when their *taifoors* were fired.

When the main body of the *taifoorchis* advanced firing, half were halted for a few seconds to fire; this done, they advanced and joined the other body, who, in turn, halted and fired. The two men who carried each *taifoor* slightly bent the back and advanced one foot. The first kept the *taifoor* in position on his shoulder by means of the cloth spoken of above, the second pressed it to his neck with his hands. Notwithstanding the great weight of the piece, the recoil after firing was still more striking. There have been cases wherein a discharge of ball cartridge has thrown down the living carriage. In order to lessen the recoil the charge has been reduced; this has, of course, diminished the range and accuracy of the weapon. Of the last little need be said, for they fire almost without taking aim. After a few rounds the numbers were changed.

Recoil very great.

Measures adopted to lessen it.

In advancing firing by sections, one *taifoor* was carried behind the other. After firing, each *taifoor* was doubled up to the head of the advancing section. The next then fired and doubled up, and so on. Some of the sections, in hurrying their firing, struck some of the crew of the *taifoors* nearest to them. The discharge was scattered amongst them, hitting the men on the back, shoulders and head.

Firing of *taifoors* by sections how carried out.

The firing of the *taifoors* ceased by signal given on a tambourine. The Chinese imagine that the shrill sound of a tambourine with its little bells can deaden the noise of the firing.

Order to 'cease fire' how given.

After thanking Dalai for the satisfaction which he had afforded us, and after praising, according to custom, his soldiers and expressing the joy which we felt on making the acquaintance of so celebrated a commander, we prepared to take leave. Dalai warmly reciprocated our good expressions. His corpselike face was lit up with a self-sufficient smile. He told us that amongst the body of men whom we had just inspected there were soldiers who for twenty years had not been out of fire, and that in any serious engagement Yakoob Bek could always rely on the strength and bravery of his *taifoorchis*.

Leave-taking with the Chinese commandant.

After listening to this boast we took leave of Dalai, carrying away at the same time the firm belief that a hundred good Cossacks would be sufficient to scatter in the open field and to overthrow all the Chinese we had been inspecting. And the loss of the Cossacks need not be especially great, since the Chinese, not having weapons of cold steel, would have nothing to defend themselves with.

Poor opinion formed by the members of the Russian Embassy of Yakoob Bek's Chinese mercenaries.

Strength of the body of *taifoors* present at the inspection.

The strength of the *taifoor* army that we had seen was approximately as follows:—

Number of *taifoors*	200
Crew of *taifoors*	800
Men with separate flags	40
Section commanders	40
Centurions	8
Sharpshooters	200
Men in advance of sharpshooters	20
Total number of men ...	1,108

Kashgarian troops on the march.

For a distance of from 50 to 100 *versts* (from 33⅓rd to 66⅔rds miles) the infantry of the Kashgarian army would march on foot. Should the distance be greater, the men would be mounted on horses, or failing these, in carts. Each cart would be drawn by three horses and would carry ten men. Part of the horses and carts would be furnished *gratis* by the inhabitants and part would be bought. In the march, for example, from Kashgar to Karashar (1,000 *versts*, 666⅔rds miles) only a small portion of the infantry rode in carts, all the rest were turned for the time into dragoons or into mounted infantry.

Rapidity of marching dependent on the necessity of the case. Average distance performed daily.

The rapidity of the movement of the Kashgarian troops would vary according to the necessity of the case. The average would be 25 *versts* (16⅔rds miles) a day. Thus, the distance from the town of Kashgar to the town of Aksu is 436 *versts* (270⅔rds miles). This would be performed in 18 ordinary marches, and in 12 forced marches.

Order of march.

During the march the troops went in *échelon*, and halted at the several posts that Yakoob Bek had constructed. In all populated districts the inhabitants had to furnish forage, fuel and cattle for the troops, and these supplies were not always paid for. When traversing roads through desert tracts, one or more traders followed the army with all the necessary provisions.

Demands made on the people of the districts through which the troops marched.

Method of supply when marching through desert tracts.

These traders entered into a sort of contract for the supply of a portion of the requisite stores. In addition to what they furnished, wheat, maize and barley were taken on State carts. As a rule, the *pansats* gave the contracts, and they, on receipt of the necessary stores, made it over to the *yuz-bashis*, who, in turn, gave out one or more days' consumption to their subordinates.

On arriving at a halting place, the traders opened their bazaar, in which the soldiers could buy rolls, meat pasties, *pilau* and tea. Generally speaking, however, the commissariat arrangements in Yakoob Bek's army were very bad, and the troops on the march were often in a starving condition. Nor was it a light part of Yakoob Bek's labours to arrange for a water-supply in traversing the waterless tracts of Kashgaria. On the road from the town of Kashgar *viâ* Aksu to Fort Karashar, Yakoob Bek, by establishing a post with wells or reservoirs to hold the spring water, succeeded in securing a watersupply for his troops whilst on the march. On this route the waterless tracts do not exceed 45 *versts* (30 miles) in length; but, on the route from Fort Karashar to Koonya-Toorfan, whereon there are two long marches through a waterless country containing some very deep and almost empty wells, Yakoob Bek used to store water in bags (*toorsooks*) made of sheep-skin, and placed two of these on every camel set apart for carrying water for the troops.

Commissariat arrangements in Yakoob Bek's army, generally speaking, very bad.

Difficulty of arranging for a supply of water for the troops on the march.

During the summer season, in consequence of the great heat, the troops halted during the day and marched at night.

During the summer season marches were made at night.

I consider it interesting to communicate some details regarding the manœuvres of the Kashgarian troops in war time.

Manœuvres of the Kashgarian troops in war time.

On approaching the enemy, the cavalry was first of all sent out to reconnoitre. The infantry left their horses and carts in the train of waggons, over which a strong escort was placed. On approaching still closer to the enemy, the cavalry rode on the flanks of the column which was composed of infantry and of artillery. The train of waggons halted in rear. The order of battle was now formed. The infantry and artillery were deployed into one or more lines. In the intervals between every two guns were from 40 to 60 infantry soldiers. The cavalry was principally held in reserve. In case of need the length of the fighting line was increased from both flanks. Until the battle became hot, the troops moved slowly forward. After this the greater portion of the troops of both sides would become mixed up in one general disorderly crowd which, like a swarm of bees, went now this way and now that. The importance of having a reserve ready at this moment, was fully understood by Yakoob Bek, and, in this way, he often got the upperhand of his more numerous but less experienced antagonists. As a rule, he held in reserve picked troops, principally cavalry.

Importance of a reserve.

Part performed by the cavalry.

The part played by the cavalry in the attack and on the halt consisted, according to the statements of Kashgarian military men, in protecting the guns from the enemy's cavalry. In order to do this, they moved in small bodies at about from 200 to 600 paces in front of the flanks of the advancing body.

The cavalry during the fight, as a rule, used its firearms. Advancing to a certain distance, it would extend like a chain of skirmishers, and open fire on the enemy.

Firing from horseback not accurate.

Firing from horseback was practised not singly but in entire ranks. The horses that we saw had been well trained to the noise of firearms. Nevertheless the fire delivered from horseback was not very accurate, so that wherever it was possible to do so, the men would dismount to fire.

Cavalry on the defensive.

When acting on the defensive the cavalry dismounted, with the exception of a fourth of their number.

Final action of the cavalry.

The real opening for the cavalry was when the enemy wavered. Then, throwing their firearms over their back (they generally held them in their hands), and seizing their sabres they dashed forward and not only routed the enemy, but sometimes caused a general massacre of the defeated foe.

Attacking an enemy of superior strength.

When attacking an enemy of superior strength, the fighting line of infantry, cavalry and artillery, formed square with guns placed at the corners.

The *taifoorchis* looked upon with suspicion.

The Kashgarians looked upon the *taifoorchis* with suspicion and said that in a hard engagement they only got in the way, that it was a difficult matter to know where to put them, and that they did no harm because they were the first to fly.

Their numbers gradually reduced.

Yakoob Bek had known for a long time of their unfitness, and he had for this reason gradually reduced their numbers. Out of the several thousand *taifoorchis* (they told us 10,000, but these figures are probably exaggerated) which he had in his army, there were only some hundreds, and these were Chinese and Doongans. We have seen above that to the Chinese *taifoorchis* flint-muskets had already been served out. A great number of the *taifoors* of the Doongan soldiers were then withdrawn, and they had given them flint-muskets in exchange, which had been returned into store after the arming of the cavalry and of the *sarbazais* with percussion and breech-loading rifles. These Doongans were then sent out on the line of advanced posts, and to form the garrison of Koonya-Toorfan.

Yakoob Bek's workshops and arms factories, &c., &c.

Yakoob Bek established in various towns of his sovereignty workshops for the preparation of uniform and equipment, also arms and powder manufactories, and magazines for the reception of military stores of all kinds. In the workshops they prepared the *kaftans* of the *sarbazais*, also head-dresses and a portion of the *khalats*. The greater portion of the *khalats* and of the underclothing of the troops was of local manufacture, and was furnished to Yakoob Bek by the several *Beks*, who took it from the people without paying for the same. Of the material used in making the uniform, it only remains to mention Russian and English cloth and Russian otter's fur for the trimming of *khalats* and head-dresses.

Arms factories.

There were three arms factories at Kashgar, Aksu[1] and Koorlia (some said there was another at Yarkend). In these were turned out percussion rifles on the Enfield pattern.

Rifles which were made therein.

These rifles were of two kinds, long and short, but mention has already been made of this when speaking of the equipment of the Kashgarian troops. Some of the rifle-barrels had three or four straight grooves varying in width.

Number of mechanics in the Kashgar and Aksu factories, and amount of work done by them.

There were 30 mechanics employed at Kashgar, who turned out five rifle-barrels in a week.

In the arms factory at Aksu, amongst the workmen, were seven Hindoos. This factory turned out only one rifle per week.

[1] The information relating to the arms factories of Kashgar and Aksu was partly taken by me from details furnished by Kalil Khan Khodja (formerly superintendent of the Kashgar factory) and which were inserted in the '*Turkestan Gazette*' for 1877, No. 10.—*Author.*

Factory at Koorlia. A Kalmuk superintended the arms factory at Koorlia. This man was an exile from Kooldja. Very good arms were turned out here.

Rifles stored after manufacture. Rifles, after being manufactured at Aksu and Kashgar, were sent to Koorlia, where they were kept in store. During our stay in the latter city, there were issued to the troops from this store from 200 to 300 percussion rifles of local manufacture.

How cannons were cast. There was no regular cannon foundry in Kashgaria. In cases of necessity, Abdrashit, a Kokan mechanic, superintended the casting of guns at Yangi-Shar. He collected for this purpose all those workmen who were engaged in the manufacture of cast-iron in the town of Kashgar. Copper was procured principally from the Aksu Circle. On one occasion one of the Turkish instructors, Mamadoo Efendi, was entrusted with the casting of rifled cannon, but his attempts were not successful, inasmuch as at the first trial one of the guns which he had manufactured burst, and the breech fell off another.

Powder manufacture. Powder was manufactured in all the large towns of Kashgaria. In the town of Kashgar five *chariks* were sent into the public store every week. In addition to this many of the *pansats* had their own small factories with two or three marking mills for the manufacture of powder for their own private use. The powder prepared in some of these factories was of very good quality. **Lead and brimstone.** Lead and brimstone were obtained in sufficient quantities from the various points of the mountainous tracts bordering on Kashgaria. The richest lead mines were situated in the Kashgar Circle. The richest brimstone beds were in the Koocha Circle. **Saltpetre.** Of saltpetre there was very often a great deficiency. There were, indeed, very small saltpetre manufactories near the town of Bai, in the village of Kooshtam and at Dan Lan Za on the road between the town of Koorlia and Fort Karashar.

Percussion cap factory. In the town of Kashgar a factory had been built under the superintendence of one of the Turkish mechanics, where they prepared percussion caps of very good quality.

Flint muskets and sabres. The manufacture of flint muskets and of sabres (*klwitchi*) was carried on by private enterprise.

English mechanics. Of the existence of English mechanics nothing was to be heard anywhere.

Cartridges for muzzle-loading rifles were also prepared by private enterprise. These were very well made and greatly resembled those used in Russian percussion rifles.[1]

Cartridges for muzzle-loading rifles.

The cartridges for the flint muskets, as a rule, held only the powder which was wrapped up in a coarse kind of paper. The bullets were kept in a leathern bag, which was attached to the waist-belt.

Cartridges for flint muskets.

Cartridges for the breech-loading rifles were imported, but there was a great insufficiency of them. They told us that in the town of Kashgar a factory was being built for the manufacture of these cartridges.

Cartridges for breech-loading rifles.

I do not know where they cast the shot for their smooth-bore guns. For the eight rifled guns which were received through India, Yakoob Bek was provided with 2,000 rounds of ammunition.

Casting of shot for smooth-bore guns.
Ammunition for Yakoob Bek's rifled guns whence obtained.

It now only remains for us to make some observations regarding those fortified posts which were inspected by me during my stay in the dominions of Yakoob Bek. These points were Yangi-Shar, Kashgar, Maral-Bashi, Aksu, Koocha and Koorlia.

Fortified places of Kashgaria.

Fort Yangi-Shar, which lies 7 *versts* (4⅔rds miles) from the town of Kashgar, is the strongest fortified point in the whole of Kashgaria, and alone deserves the name of a fortress. Yangi-Shar was built by the Chinese, who called it their citadel. In form it is an irregular square with faces of about 700 yards in length. Its defences consist of ramparts, surrounding walls and a ditch with water.

Yangi-Shar.

The ramparts are of beaten earth and have a thickness of 5 *sajens* (35 feet). They consist of a *terre-plein*, along which a cart can pass, and of a castellated wall with towers. The height of the *terre-plein* is 4½ *sajens* (31½ feet). Clay walls of a thickness of 1 *sajen* (7 feet) rise to a height of 2 *sajens* (14 feet)

[1] In the town of Koorlia, at the request of the Kashgarian *djigits*, who were attached to our suite, I gave 36 cartridges belonging to rifles that were formerly in possession of Siberian Cossacks. These cartridges the *djigits* presented at the inspection held by Yakoob Bek, instead of those of their own which they had expended on the road.—*Author.*

above the *terre-plein.* The base of the exterior and interior slopes of the ramparts is equal to half their height.

The ditch has a width of 4 *sajens* (28 feet) and a similar depth. At the bottom of the ditch there is a cistern, about 5 feet deep. The sides of the ditch are of such a shape as to admit of easy descent into it, and of an escalade of the defensive walls. The water is supplied from the Igiz canal and is introduced into the fort from the western side. The canal supplies the fort with running water and fills a large reservoir which has been excavated inside. It seems that there are wells also in the fort besides this reservoir. The Igiz canal passes along an aqueduct which could be easily destroyed. The defence of the ditch is provided by two projecting towers. At the angles this defence is very weak.

On the top of the scarps a wall has been built about seven feet high, but of insufficient thickness to resist even a bullet fired from a rifle. In this wall embrasures have been cut. Without having made a breach in this wall it would be difficult to storm the principal works.

On the other side of this wall there is a *banquette* with a width of 70 feet.

Plan and profiles of Yangi-Shar prepared in 1872 by Colonel Kaulbars and Second Captain Startseff of the Russian army.

One gate on the north side leads into the fort. During the year 1872, when our Embassy was at Kashgar, Colonel Kaulbars and Second Captain Startseff prepared a plan and very good profiles of Fort Yangi-Shar. Judging from this plan, Yangi-Shar had in the year 1872 a better glacis than in 1876.

The glacis of the works much obstructed since that time.

We found a number of newly-constructed buildings on the Igiz canal, at a distance of 50 paces from the fort. On the north side too barracks which before were 200 paces from the ditch have now been moved to within 100 paces of the gates and in some places to 60. These erections are numerous and could not be easily thrown down from the fort. They, therefore, present several favourable points for the erection of batteries without great loss.

Ordinary garrison of Yangi-Shar.

The ordinary garrison of Yangi-Shar amounts to 1,000 men. Besides these there are in the surrounding barracks about 3,000 more; no guns were mounted on the walls. Inside the fort we only saw eight guns of various patterns and one large mortar.

Another fortified point is the town of Kashgar, distant 7½ *versts* (4½ miles) north-west of Fort Yangi-Hissar. The town is surrounded by a wall of Chinese construction, with a circumference of 3 *versts* (2 miles). In shape the wall is an irregular polygon. Numerous towers form the flanking defences of the ditch. The wall, during our stay at Kashgar, was kept in good order, but throughout almost the whole of its extent it was without a *banquette*, so that its defence was only possible from the towers. The defences of the town of Kashgar have no *glacis*, and admit of an approach to within 50 paces of its walls. **Kashgar.**

The armament of the defences of Kashgar consisted only of *taifoors*.

After taking Fort Yangi-Shar, the surrender of the town of Kashgar without a fight might be reckoned upon.

The third of the important defences of Kashgaria is Maral-Bashi, which is a point of very great strategical importance, as the meeting place of the roads which lead to the town of Aksu from Khotan, Yarkend and Kashgar. It lies on the river Kashgar-Darya (which in its upper course is called the Kizwil-Su), half-way between the towns of Kashgar and Aksu. **Maral-Bashi (a point of very great strategical importance).**

Maral-Bashi was also built by the Chinese. It is in shape a pentagon with faces about 120 *sajens* (280 yards) long. The thickness of its earthen ramparts is about 21 feet and their height about the same.

At the corners there are high projecting towers, and in the middle of each face there is a small covered lodgment (caponnierè).

Below the counter-scarp a defensive wall has been built. The ditch, which is fourteen feet wide, is furnished with an apparatus for filling it with water. At the bottom of the ditch stakes have been placed. No guns were visible, although each of the towers at the angles had embrasures.

The gates are on the eastern face. Opposite them and outside the fort stands a caravanserai, which was built for Yakoob Bek's reception on the occasion of his visits to the place. This caravanserai and the mosque attached to it greatly obstruct the *glacis* of the work and afford suitable points for the erection of batteries.

The fort, which is large enough to hold a garrison of 1,000 men, was occupied, during our stay there, by a hundred *sarbazais* armed principally with flint muskets. Several *taifoors*, which have been placed on the walls, would have to make way for artillery were any useful purpose in view.

Aksu. The fourth of the fortified points of Kashgaria is the town of Aksu, which is surrounded by a small wall about fourteen feet high, with a *banquette*. The whole is in a good state of preservation. Along the western side of this wall there is a small ditch, at the bottom of which runs a small canal. There is no *glacis* at all outside the walls. Four gates lead into the town. Outside the city walls stand two citadels, an old one built by the Chinese and a new one built by Yakoob Bek.

The old citadel lies to the north of the town on an eminence underneath which stands the town of Aksu, and hence this citadel commands both it and the new citadel. The old citadel has now been abandoned on account of its being found impossible to carry water up to it. It would not, therefore, be difficult to gain possession of it. This commanding point once held, both the town of Aksu and the new citadel could be gained after a single bombardment.

The new citadel, which lies to the west of the town, has been recently built. Part of its walls are composed of burnt brick. Nevertheless the fire from 3-pounder mountain guns would soon overthrow them. The gates which lead into the citadel from the town are massive. There is no *glacis* to the works. Inside are the residence of the Hakim, stores, an arms factory and a portion of the garrison. Outside and close to the citadel there are two barracks. Beyond these again stretches a vast cleared space, which is used as a parade ground.

In Yakoob Bek's time Aksu was defended by from 200 to 400 *sarbazais*, two guns and 1,000 of the latest joined recruits.

Koocha. The fifth of the most important fortified places of Kashgaria is the town of Koocha, which has lately been encircled with a new clay wall, in which embrasures have been cut, and to which flanking towers have been attached. The wall is not thick. The ditch is about 28 feet deep and about 21 feet wide. On the top of the scarp there is a defensive wall, and on the other side of it a wide *banquette*. The town is entered by two gates, on the west and east respectively. The second of these is badly defended and could be taken with a rush. On the western side the ditch has somewhat fallen in, so that here it could be crossed without a ladder. At the bottom of the ditch on this same face a small cistern has been sunk, which has been filled with water.[1]

There is no *glacis* on the north-east and south faces. On the northern face there is a cemetery, whence part of the walls can be completely commanded. In front of the west face stretches a vast extent of ground forming a splendid *glacis* on this side.

Inside the town and at about from 120 to 150 paces from the new wall is the old wall, which in places is almost entirely in ruins.

The garrison of the town during our visit consisted of 1,500 men and two guns. Of these 1,000, who were uniformly clad and well-armed notwithstanding that many had only flint muskets, came from the town of Khotan and were going to start in the ensuing spring [2] for the advanced posts, leaving 500, who were for the most part recruits.

Koorlia.

Lastly, the sixth of the fortified points of Kashgaria is the town of Koorlia. This some years ago was encircled by a wall of very good construction, but thin and without flanking defences. The diameter of the town of Koorlia is about $\frac{1}{2}$ *verst* ($\frac{2}{5}$ths mile). The river Hoidwin-Kooya washes the western and part of the southern face of the city walls. At $1\frac{1}{2}$ *versts'* (1 mile) distance to the east of the town is the citadel, quadrangular in shape with faces of about 160 yards in length. This is encircled by a wall with projecting towers at the angles. The height of this wall is about seven feet and of the towers about fourteen feet. The wall is very thin. Two gates facing the city lead into the citadel.

[1] During our visit this water was frozen.—*Author.* [2] In the year 1877.—*Author.*

The garrison of the citadel in the year 1877 consisted of 600 soldiers with three guns.[1]

Line of posts from the river Kok-Su to the town of Kashgar.

Besides the places named, we inspected also the line of posts from the river Kok-Su, which is the boundary between the province of Fergana and Kashgaria, to the town of Kashgar. We refer to Irkeshtam, Yegin, Nagra-Tchaldwi, Mashroop, Ooksalir, Kan-Djoogan and Min-Yul. These are all of the same type and are quadrangular in shape, with faces of from 35 to 70 yards long with projecting towers at the angles connected by a defensive wall. Some have also a ditch. The walls are of clay and very thin. Their armament consists of some *taifoors*, and they have a garrison of from 20 to 80 men.

Oloogchat stronger than the rest.

In order to take possession of each of these posts in turn, a company of infantry furnished with a beam for battering down the gates or the walls would be sufficient. The post of Ooloogchat is somewhat stronger than the others and may almost be called a fort. It is of the same type, but the length of its faces is from 9 to 115 yards and its garrison numbers 150 men.

The town of Bai not fortified.

Of all the towns which we visited Bai alone is not fortified.

Numerical strength and distribution of the Kashgarian army in the year 1877.

Let us now turn to an examination of the numerical strength and distribution of the Kashgarian army during our residence in the country in the year 1877.

Below will be found authentic details of the numerical strength of that army arranged in two categories. The strength at those points where we were ourselves and where we saw the troops mentioned, and the strength at those points which we did not ourselves visit. To the first category relate particulars as to the numerical strength of the troops at Kashgar, Fort Maral-Bashi, Aksu, Bai, Koocha, Koorlia and Fort Karashar, and at the posts between Fort Gultcha and Kashgar. To the second category belongs the information supplied in answer to questions put on the subject of the numerical strength of the troops in Yakoob Bek's advanced line of posts, *viz.*, at Togsoon, Divantchi, Koonya-Toorfan and in the Circles of Yarkend and Khotan.

[1] During our stay at Koorlia there were, besides these, in camp 2,500 *djigits*, brought by Yakoob Bek from Fort Togsoon on account of the deficiency of supplies at that place.—*Author*.

A.—Points which we visited.

The Town of Kashgar.		
Under the command of Yakoob Bek's eldest son, Bek Koolwi Bek:		One *tabor* of infantry was armed with rifles, the rest had firearms of various kinds, and amongst them many flint muskets. Most of the cavalry had percussion and even breech-loading rifles. Part of Aldash's force had breech-loaders (we saw about 30 such). The rest had firearms of various kinds, and amongst them were flint muskets.
Sarbazais ...	From 2,000 to 2,200 men	
Djigits ...	1,000 "	
Chinese and Doongan *taifoorchis* ...	1,000 "	
Sarbazais and *djigits* under Aldash, Hakim of Kashgar, forming the ordinary garrison of the town ...	600 "	
	Total from 4,600 to 4,800 men, with 20 guns.	
Fort Maral-Bashi.		
Djigits ...	300 men.	The *sarbazais* were armed with flint muskets. The *djigits* were away with the Hakim of Maral-Bashi at the advanced posts, and I do not know of what their armament consisted.
Sarbazais ...	100 "	
	Total ... 400 "	
The Town of Aksu.		
Sarbazais ...	1,000 men.	Of these only 300 were old soldiers, the rest being recruits. Their armament was composed partly of percussion and partly of flint firearms.
Djigits ...	100 "	
	Total 1,200 " with 2 guns.	
The Town of Bai.		
Djigits & sarbazais ...	400 men.	Three hundred of these were recruits, and they were armed for the most part with flint muskets.
The Town of Koocha.		
Sarbazais ...	500 men.	Amongst the *sarbazais* were 200 recruits. The 1,000 *djigits*, who were well trained and uniformly clothed, came from Khotan, and were to winter only at Koocha, departing in the spring for the advanced posts. Amongst their armament were many percussion rifles and some flint muskets.
Djigits ...	1,000 "	
	Total 1,500 " with 2 guns.	
Town of Koorlia.		
Sarbazais composing the garrison of the citadel	660 men. with 3 guns.	The *djigits* had been brought from Togsoon by Yakoob Bek for commissariat reasons. Of these 600 men were sent with us to Koocha for the same reason. In the spring the whole were to go again to Togsoon or to Koonya-Toorfan.
Djigits in camp ...	2,500 men.	
	Total 3,160 " with 3 guns.	

B.—Points which we did not visit.

In posts and forts of the mountain tracts.		
Djigits & sarbazais ...	1,500 men.	The armament of these men consisted partly of flint muskets and partly of percussion rifles.
(The posts which we visited were: Irkeshtam, Yegin, Mashroop, Ooksalwir, Kandjoogan, Min-Yul and Fort Ooloogchat. The garrison of each of these places numbered from 20 to 100 men, whilst that of Ooloogchat was 150.)		

Collected by Yakoob Bek at the advanced posts to oppose the Chinese.

At Fort Divantchi.		
Djigits ...	900 men and 2 guns.	These were armed with breech-loaders on the Snider system. Of the guns one was a breech-loader, the other a muzzle-loader. Both were rifled 3-pounders, and each was carried on a horse.
In the Town of Koonya-Toorfan.		
Under the command of Hakim Khan Turya:		A portion of the cavalry was armed with breech-loaders and a part of the infantry with percussion rifles (some of these were of local manufacture). The rest, both cavalry and infantry, had flint muskets.
Djigits ...	3,500 men.	
Sarbazais ...	5,000 „	
	Total 8,500 „ with 20 guns of different patterns.	
Doongan levies ...	10,000 men.	These Doongans had been recently collected for the defence of the town, they were little to be depended on, were badly armed and ill-disciplined.
At Fort Togsoon.		
Under the command of the *Badaulet's* second son, Hak Koolwi Bek:		A portion of the cavalry was armed with breech-loaders, but the majority of the infantry with muzzle-loaders. The guns were of no use, either because the breech mechanism was out of order or because of an insufficiency of ammunition.
Djigits ...	4,000 men.	
Sarbazais ...	2,000 „	
	Total 6,000 „ with 5 breech-loading guns.[1]	
In the Yarkend and Yangi-Hissar Circles.		
Djigits & sarbazais ...	4,000 men.	These figures are only approximate, and should be received with caution.
In the Khotan Circle.		
Djigits & sarbazais ...	3,000 „	
	Total 7,000 „	

[1] According to other information two of these guns were muzzle-loaders. The whole were rifled.—*Author.*

TOTAL.		
Djigits ...	13,300 men.	With these troops were 54 guns of different apterns.
Sarbazais ...	11,560 „	
Djigits and sarbazais together ...	9,500 „	
Chinese and Doongan *taifoorchis* ...	1,000 „	
Doongan levies ...	10,000 „	
GRAND TOTAL ...	45,360 „	

These figures show the *maximum* force which Yakoob Bek could muster for the maintenance of peace in his own vast sovereignty, for the preservation of his frontier line towards Russian territory and for a struggle with the Chinese. Against the latter he had placed in the town of Koonya-Toorfan and in Forts Togsoon and Divantchi forces of the following strength: *sarbazais* 7,000; *djigits* 7,500, with 27 guns and levies of Doongans amounting to 10,000 men.

Maximum force at Yakoob Bek's disposal.

These forces had, on the 1st March or 1st April (old style), to be increased by 1,500 *djigits* from Koorlia and 1,000 *djigits* from Koocha.

In November 1876, in consequence of a famine in the Koonya-Toorfan District, Yakoob Bek was obliged to withdraw a considerable portion of his forces from the advanced posts to Koorlia and even to Koocha.

On the $\frac{1st}{13th}$ January 1877, the troops in the advanced posts were distributed, on account of the difficulty of provisioning them, at the following points: At Divantchi, Koonya-Toorfan, Togsoon, Fort Shag Tal, Oortantcha-Taulga (the last two are on the road between Togsoon and Karashar), Fort Karashar and Koorlia.

The *Badaulet* brought with him to Koorlia 3,000 *djigits*. Of these 600 were sent to Koocha, and after taking to the advanced posts provisions for 1,000 men up to $\frac{1st}{13th}$ February, they returned to Togsoon.

The condition of the troops at the advanced posts during the winter was woeful. The greater portion of them lived in tents made of *mata*, with 20 degrees of frost on the ground. They had not sufficient warm clothing and scarcely any fuel.

Condition of the troops at Yakoob Bek's advanced posts.

Advanced point of the Chinese in the beginning of 1877.

The advanced point of the Chinese on the $\frac{1st}{13th}$ February 1877 was the town of Ooroomtcha, where they had a force of 6,000 men.

Yakoob Bek's army not to be compared with any European army.

After casting a rapid glance over all that we have said, one cannot but come to the conclusion that the army which Yakoob Bek had, could in no sense be compared with a European army. Hence it is only possible to compare it with those of other independent Asiatic potentates, with whom we had come into collision.

Heterogeneous nature of Yakoob Bek's army.

In its organization Yakoob Bek's army was more heterogeneous than, for example, the army of Bokhara. In its armament and training it stood perceptibly higher than the forces of the Central Asian Khanates. Especially good was the Kashgarian cavalry in comparison with those disorderly and badly equipped bands of horsemen with whom we had come in contact in Central Asia.

Spirit of his troops bad. Causes.

The spirit of Yakoob Bek's troops could not be considered favourable for undertaking a stubborn fight. Abuses in recruitment (compulsory enlistment), the withholding of stipulated pay, the privations which the men had to undergo at the advanced posts, the presence of masses of Andijans (who were ready after the first failure to abandon their employer, and to make off to their own country with the goods which they had plundered in Kashgaria), lastly, a struggle with the Chinese, the issue of which could scarcely be doubted by any,—all these were the causes which called forth in the ranks of Yakoob Bek's army that inducement to desert which increased day by day.

Forecast of the struggle between Yakoob Bek and the Chinese.

We have not seen the Chinese army which is opposed to that of Yakoob Bek, and we, therefore, cannot judge of its merits, much less settle the question as to which will come out victorious in the struggle which has commenced. This much only is clear to us, that whereas Yakoob Bek has already made every effort to bring together all his forces for the fight, the strength of the Chinese forces must increase with every month. We can in like manner confidently predict that the first serious engagement of the *Badaulet's* force with those of the Chinese will call forth a rising of the people against Yakoob Bek, because they are burdened with intolerable imposts, and because the existing order of things in Kashgaria is too oppressive to last.

Opposition to a Russian force entering Kashgaria.

With regard to the opposition which at this particular epoch a Russian army marching on Kashgaria would encounter, it may be said, that such an opposition would detain us only during the time that it would take to march through the mountainous tracts for the purpose of capturing Yangi-Shar and certain other fortified points. In the open field Yakoob Bek's army could be as easily defeated and scattered as have been the hosts of Kokan, Bokhara and Khiva, when these have met our Turkestan troops at Irdjar, Tchapanata, Zeraboolak, Chandir and Makhram.

CHAPTER VIII.

Glance at events in Kashgaria from February 1877 up to the present time — Death of Yakoob Bek — Internal dissensions — Struggle amongst Yakoob Bek's sons — Bek Koolwi Bek — Advance of the Chinese — Capture of Koorlia, Koocha, Aksu, Maral-Bashi and Kashgar by the Chinese — Bek Koolwi Bek's unsuccessful campaign against Khotan — Policy of the Chinese commanders towards the population of Kashgaria.

Yakoob Bek's advanced posts.

AT the time of our stay in Kashgaria, *viz.*, from October 1876 to March 1877, Yakoob Bek's advanced posts were the following:—

Koonya-Toorfan, which was held by Hakim Khan Turya with a force of some thousand *sarbazais* and levies.

Togsoon, which was held by Hak Koolwi Bek, Yakoob Bek's youngest son, with a force of 6,000 *djigits* and *sarbazais*.

Fort Divantchi, the most advanced post, which was held by 900 *djigits* armed with breech-loaders.

Chinese advanced point. Lowering of the *morale* of Yakoob Bek's army and the desertion therefrom.

The small range of the Divantchi hills separated the combatant forces. Ooroomtcha was the most advanced point held by the Chinese. In it they had 6,000 men. The winter of 1876-77 had lowered the condition of Yakoob Bek's army, especially in regard to its *morale*. Desertion had begun to rapidly spread even amongst those persons on whose devotion Yakoob Bek had always depended.

Chinese treatment of deserters.

The Chinese received deserters very kindly and nominated them to various posts in the towns of Djitwishar.

Return of the Russian Mission before Yakoob Bek's overthrow.

We ourselves did not happen to be spectators of the events which led to the rapid and unexpected overthrow of the Kashgarian sovereignty, since our Embassy had started on the $\frac{\text{24th March}}{\text{5th April}}$ 1877 on its return journey, one week before the advance of the Chinese to their attack on Yakoob Bek's army.

Below will be found some interesting particulars obligingly communicated to me by Major Ionoff, Commandant of the Osh District, and by Zaman Khan Effendi.[1]

---

[1] Zaman Khan Effendi, an exile from the Caucasus, and a man of some education, came from Constantinople to Kashgaria, where he succeeded in obtaining a prominent position under Yakoob Bek. During the period of our

According to the testimony of these two persons, the march of events in Djitwishar, from April 1877, went on in the following order:—

On the $\frac{3rd}{15th}$ April 1877, the Chinese, to the number of 4,000, marched from Ooroomtcha to Fort Divantchi, to which they laid siege. The garrison, numbering 1,300 men, after a poor defence, which lasted for three days, surrendered to them.

The Chinese advance from Ooroomtcha to Fort Divantchi, which surrenders to them.

At the same time as they moved from Ooroomtcha to Divantchi, the Chinese made a demonstration from the town of Hami (Komool) towards Koonya-Toorfan. 2,000 armed inhabitants held this place, and they surrendered to the Chinese without firing a shot. Hakim Khan Turya just succeeded in getting off with a handful of soldiers to Togsoon, where he joined Hak Koolwi Bek. The detachment, then under the command of the latter, was composed of 4,000 *djigits* and *sarbazais* and of 6,000 armed inhabitants.

They make a demonstration also from Hami towards Koonya-Toorfan, which also surrenders to them.

On hearing of the advance of the Chinese, Hak Koolwi Bek sent to his father, who was at Koorlia, for permission to forward reinforcements to Divantchi and Koonya-Toorfan, but before an answer could be received these places had already fallen, and Hak Koolwi Bek, who was, in turn, without reinforcements, retreated with his whole force to the town of Karashar, fearing that he would be cut off from the Soo-Bashi pass.

Hak Koolwi Bek retreats to Karashar.

Loo Tcha Darin, the Commander of the Chinese forces, acted very judiciously with regard to the prisoners whom he took at Divantchi. His treatment of these men was calculated to have a good influence in favour of the Chinese.

Judicious conduct of the Chinese Commander Loo Tcha Darin towards his prisoners.

All of such as were inhabitants of Djitwishar, amounting to 1,000, he treated kindly, furnishing them with money for road expenses and with passes, and then releasing them.

He further announced that he was fighting only against the Andijans, *i. e.*, the *parvenus* from Fergana and Tashkent; that he

stay at Koorlia, Zaman Khan shewed many civilities to us. In like manner he did much to lighten the position of our traveller Prjevalski, whom he accompanied to Lob-Nor. Zaman Khan remained with Yakoob Bek till his death, and was present at the fall of the Kashgarian monarchy. He then, with other adherents of Yakoob Bek, fled to Russian territory, where he met with a hearty reception.—*Author.*

held no doubt as to the devotion of the inhabitants of Djitwishar to the Chinese Government, and that in a short time he would endeavour to free them from the extortions of Yakoob Bek.

The remaining prisoners, who were natives of other parts of Turkestan, were sent to Ooroomtcha.

Effect of this mild treatment.

The released prisoners came to Karashar, and the rumour of the details attending their release reached the *Badaulet.* Esteeming the course of action adopted by the Chinese to be very pernicious to himself, Yakoob Bek, in order to neutralize the Chinese influence over the released prisoners, resorted to a measure, which did himself still greater harm, whilst it increased the general sympathy for the Chinese. He sent directions to his son Hak Koolwi Bek to deprive the released prisoners of all further power of spreading the story as to their deliverance. Hak Koolwi Bek, in fulfilment of his father's orders, massacred the greater number of these unfortunate persons. The remainder effected their escape and returned to the Chinese.

Yakoob Bek in endeavouring to neutralize the Chinese influence resorts to a measure which does himself still greater harm.

This measure, as might have been expected, produced a result entirely opposed to that anticipated by Yakoob Bek. The report of this atrocity swiftly spread throughout the whole of Kashgaria, and not only revealed the weakness of the Andijans, but made them more detested than before. The clemency of the Chinese towards their prisoners was exaggerated in the narration and served to strengthen the party opposed to Yakoob Bek. The Chinese were thus benefited and a machine was set in motion, which, aided by a course of energetic action, tended to the overthrow of Yakoob Bek's authority.

Causes of the rapid successes of the Chinese.

Certain it is that the effect of this story acting in combination with the general discontent of the people against Yakoob Bek, is the only explanation of the subsequent and extraordinarily rapid successes of the Chinese, of which we shall speak below.

Yakoob Bek in a fit of anger slays his secretary, Hamal

At 5 o'clock in the afternoon of the $\frac{16th}{28th}$ May 1877, the 'Badaulet' became greatly exasperated with his secretary Hamal, whom, for some inexact discharge of a certain duty, he killed with a blow delivered with the butt-end of his gun.

And then attacks his treasurer

Having killed Hamal, he set upon his treasurer, Sabir Akhoon, whom he also began to beat. In the struggle with him he

Sabir Akhoon. In the struggle he receives a blow, which deprives him of his senses. Death of Yakoob Bek.

received a blow which deprived him of his senses. After remaining in this condition for some time the 'Badaulet' died at 2 o'clock in the morning of the $\frac{17\text{th}}{29\text{th}}$ May. The stories that Yakoob Bek was poisoned by his son Hak Koolwi Bek, and that he himself took poison in consequence of his want of success against the Chinese, are devoid of foundation.

I will here insert *verbatim* an account of Yakoob Bek's character as related by Zaman Khan in a letter to my address:

Account of Yakoob Bek's character.

"The deceased Yakoob Bek was an intelligent and energetic man, possessed of a surprising memory. He was at the same time both cunning and sly. The truth he scarcely ever spoke. He was an egotist in the fullest sense and respected the opinion of no man. As a military man he of late shewed himself to be very inferior. As a polygamist he surpassed the Persian Fatali Shah. In his private life he was simple, without any pretensions, and was satisfied with little. At times he was kind and courteous to all. He observed the ceremonies of religion in a conscientious manner. During the 24 hours he rested only for four hours,[1] being occupied during the remainder of the day. He trusted no one. In all matters, whether relating to the stable or the cook-house, or to the most important affairs of State, he looked after everything himself.

"Three secretaries formed his entire council. Yakoob Bek was not an educated man, and yet those who did not know him would imagine him to be learned; for oftentimes he would quote, either for the sake of eloquence, or in illustration of what he was saying, such texts from the Koran as might be apposite to his remarks, or couplets from verses by well-known Persian poets. In the Persian language he conversed with freedom. His orders as issued to his subordinates were written out at his dictation, and their reports were returned with his remarks noted thereon. Letters, however, which he received from Russia or from other States he kept together with the copies which were made of the same.

[1] Probably in this period the time which he devoted to sleep is not reckoned.—*Author.*

"Yakoob Bek took nothing from the rulers of towns except the yearly offering. Such officials were, however, obliged to keep up a certain number of troops. With regard to the taxes exacted by the provincial rulers from the people under their administration, they had no control over such demands. It was only at uncertain periods that he called upon his officials for considerable sums of money, and these had to be paid without demur. Niaz Bek, Hakim of Khotan, besides a yearly offering, sent every week 11 *yambas* of silver (1,200 roubles or £150) and 44 seers of gold = about 1,800 roubles (£225), or about 3,000 roubles (£375) a week."

Hak Koolwi Bek goes to Koorlia on the day of Yakoob Bek's death.

On the day of Yakoob Bek's death, *i. e.*, on the $\frac{17th}{29th}$ May, Hak Koolwi Bek came to Koorlia from Karashar. For three whole days he told no one of his father's death. During this period all the troops at Karashar were called back to Koorlia.

He announces the event to his troops.

Having collected his forces at Koorlia, Hak Koolwi informed them on the $\frac{20th\ May}{1st\ June}$ of the death of their sovereign and declared that it was his wish to go with his father's body to Kashgar, where his elder brother Bek Koolwi Bek was, who, he said, had taken the place of a father to him and without whose permission he would undertake nothing. Having contented the army with the issue of two months' pay, and having appointed Hakim Khan Turya his deputy for the time being, Hak Koolwi Bek set out on the $\frac{25th\ May}{6th\ June}$ for Kashgar.

Appoints Hakim Khan Turya as his deputy at Koorlia and proceeds to Kashgar.

Report as to Yakoob Bek's wishes with respect to the succession to the throne. Sympathy of the army and of the people respectively.

According to report, it was Yakoob Bek's wish to appoint not his eldest but his youngest son, Hak Koolwi Bek, his successor, the latter being more warlike and more liked by the army. All the officers of the army were also on his side. With regard to the sympathy of the people, especially of Kashgar and particularly of the merchant class, that was on the side of Bek Koolwi Bek.

Real motive for Hak Koolwi Bek's departure for Kashgar.

According to the same information, Hak Koolwi Bek set out for Kashgar with the object of proclaming himself ruler. The taking of his father's body to that place was a mere pretext.

Bek Koolwi Bek's feelings towards his brother.

It is equally certain that Bek Koolwi Bek recognized in his brother a dangerous rival, of whom he hoped to rid himself with the aid of an assassin.

On the $\frac{\text{26th May}}{\text{7th June}}$, *i. e.*, the day after Hak Koolwi Bek's departure from Koorlia, all the troops assembled in that town and proclaimed Hakim Khan Turya, Khan. The latter immediately sent off a certain Kipchak, Dash Bek by name, with 500 horsemen, in pursuit of Hak Koolwi Bek, with orders to prevent his seizing the treasury at Aksu.

The troops at Koorlia proclaim Hakim Khan Turya Khan of that place.

On the $\frac{\text{11th}}{\text{23rd}}$ June, Hak Koolwi Bek, with 30 attendants, left Aksu for Kashgar. At 80 versts' (53⅓rd miles) distance from that town, near the station of Koopruk and at the bridge over the Kizwil-Su, Hak Koolwi Bek was treacherously slain by Mahmed Zia Pansat, who was sent by Bek Koolwi Bek to meet him.

Hak Koolwi Bek is slain at the instigation of Bek Koolwi Bek.

According to another story, less worthy of credence, Bek Koolwi Bek personally met Hak Koolwi Bek and shot him with a revolver at the very moment of their meeting. He at the same time ordered all Hak Koolwi's followers to be slain.

In consequence of these events the Kashgarian sovereignty became divided into three parts, each of which had at its head a separate ruler. In Kashgar there was Bek Koolwi Bek; in Aksu, Hakim Khan Turya; and in Khotan, Niaz Bek. These three began to fight amongst themselves. Bek Koolwi Bek proved himself the most powerful and the most energetic. Having collected a force of 5,000 men he advanced against Aksu. Hakim Khan Turya, on his part, collected a body numbering over 4,000 men and went out to meet him. Near Yaida (Djaida), between Maral-Bashi and Aksu, the respective advanced guards had a skirmish, in which the Kashgarians were defeated and pursued as far as Tchool-Koodook (Shoor-Koodook). Three days afterwards Bek Koolwi Bek concentrated his forces at the place last named, whilst Hakim Khan Turya's main body was at Yaida. Between these two places a decisive battle took place that lasted for five hours. Hakim Khan suffered a defeat and saved himself by escaping to Russian territory. His army surrendered to Bek Koolwi Bek.

Division of the sovereignty of Kashgaria into three parts, under Bek Koolwi Bek, Hakim Khan Turya and Niaz Bek respectively.

Bek Koolwi Bek advances against Aksu.

Hakim Khan Turya's forces are defeated and he flies to Russian territory.

On the $\frac{\text{1st}}{\text{13th}}$ August, Bek Koolwi Bek entered Aksu in triumph. Having stopped there two weeks, he started on the $\frac{\text{24th August}}{\text{5th September}}$ on his return journey to the town of Kashgar, where he gave

Bek Koolwi Bek enters Aksu in triumph.

He advances to Khotan.

his troops a month's rest, after which he set out, on the $\frac{\text{22nd Septr.}}{\text{4th October}}$, with 5,000 men for Khotan.

On the $\frac{\text{8th}}{\text{20th}}$ Octoter he was met at Zava by the Khotan army under the leadership of Emin Bek, brother of Niaz Bek. The Khotanese fled on the first charge of the Kashgarian cavalry. Niaz Bek, who was at the time in Khotan (Ilchi), 30 versts (20 miles) distant from Zava, hearing of his brother's defeat, had no desire to prolong the contest, so he took his family and his belongings and set out for Tchar-tchak, whence, in all probability, he intended making his way to the Chinese by the river Khotan-Darya and across Lob-Nor.

Niaz Bek's forces having been defeated he flies to Tchar-tchak.

Bek Koolwi Bek enters the town of Khotan.

The next day Bek Koolwi Bek entered the town of Khotan and sent men to pursue and to catch Niaz Bek, but those whom he sent returned without success.

The Chinese capture Koorlia, Koocha and Aksu and the Kashgarian garrisons retreat to Kashgar. Effect of this news on Bek Koolwi Bek.

On the $\frac{\text{18th}}{\text{30th}}$ October Bek Koolwi Bek received news of the capture of Koorlia, Koocha and Aksu by the Chinese, and of the retreat of the Kashgarian troops towards Kashgar. Under the influence of this news he sent a messenger to Kashgar for his family, directing that they should be escorted to Yarkend. On the $\frac{\text{25th October}}{\text{6th November}}$ he himself went to Yarkend, where he found his family. But meanwhile still sadder news had reached the same place. Those Chinese soldiers who had been made Mussulmans by Yakoob Bek, forced their way into Fort Yangi-Shar (citadel of the town of Kashgar) and shut themselves up in it. This intelligence produced a great impression on all Bek Koolwi Bek's followers, for the families of very many of them were living in Yangi-Shar, and had, therefore, been seized by the Chinese. They, therefore, began to publicly reproach Bek Koolwi Bek, saying that if he had not sent for his own family from Yangi-Shar, the Chinese would not have dared to resort to such an extreme measure.

The Chinese troops in the service of Kashgaria shut themselves up in Yangi-Shar.

Effect of this news on the followers of Bek Koolwi Bek.

Flight of the whole of Bek Koolwi Bek's infantry.

A little before this, Bek Koolwi Bek had sent all his infantry from Yarkend to Maral-Bashi by the direct road, but on the way they all fled. Seeing that his affairs had now become desperate, he, accompanied by the Hakim of Yarkend and by his own family, started on the night of the $\frac{\text{4th}}{\text{16th}}$ November for the town of Kargalwik, which lies on the road to Khotan. But

Bek Koolwi Bek endeavours to make

certain persons, whose families had been detained in Yangi-Shar, stopped the intending fugitive, and demanded that he should go with them to try and recapture this fort.

for Kargalwik, but is prevented and made to undertake measures for the recapture of Yangi-Shar.

Bek Koolwi Bek was consequently obliged to consent and to return to Kashgar. Having arrived at Yangi-Hissar, which is half-way between Yarkend and Kashgar, he out of pure spite to the Chinese gave orders that all the Chinese boys in the service of various persons should be slain.

Bek Koolwi Bek's massacre of a number of Chinese boys.

Two hundred were the victims of this order. At the same time Aldash Datkha, Governor of Kashgar, killed 400 Chinese of both sexes and of various ages who had not gone into the citadel of Yangi-Shar.

Aldash Datkha, Governor of Kashgar, slays 400 Chinese.

On the 24th November / 6th December Bek Koolwi Bek came to Kashgar and took up his abode in a garden, distant about 3 versts (2 miles) from Yangi-Shar. Those of his troops and some Doongans who had come to him from Aksu, to the number of more than 10,000, laid siege to the citadel and began to prepare to storm it. All their efforts were fruitless. The garrison of 500 Chinese defended itself heroically, for not only were all the assaults repulsed, but almost every night the Chinese made sorties and inflicted sensible loss on the besiegers.

Bek Koolwi Bek arrives at Kashgar.

Failure of his attempts to retake the citadel of Yangi-Shar.

On the 4th / 16th December reports were circulated throughout Bek Koolwi Bek's camp that the Chinese were close to Faizabad, 60 versts (40 miles) distant from Kashgar. Aldash Datkha was sent with a force against them, but he, after firing a few shots, retreated. This retreat was the commencement of a general retirement.

The Chinese said to be at Faizabad.

Aldash Datkha's force retreats.

A panic seized Bek Koolwi Bek's troops, and they fled into Russian territory, some to Fergana through the Terek-Davan pass, some to Narwin by Chakmak and Artoosh. Bek Koolwi Bek was the first to give the signal for the flight.

Bek Koolwi Bek's troops fly in various directions, whilst he himself goes too.

At seven o'clock the same evening a small reconnoitring party sent by the Chinese from Maral-Bashi entered the town of Kashgar without a blow.

The Chinese occupy Kashgar.

After Bek Koolwi Bek's troops followed thousands of the inhabitants of Kashgar and their families, for they feared a

Exodus of the inhabitants of Kashgar.

repetition of those atrocities which had on every occasion attended the appearance of the Chinese after the expulsion of the Khodjas Djengir, Valikhan and Katta-Turya.

These unfortunate people set out for the Terek-Davan and crossed the range of mountain bordering it at a time when there were 30 degrees of frost.

Their sufferings.

There now began a repetition of the horrors which attended the flight of the Kashgarians after Katta-Turya's expulsion, when tens of thousands perished from frost and hunger.

Measures adopted by the Russian forces for the relief of the fugitives.

Happily for the fugitives on the present occasion, Major Ionoff, an energetic and experienced Turkestanian and Commandant of the Osh District in which the Terek-Davan pass is situated, adopted measures for their safety. He himself accompanied by his second-in-command, Captain Roselein, set out for the pass and at once organized measures for the relief of those Kashgarians who reached Russian territory almost frozen and perished from hunger.

The fugitives were warmed and fed and then sent on horses to the town of Osh. All who crossed Russian territory were saved. The District Commander of the province of Sermiraitchia likewise did all he could to lighten the sufferings of those fugitives who sought safety in Russian territory.

The Sari-Kol Kirghiz prevent fugitives from Tashkent entering their territory.

The inhabitants of Yarkend tried to fly to Sarwikol and even to Shignan, but the Sarwikol Kirghiz made them go back and gave them into the hands of the Chinese.

Altered behaviour of the Chinese towards the people of the country.

On this occasion the Chinese, taught by bitter experience, kept themselves at first under comparative restraint. The people were appeased. Mussulmans were appointed as headmen of the towns. Trial by the Code of the Shariat was permitted, and religion was not interfered with.[1] About ten men were executed during the first day of their return. But the Chinese had only just come. They let the people remain in peace and turned their attention, amongst other matters, to the horses.

The inhabitants of Kashgaria are not permitted to possess horses.

Rumour tells us that the Kashgarians were forbidden to keep horses. Those who disobeyed this order were executed, or,

[1] The Chinese always strictly adhered to non-interference in religious matters. —*Author.*

according to other reports unworthy of credence, they were starved to death and even blown from guns.

In the horses which had given the Kashgarians the power of moving rapidly over vast tracts, the Chinese saw one of the principal causes of their former defeats. Reason for this prohibition.

The further events which took place during the present year are but little known to us. We only know that with the occupation of Kashgar by the Chinese, the struggle is not yet over. Certain towns have not acknowledged the supremacy of the Chinese, and continue to fight with them up till now. Amongst these towns, Khotan and Ootchtoorfan maintain the lead. The Chinese have undertaken to occupy the country with too weak forces, which must perforce be scattered about. If, therefore, there should appear in Kashgaria an energetic opponent of the Chinese, he might hope to give them much trouble and might even defer the pacification for some years until sufficient reinforcements from the Celestial Empire should arrive to overcome all opposition, and be in a position to uphold the order of things once more re-established. Further events in Kashgaria after the return of the Chinese.

From the latest intelligence it is apparent that the mild behaviour of the Chinese towards the natives has ceased. The people, as of old, are burdened with intolerable exactions in the shape of money, provisions and forced labour. Executions have begun. Dissatisfaction increases and many have come to dwell on the memory of Yakoob Bek with regret. The Chinese alter their behaviour towards the natives, who begin to regret the removal of Yakoob Bek.

THE END.

HISTORY OF AFGHANISTAN, from the Earliest Period to the Outbreak of the War of 1878. By Colonel G. B. Malleson, C.S.I. Second Edition. Rs. 12-14.

LIFE OF LIEUT.-GENERAL SIR JAMES OUTRAM. By Major-General Sir Frederic J. Goldsmid, C.B., K.C.S.I. Two vols. 8vo. Rs. 23.

SIR GEORGE POLLOCK. The Life and Correspondence of Field-Marshal Sir George Pollock, Bart., G.C.B. By Charles Rathbone Low. 8vo. Rs. 12-14.

KAYE (SIR W.) History of the War in Afghanistan, from the unpublished letters and journals of Political and Military Officers employed in Afghanistan throughout the entire period of British connection with that Country. Three vols. 12mo., cloth. Rs. 18-10. (1874.)

SHAHAMAT ALI. The Sikhs and Afghans immediately before and after the death of Runjeet Singh; from the Journal of an Expedition to Kabul through the Punjab and the Khaibar Pass. By Shahamat Ali. Rs. 7-8.

HOUGH (MAJOR W.) March and Operations of the Army of the Indus in the Expedition to Afghanistan, 1838-39. By Major W. Hough. 8vo. Rs. 10. (1841.)

TURKISTAN. Notes of a Journey in Russia, Turkistan, Khokand, Bukhara, and Kuldja. By Eugene Schuyler, Ph. D. With Maps and Illustrations. Two vols. 8vo. Rs. 30.

ENGLAND AND RUSSIA IN THE EAST; a series of Papers on the Political and Geographical Condition of Central Asia. By Major-General Sir Henry Rawlinson, K.C.B. 8vo. Rs. 8-8.

CENTRAL ASIA AND THE ANGLO-RUSSIAN FRONTIER QUESTION; a series of Political Papers. By Arminius Vámbéry. Crown 8vo. Rs. 6-8.

THE RUSSIANS IN CENTRAL ASIA. A Critical Examination of the Geography and History of Central Asia by Frederick Von Hellwald. Translated by Col. Wiegman. Crown 8vo. Rs. 8-8.

CAMPAIGNING ON THE OXUS AND THE FALL OF KHIVA. By J. A. MacGahan. With Illustrations. Crown 8vo. Rs. 5-6.

KHIVA AND TURKISTAN. Translated from the Russian by Capt. H. Spalding, F.R.G.S. With a Map. Crown 8vo. Rs. 3-8.

BANNU; OR, OUR AFGHAN FRONTIER. By S. S. Thorburn, Civil Service. 8vo. Rs. 12-14.

TELEGRAPH AND TRAVEL. A Narrative of the Development of Telegraphic Communication between England and India. With incidental notices of the countries traversed by the lines. By Col. Sir Frederic Goldsmid. 8vo. Rs. 13-8.

CLOUDS IN THE EAST; Travels and Adventures on the Perso-Turkoman Frontier. By Valentine Baker. With Map and Illustrations. 8vo. Rs. 12-14.

www.ingramcontent.com/pod-product-compliance
Lightning Source LLC
Chambersburg PA
CBHW030351270326
41926CB00009B/1057

* 9 7 8 3 3 3 7 2 9 1 9 3 8 *